The

CAPE COD
GARDEN

The
CAPE COD
GARDEN

by
C.L. FORNARI

Paraphyses Press

First printing, 1996 Parnassus Imprints ISBN 0-940160-65-X

Paraphyses Press
P.O. Box 50
Osterville, MA 02655

Front cover photo:
Annuals and perennials bloom in the author's Cape Cod garden.

Back cover photos:
(Top) Bonica roses and perennials in John and Ann Bennett's sea-side garden in Orleans.
(Middle) A stone path made by Elizabeth Ann Wolff in her South Yarmouth garden. *(photos by C.L. Fornari)*
(Bottom) C.L. Fornari in her garden *(Photo by Eileen Friedenriech)*

Library of Congress Cataloging-in-Publication Data

Fornari, C.L., 1950-
    The Cape Cod Garden – revised / C.L. Fornari — 2nd edition
    p. cm.
    Includes bibliographical references (p.   ) and index.
    ISBN 0-9718220-0-X (pbk.)
1. Gardening—Massachusetts—Cape Cod   I. Title
    SB453.2.M52F67   2002
    635 .09744 '9—dc21   2002090552 CIP

Manufactured in the United States of America

For Dan, with love.

ACKNOWLEDGMENTS

As I finish the revisions on *The Cape Cod Garden*, I am once again truly grateful to the many people who helped make this book possible. Wally Exman believed in my ability to be an author, and because of his help and expertise, this book came into being. This second edition would not have been possible without Katherine Joyce and Cia Elkin; because of their help, the process of taking it from manuscript to printing has been less overwhelming.

As before, I thank the people at the Barnstable County Cooperative Extension. I am especially indebted to Roberta Clark, Extension Specialist, for her comments and suggestions; she has been an invaluable source of wisdom and advice. She and her colleague, Bill Clark, and all of the Extension staff, are truly an asset to everyone involved in horticulture in Barnstable County. They have my deepest gratitude.

My thanks and appreciation also go to all of the gardeners on Cape Cod and the Islands who have so generously shared both their gardens and their experiences; this includes those I met while photographing their gardens, Master Gardeners, and other diggers of dirt. I thank you all for the information and lovely garden pictures, and for your insights and good-spirited friendship.

The staff at Country Garden in Hyannis deserves mention for so graciously putting up with both my erratic schedule and my plant mania. All who work there - Dave Lane, Marsha Potash, and Dave Griffith in particular - have always been willing to share their knowledge and experience, not to mention a good laugh. I have especially appreciated working with Donna Andrews-Maness; we share a passion for plants, if not their pronunciation.

Pamela Phipps (The Handy Woman) has my continuing appreciation for her help with my garden; my garden remains beautiful because often, while I am at the computer, she is dealing with the weeds and more.

I thank and acknowledge the following people for their help, support, and encouragement: my in-laws, Harry and Misa Fornari;

Jeanie Gillis, Horticulturist at the Heritage Plantation; the staff at the Osterville Public Library; and the folks at the Cape Cod Community Media Center in Yarmouthport. Love and thanks to my mother, Janice Albertson, who was the first gardener I knew; she is a woman who has a special communication with plants.

Most importantly, my love, appreciation, and gratitude go to the folks at home: first and foremost to my husband, Dan, who puts up with my plant obsession, and has always been supportive of all my schemes and dreams. Thanks and love always to my sons, Sasha and Simon, for their patience and encouragement. You are the most wonderful things growing in my garden.

TABLE OF CONTENTS

INTRODUCTION

I must confess up front that I have Ron Dier Disease. Before you rush to give me sympathy (or plan my funeral) let me explain that Ron Dier Disease is not an illness, but my name for being hopelessly obsessed with plants. I named this condition after Ron Dier, an artist and plantsman I know who cannot drive by a nursery without stopping to buy a plant. He got the honor of having this condition named after him because his last name starts with a "D", and so it sounds good with "disease." I hope he has a sense of humor about this.

Having loved plants all my life, I already had Ron Dier Disease when I moved to Cape Cod, but it was here that it completely exploded. Perhaps the escalation was caused by moving from the cold-winter foothills of the Berkshires to the comparatively mild winters on Cape Cod. Or perhaps it was inevitable; an obsession with plants has to *grow* I suppose.

I have been fortunate throughout my involvement with plants to have many teachers. I have enjoyed gathering information from books, other gardeners, the Master Gardener program at the Cooperative Extension, and most importantly, from the plants themselves. When I am speaking or hosting a radio program, I welcome questions that I don't know the answer to; in finding the answer I always learn something new. My goal in writing this book was to compile the information that I have found most helpful in my own gardening, along with the answers to questions that I have heard other gardeners ask.

In the process of revising this book, I have been reminded that I continue to expand my knowledge of plants and plant care. Some of the advice that I gave in the first addition has been changed; new research, further exploration, and several seasons of gardening have altered my thinking about some garden practices and plants.

Throughout this book I use two terms that may be unfamiliar to some gardeners. "Cultivar" is a term for a "cultivated variety"; that is a plant that was grown in cultivation, not in the wild. When I refer to a plant's "cultural conditions" I am speaking about how that plant is cared for. The way the plant was first planted, the way it is watered, or the amount of fertilizer it is given are all examples of cultural conditions.

While striving to keep the information in this book as complete as possible, I have also tried to be brief. I assume that time is as precious to all of you as it is to me. There will always be more that can be said, and if I have left out methods or plants that are dear to your heart, it is not because the plants aren't wonderful, or the information not valuable. I am pleased to say that there is always more for me to learn, and there is rarely only *one way* to do anything; you may have had great success using a plant or strategy that I haven't included. Diversity in life keeps things from ever being boring. While giving enough information to help the gardener and home landscaper plant and maintain a beautiful garden, I also hope to steer anyone motivated to learn more about a particular subject toward sources of that information.

It is important to say that even I do not follow my own advice all the time. Sometimes I must take the expedient approach, knowing that it may not be the best thing for the garden. Just ask my neighbors. They may have noticed that I am watering the garden at five in the afternoon even though I *know* that I am encouraging leaf spot fungi by doing so. If I have been out all day and come home to find wilted plants, I will not keep them thirsty because it is the wrong time of day to water. Sometimes we have to be as practical as possible and hope for the best.

I try not to let expediency harm other creatures in my yard and garden, however. I believe that gardening should always, always, be an activity that draws us back to nature, not one that pits us against the natural world. For this reason I have stressed using the least-toxic solutions to garden problems, and on this matter I will not take the easy way out. I see no reason to use harsh chemicals as there are so many plants that thrive without the use of them. I have observed that gardens thrive for those who listen to nature instead of trying to control it.

In gardening, as in life, you will probably be most content if you stay flexible and are willing to be gracious about surprises. There are no guarantees and seldom are there easy answers. Even the most experienced gardeners have plants die for no apparent reason, or suddenly have problems with a tried and true method that they have used for years. Sometimes nature is inconsistent...a plant may bloom like crazy one year, and never perform the same way again. One year we may have a plague of locusts, the next year clouds of butterflies. Knowing this, we realize that any "cure" to a gardening problem won't work 100% of the time; if a plant dies in spite of all your efforts, remember (as you plant something else) that your ability to be flexible is just being exercised.

Most of the information in this book could be applicable to gardens throughout the country, but I have made it a point to address growing conditions on Cape Cod, Nantucket, and Martha's Vineyard within the general information. The excellent drainage (read: sand) that most of us garden in presents special opportunities and challenges, as does the moist, off-the-ocean air.

In addition to the highlighting of local growing conditions and the wisdom of working with nature, you will find two other things stressed again and again throughout this book. They are the importance of: 1) following the directions that come with any product used in the yard and garden, and 2) choosing the right plant for the location. All too often the garden is no different than politics, I'm afraid, and Pogo was right: "We have met the enemy and he is us." If we give our plants the location and growing conditions that they thrive in, and use all products - be they organic fertilizers or pesticides - as they were meant to be used, we solve many problems before they start.

As we give our time and attention to our plants we are rewarded with beautiful flowers, sweet scents, cooling shade, privacy in small backyards, delicious fresh vegetables and fruits, and homes and food for a variety of lovely wildlife. In fact, the rewards of gardening extend beyond the tangible by giving us a place for physical exercise, artistic expression, and spiritual renewal. With all of this to gain, it is no wonder that I have a chronic case of Ron Dier Disease. With all of this to gain, let's hope that it's contagious.

~1~

GARDENING ON THE CAPE AND ISLANDS

GARDENING ON THE
CAPE AND ISLANDS

The love of gardening thrives on Cape Cod and the Islands, and with good reason. We are blessed with a climate that allows a wide variety of plants in our gardens, and the growing conditions are generally hospitable. Our beaches and woodlands provide us with inspiration. Like gardeners everywhere, we celebrate the advantages of planting in our particular area, while at the same time we develop strategies for coping with regional challenges. In this chapter I answer questions about the growing conditions that we appreciate, as well as those we struggle with. Basic gardening information dealing with topics such as fertilizing and composting is also included; when we garden we truly start from the ground up, so it is appropriate that this book should start with the soil and grow from there.

Q. We just moved to Cape Cod, and my neighbors all say that gardening on the Cape and Islands is so *different* than anywhere else. What makes it so unlike other areas?

A. For many people in Southeast Massachusetts, gardening is different because of the sandy soils. You can't just plunk something in the ground and expect it to grow. In addition, the proximity to the ocean means a colder delayed spring and a warmer extended fall. Add to that mix the potential for strong winds, summer drought, and humid off-ocean air, and you have somewhat unique growing conditions.

3

Q. I am going to be planting some shrubs and starting a flower and vegetable garden. What is the most important thing I should know as I start this process?

A. Two words: soil amendments. If ever there was a gardening term that Cape Cod gardeners should know about, it is "soil amendment." It means adding to the soil what is naturally lacking, and for most of us this means organic matter. The organic material we add to our gardens can be homemade compost, composted manure, rotted leaves, seaweed, or peat moss.

Many gardeners on the Cape and Islands have sandy soil; dig down through the few inches of humus on the surface and you hit a beach. Other gardeners in Southeast Massachusetts have clay soils. Both clay and sand need organic matter added to them, but for different reasons. There are also a few locations in our region that have a deep layer of loam, which is the perfect mix of sand, silt, and clay particles. If you garden in such an area please keep your mouth shut about it...the rest of us are deeply jealous! We are consoled only by the thought that adding organic matter is always a good idea, but for clay and sandy soils it is essential.

Clay particles are thin and disk shaped, so they pile up flat sides together, like a stack of pancakes. (Think of a stack of millions, not six.) Because the particles are this shape they can pack together tightly; so tightly that there is little space for air in between the particles. This is why clay soils are so poorly drained. It is also why those wanting to plant a shrub in clay will need a strong back and a pickax. There is little air space in clay so it is *heavy*. Adding organic matter to clay breaks up those tightly stacked disks allowing water to drain down through the soil more quickly. A plant's roots can penetrate such clay more easily when there is a good deal of organic matter worked into it. Compost gives clay soils some breathing room.

Sandy soils need organic matter too but for almost the opposite reason. Sand grains are round or irregularly shaped and do not stick together. There is so much air space between them that water runs right through sandy soils. Organic matter acts like sponge material here, holding onto the water as it rushes by the sand. Water retention alone is reason enough to add it to sandy gardens.

Every gardener wants to conserve our water supply, *and* keep his or her water bill as low as possible, but water isn't the only thing that rushes through sandy soil. The water is only too happy to take nutrients, such as nitrogen, along for the ride. Without organic matter in the soil there is nothing to hold the nutrients in place, and there is no point in adding fertilizer if it is going to wash away before the plant can use it.

The easiest time to amend the soil is when you first prepare your planting beds. Add as much compost (homemade or purchased from your garden center) or composted manure to the bed as you can. Peat moss can be purchased as well, although there is a growing (no pun intended) movement to avoid the use of peat. Peat is a nonrenewable natural resource, and many people, including myself, think that we should take full advantage of the organic materials available to us closer to home before we dig up and transport peat.

Many communities are composting their Christmas trees and such shredded plant refuse as municipal leaves and lawn clippings. Check to see if your town has such compost available. If you buy a load of manure, or have access to someone's stable-cleanings, make sure that you let it sit for a few months (four to six) before adding it onto your established beds. New beds can have fresh manure added to them as long as you let them sit unplanted over a winter to give the manure time to mellow in the bed. (Mulch to discourage weed growth during that time.) Composted seaweed, grass clippings, and leaves are also excellent sources of organic matter. (See the questions on Compost for more information.) No matter what type of organic matter you choose, mix it in as thoroughly and as deeply as you are able, either with a shovel or a power tiller.

Q. My yard is a real sandbox so I always add cow manure or peat when I plant a shrub or perennial. Do I need to add more as time goes on?

A. The good news is that the sand has provided you with excellent drainage. The bad news is that you need to constantly be adding organic matter to the soil. After organic matter is dug into your garden, it continues to break down; in order to continue to reap the benefits of having it in the soil you must continue to replace it. A good general rule is to top-dress gardens and the area around shrubs with two inches of compost or composted manure every year. Yes, I know, that's a lot of compost. Do what you can. If you are mulching around your shrubs and in your flower beds (and I hope that you are), consider putting down a layer of compost before the mulch goes on. As the mulch decays it also adds organic matter to the soil. You can work your way around your yard in the late fall or early spring, laying two inches of compost down and then adding mulch on top of it. An alternative approach is to put amendments down in the fall and your mulch layer down in the spring.

As I read over the last paragraph I realize that the process of soil amendment sounds like a lot of work. All gardening sounds like a great deal of work when the process is written out, but as it's being done it's just part of the process of tending the garden. Well all right ... it *is* work. But taken one job at a time it isn't nearly so overwhelming as the description makes it sound.

A garden is never finished. A gardener will be happy as long as he or she can enjoy the garden just as it is at the present moment, while at the same time planning for the future. Spreading compost is one of the many chances we have to be up-close-and-personal with the garden; while working with the plants and soil we can enjoy the garden as we currently find it. Continuing the amendment of the soil is the investment in the garden's future.

Q. If my soil seems good, why do I need to continually add soil amendments? Can't I just fertilize?

A. Regular additions of organic matter are not only important because what is in the soil breaks down over time, but also because such organic materials are vital to the host of microorganisms that make a healthy soil community. There are many beneficial fungi and bacteria that help plants grow; some break down organic materials so that it gets incorporated in the soil, some help the roots of plants absorb nutrients, and others keep destructive pathogens away by out-competing them in the environment. This living soil community is as important to plants as the nutrients in fertilizers.

Compost or composted cow manure can be spread over the surface of established perennial gardens and around shrubs and trees.

A two-inch layer is perfect. Most perennials won't mind if some of the compost is put over the crown of the plant, but in general you should try to spread it thinly over the clump itself.

Q. The plants in my garden seem to dry up so quickly. Several bushes and perennials that I planted last year died. My soil is very sandy. Could this be the problem?

A. Those who have sandy soil learn that the rapid loss of water is the "flip side" of good drainage. We want good drainage, but the water runs right through the sand. Amending your soil with lots of organic matter will help. A layer of mulch will also help keep the soil moist. Of equal importance is your awareness of how much rain has fallen in the recent past. Many times people forget that if it hasn't rained in a week or so they may need to water the plants. This is especially true of newly planted shrubs, trees, and perennials. Older shrubs and trees will also need a good *long* soaking if there has been a two-week period with no rain, especially if it has been hot and sunny. It may sound overly obvious to say "be aware of how much rain has fallen," but it's surprising how quickly we can forget what the weather was like just eight or nine days ago. It is also easy to be fooled by a short heavy downpour; we think that a great deal of rain has fallen because we remember it *pouring*, but in truth that downpour may have just moistened the surface of the ground, leaving the plants thirsty. Placing a rain gauge in an open part of the garden, and checking it regularly, is an easy way to be accurate about the amount of moisture a garden has received.

How much rain is enough? Just over an inch of rain per week, preferably in one 24 hour period, is considered sufficient for plants growing in good soils. Plants in sandy soils may need an additional soaking mid-week if the temperatures have been above 80 degrees and it has been sunny.

Q. How can I make the compost I need to amend my soil?

A. A compost pile is nothing more than a pile of organic matter, contained or not. You can either construct a bin or purchase one; compost bins are for sale at most garden centers, and some towns make them available to town residents for a small fee. There are also a variety of whiz-bang models available from catalogs, most of which are so expensive that I think that they should *cook* our dinner as well as compost the remains! Compost can be made in open piles on the ground, but contained piles make it possible to expose more of what you are composting to the air, as well keep any foraging wild life out.

All organic material that you add to the compost pile eventually breaks down, but some materials break down more quickly than others, and certain conditions and practices speed it along. The ideal compost pile needs a combination of moisture and oxygen along with organic materials high in both nitrogen and carbon.

The moisture comes from the rain or your garden hose. Oxygen comes from the air, but if the pile is deep and undisturbed it won't get enough oxygen to the center; mixing it up with a pitch fork, or turning a tumbler-style bin, are ways to get oxygen to where it's needed. Nitrogen is supplied every time you put something fresh and green into the compost heap. Grass clippings, kitchen waste, and fresh manure all supply nitrogen. Dead brown things like leaves and sticks are mostly carbon, and nitrogen is needed to break these down.

Basically, we are looking for a balance of materials high in nitrogen (fresh greens) and those high in carbon (dried browns) when filling a compost pile. If your compost pile is filled with "carbons," you will need to add green plant material, kitchen waste, or some blood meal to supply the nitrogen necessary to get it cooking. If the pile is composed of mostly fresh greens or kitchen scraps, it is likely to smell.

Q. Composting seems so complicated to me. Is there a simple way of doing it?

A. I guess you could say about composting the same thing that people have long said about housework...that it expands to fit the time available. If you have the time and the interest you can run all your leaves and sticks through the shredder, and grind all food scraps in the blender to speed the breakdown. You can layer the pile with alternating layers of grass clippings and kitchen waste (for nitrogen) and leaves and sticks (carbon). The pile can be watered and turned regularly in order to speed things along. But none of these steps are absolutely necessary. How much time and energy you want to invest in your compost is up to you.

One of the easiest and most sensible methods I've seen for composting was at Connie LeClair's garden in East Orleans. Connie is a retired Landscape Designer and she and her husband maintain extensive gardens. Her method of composting starts with a bin that is four feet deep, twelve feet wide, and four feet tall. She explained that she mentally divides the bin into thirds, and always adds new material to the left side. When that side starts looking full she moves it with a pitchfork to the middle "third," and when that area gets full she moves it to the right side of the bin. She is always putting new material in the left side, letting it compost in the middle, and taking it out of the right. The movement from section to section keeps the pile turned, and by the time it reaches the section on the right it is about "cooked." This method may not be the fastest or the hottest method of composting but it is simple and very easy to manage for the average home gardener.

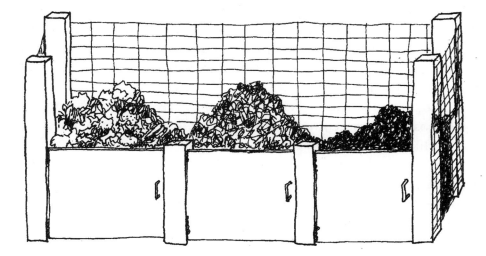

NEW MATERIAL   COMPOSTING   FINISHED COMPOST

Q. Can I put *any* organic material in my compost?

A. The short answer to this question is "almost." Grass clippings, leaves, small branches, and other yard waste are all fine as are plants cleared from your garden. The exceptions are any plant material that has a fungal problem such as the Phlox leaves with mildew, or Roses with blackspot, and any weed or flowering plants that set seeds. Most home compost piles are not hot enough to destroy seeds, so those that readily germinate will do so when the compost is spread. Most gardeners have had the experience of putting the spent Cleome plants in the compost only to see hundreds of Cleome sprout where the compost was spread the next year. I have spent time weeding tomato seedlings from my shrub border for the same reason.

The organic waste from your kitchen can go into the pile with the exception of any meat, cheese, and fish. Meat and fish attract animals to your compost and cause the pile to smell. Fruit peels, vegetables, eggshells, and bread crusts are all fine. You can also throw in that moldy leftover pasta or that forgotten piece of tofu from the back of the fridge. Coffee grounds and tea leaves are excellent compost material, as are the paper filters and tea bags.

Manure from cows, horses and chickens can go into your compost but *don't* add dog poop or the contents from your cat's litter box. You *can* add the hair that you clip or brush from your pet, however, as well as the hair you cut from your children's heads. Those who live near the sea have an excellent source of compost material if they are willing to gather seaweed and eel grass. Sawdust from the workshop is good compost material as are any potted plants that have died. (Add the dirt too.)

Packing materials, such as excelsior, are sometimes good for composting. Some companies are using a new packing material that *looks* like those horrible Styrofoam packaging peanuts, but it actually is made of cellulose or cornstarch. To tell if you've gotten one of the bio-degradable types just hold one under the faucet. If it dissolves in the water it is the newer type and you can dump them in your compost. If it is the older type it won't dissolve and you'll need to recycle it. Note: I have received some packages recently that have the old and new types mixed together, inevitable, I suppose, now that people are making an effort to recycle the stuff. Look at yours closely to make sure it is all the same before dumping it into your compost bin!

Q. I have many oak trees, and rake up lots of oak leaves every fall. Last fall I put them into a compost pile, but they are still sitting there this spring. When will they break down?

A. Oak leaves, being high in carbon, need to be composted with something high in nitrogen if you want them to decompose quickly. The addition of grass clippings, kitchen waste, or blood meal will help the leaves break down. Most home compost piles aren't very active over the winter anyway, because it is too cold. Composting is most rapid when the day and night temperatures are warm, so even with added sources of nitrogen, your leaves may not do much until late spring. Sometimes leaves are slow to decompose because their flat shape allows them to get pressed into a flat, wet mat. When this happens it keeps out the oxygen necessary for decomposition. Chopping the leaves up before adding them to the compost is one way to avoid the matting, thereby speeding the composting process. Leaves can be raked into a thick layer on the lawn, and run over two or three times with a lawn-mower to shred them. Periodic movement of the pile, or turning it with a pitchfork will also give it the air that it needs.

Products are available at garden centers to help speed the composting process, but you might consider that complete decomposition is not really necessary. Half-rotted leaves, called "leaf mold," are as valuable for the garden as fully finished compost.

I have constructed a large bin on my property just to hold leaves. I try not to put other plant material in that bin, and after it is filled I don't turn it, make additions, or add water. In the fall, shortly before the leaves fall again, I empty that leaf-bin and put its contents on the garden. Although the outer layer of leaves are still whole and crispy, the inner part of the pile is half-composted, black leaf mold that is *gold* for the garden.

● ● ●

Q. How do I know when my compost is ready to be used?

A. Finished compost resembles dark soil, but frankly, most home-made compost is not as homogeneous as that. Most compost has a mix of black, crumbly material, items half-rotted but still recognizable, and the occasional not-composted peach pit or eggshell. Not to worry. Partly finished compost is actually better for the garden than the fully finished product, because it is teaming with all the microorganisms that break organic matter down, and these microorganisms are good for the soil. So, there is no need to wait until your compost looks fully finished.

Q. I add compost to my garden; do I still need to fertilize?

A. The answer to this question partly depends on what has been put into the compost pile, and what your soil is like. A compost pile heavy in manure will contain more nutrients than one made completely of vegetable matter. In general, however, compost is not fertilizer. Compost and composted cow manure have some nutrients but the primary reason for adding it to your soil is because you want the organic matter and the microorganisms that come with it. Research shows compost to be a good source of many beneficial microorganisms that help keep pathogens (the bad guys) in check. The compost is also a veritable worm farm, so when you spread compost onto your garden you are adding many of those small squiggly workers to your soil. I would plan to continue to fertilize your plants even though you add compost, particularly if your soil is naturally sandy. There are many slow-release, organic fertilizers on the market now, and although you shouldn't overdo the use of fertilizers, a yearly application of both fertilizer and compost will help keep your garden growing. If you somehow think you can only manage to either fertilize or add compost, add the compost.

Q. Do I need to buy a different fertilizer for the shrubs, flowers, vegetables, and lawn?

A. The labeling of fertilizers as shrub food, flower power, or lawn magic is partly the result of research into individual plants' needs for nutrients, and partly a matter of marketing. Fertilizers are labeled and promoted in this matter partly for the ease of the customers, and partly to sell more packages of fertilizer. A general discussion of fertilizers is in order.

Plants require seventeen nutrient elements for growth. Of these, the main three are nitrogen, phosphorus, and potassium. Magnesium, calcium, and sulfur are secondary elements, and boron, chlorine, cobalt, copper, iron, manganese, molybdenum, and zinc are the trace elements. Plants also need carbon, hydrogen, and oxygen, but fortunately these are supplied by the air and water, so there are at least three that you don't have to worry about! Nutrients must be present in balanced proportions for healthy plant growth, so buying large quantities of these elements and dumping them around your plants may make them less healthy, not more. The primary three (nitrogen, phosphorus, and potassium) are the nutrient elements of concern to most gardeners, and most fertilizers are a combination of these.

In a nutshell, nitrogen encourages vegetative growth, stimulating leaf production. Phosphorus promotes stem and root growth, as well as stimulating the formation of flowers and fruit. Potassium encourages plant vigor and helps the phosphorus to do its job. (Potassium is sometimes called potash.) Fertilizers that have all three of these elements -nitrogen, phosphorus, and potassium- are called "complete" fertilizers.

The three numbers on a fertilizer package tell you the ratio of these three elements to each other. The first number tells you the percentage of nitrogen, the second of phosphorus, and the third potassium. A label that says 5-10-5, for example, has twice as much phosphorus as nitrogen and potassium. A label that reads 10-0-0 is all nitrogen with none of the other two. If you buy a 10-10-10 fertilizer there are equal amounts of the three. A 10-10-10 fertilizer is the same as one labeled 1-1-1, only it is ten times more concentrated. You would need to use more of a 1-1-1 fertilizer to get the same effect as a 10-10-10. Is it better to buy a 1-1-1 (if such a product exists) or a 10-10-10 or even a 20-20-20 fertilizer? If the product is used according to directions you will be putting more or less the same amount of nutrients onto your plants, but you will be using more of the 1-1-1 fertilizer than the other two. Practically speaking, what does this mean? If the fertilizer you have chosen is a concentrate that gets mixed with water, you will be mixing more of it into the water if you use a fertilizer with lower percentages.

It is very important to use fertilizers according to directions. More is *not* better! If you have chosen a concentrated powder that needs to be mixed with water, be sure to do this according to directions. Follow the product's recommendations for the type of plant being fertilized as well. Products that are targeted at plants that flower or produce fruit often have higher levels of phosphorus than of nitrogen and potassium. Lawn fertilizers, however, have a higher percentage of nitrogen. It wouldn't be smart to use a fertilizer high in nitrogen on your vegetables or flowers, because this would stimulate the plant to grow a lot of leaves but not much else.

It is wise to buy a lawn fertilizer that is made for the lawn. There is a wide range of choices, from organic to chemical, from fertilizers to use in the spring to those made to be applied in the fall. There are products that have weed inhibitors or insecticides mixed with the fertilizer, but they shouldn't be used unless they are actually needed. Remember that every time you use an insecticide, many bugs are killed. Some of those bugs aren't pests but in fact are our allies, feeding on those insects that *are* pests. When you apply an insecticide you are upsetting the balance that exists and therefore may be making more problems for yourself in the long run. Applying a pesticide if you don't have an insect problem is rather like going in for chemotherapy even though you don't have cancer. If it ain't broke...

A general fertilizer such as a 10-10-10 is fine to use on shrubs, trees, or flower beds, especially in the spring. Choosing a general fertilizer that has a higher percentage of phosphorus and potassium is also acceptable, especially if you are using it on flowering plants. Remember that balance is important, so don't go overboard. Adding too much of anything will upset something else.

If you are concerned that your plants are not doing well, and you want to know if you are under-fertilizing or over-fertilizing, it would be wise to invest in a soil test. (See Chapter 8 for information about sending your soil to be tested.) A soil test can also tell you if your soil needs any of the micro-nutrients as well. Sandy, acidic soils are sometimes short of calcium, magnesium, or iron.

Q. Do I need to dig the fertilizer into the soil in my flowerbed, or apply it differently around shrubs and trees?

A. If it is possible to dig the fertilizer in without disturbing nearby roots then it's fine do so, but it isn't really necessary. Fertilizer can be spread onto the surface of the soil and then watered in well. (Concentrates made to be mixed with water should be diluted with water as directed.) When applying fertilizer to perennial beds, be sure not to scatter it next to the stems or onto the crowns of plants; apply it to the soil a few inches away from the stems.

Fertilizers can be put on the soil surface under shrubs and trees in the same manner, spreading it on the soil surface under the drip line, keeping it away from the stems and watering it in well. The drip line is the area under the foliage of a plant. Think of the place where the rain that drips off of the outer leaves will fall on the ground.

Older trees with large root systems, and those with grass or plants under them, will benefit from applying the fertilizer into holes. This takes the fertilizer past competing plants and places it in the area where the trees' roots can reach it. The holes needn't be too deep ... six to eight inches is fine. (The use of a "deep root" feeder is unnecessary since 90% of a tree's feeder roots are within the top twelve inches of the soil.) Using a crowbar, auger, or metal pipe, make several holes under and around the drip line of the tree. Space the holes two or three feet apart, starting a foot or two from the trunk of the tree. After putting the fertilizer in the holes, fill them with water a few times, allowing it to soak in before filling the holes with topsoil or compost.

Q. Is organic fertilizer better than chemical fertilizer?

A. I am tempted to answer that it depends on who you ask, but since you've asked me I'll tell you what I think. There has been some discussion about synthetic fertilizers being toxic to soil microorganisms, but if used properly (repeat after me, *read and follow the directions*) synthetic fertilizers are not harmful to these microorganisms. Fertilizers that are made from plant and animal sources are generally not as concentrated, so it is less likely that they will burn the roots of your plants. An added benefit of organics, aside from their nutrients, is that they improve soil structure; this enhances the ability of soils to hold onto nutrients and water. Organic fertilizers also tend to be slower to release their nutrients, so they aren't a quick fix. (The nitrogen in fish meal and emulsion, as well as in bloodmeal, is the most immediately available organic nutrient.) Organics are in for the long haul, which is where you want them to be. Some, such as liquid seaweed, also contain micro-nutrients. I believe that a wise gardener uses organic fertilizer whenever possible, but if a quick shot of liquid is needed to give a plant a boost I am not a complete purest about it. My garden shed contains an organic granular fertilizer, bottles of fish fertilizer and seaweed extract, and a foliar feed made of fermented salmon. It also contains two or three tubs of various brands of concentrated inorganic fertilizers, one of them used only on the orchids. I use the liquid synthetic fertilizers mainly on my potted plants and annuals, and the organics on the shrubs, trees, and perennial beds. I also use an organic lawn fertilizer.

If you want to use organic nutrients but desire the convenience of a "complete" fertilizer, you will find several products available at your local garden center. The packages will be labeled with the same three numbers that are on all fertilizer products. If used on a regular basis according to directions they will provide a constant source of nutrients to your plants.

Q. How does too much fertilizer burn my plants?

A. If you are tempted to make your fertilizer mix more concentrated than the directions advise, just remember a time when you took a bite of food that had too much red pepper in it. "Water! I'm burning up!" you may have cried. You weren't really burning up, but you did need water to dilute the effects of all that red pepper. Too much fertilizer does not actually burn the plants, but it dries up the root cells, which prevents them from getting the water that they need.

Plants are constantly taking up water which moves from the soil into the cells of the root hairs. Small amounts of nutrients travel along in the water, but it is mainly water that is taken into the plant.

If too much fertilizer is mixed into the water those root cells get fertilizer not water, which causes them to dry up; if the roots are dried the plant can't support all the leaves on top, so they become parched too. For this reason it is better not to fertilize a thirsty plant. If you think that your plant could use a shot of nutrients, water it well first. You can give it the fertilizer after it has had an hour or two to absorb some water, and always use at the recommended rate. Too much is worse than none at all.

Q. My property looks out onto the ocean and I want to plant some new shrubs and trees. Are there some that will do better than others?

A. There are plants that are known to be tolerant of seaside conditions. Although it is stretching it to say that they thrive in windy salt spray, they are at least good-natured about it. There is a list of plants recommended for seaside plantings in Chapter 9, and two books on the subject are listed in the bibliography. I encourage you to do some on-the-spot research as well.

When you drive around the area or are visiting your neighbors begin to notice what plants are thriving in other coastal plantings. This is also an opportunity to see what various plants look like when they are established and of mature size.

All oceanfront conditions are not the same however, and before you choose plants and go to the trouble and expense of planting them it would be worthwhile for you to notice what the specific characteristics of your location are. Is the salt spray an occasional condition or is there often saltwater in the wind. (Notice if your windows have traces of salt on them that need to be washed off frequently.) Is the wind always blowing or are existing trees, rocks, or buildings providing shelter? Remember that the wind will contribute to drying, so be sure that you can keep new plantings watered; if you will not be there to monitor the watering in the future you will do well to choose drought-resistant plants. Hydrangeas, for example, will tolerate some wind and salt spray but even established plants need watering if there is a period of drought.

Finally, notice what plants are already there. Which ones are doing well and which plants are just staying alive through sheer stubbornness? If all the trees on your property are short, for example, it may be that a tree that gets very tall will not survive the high winds. Looking at what is already thriving will give you a clue to what new plants will flourish.

Q. I live on the water in a very windy location. Is it possible for me to have a perennial garden?

A. Success depends on choosing your site and plants carefully. Make note of plants that are listed as both tough and tolerant of seaside conditions. (List in Chapter 9.) Plants with fragile stems, such as delphiniums, or high, top-heavy plants such as the tall Oriental lilies, would *not* be good choices. Even sturdy plants will be better off if you are able to plant them in a sheltered location. Consider locating your garden behind or next to a building, or plant a low shrub border in between the garden and the water. A shrub border will provide a windbreak as well as a pleasing background for the perennials. If you don't want to plant shrubs, consider a sunken garden, with stone walls. A garden that is three or four feet down will provide shelter for the plants and create a charming garden "room." (If you decide to go to the trouble and considerable expense of digging a sunken garden, be sure to dig out an extra foot or two so that the soil can be amended with manure and topsoil bringing it back up to the desired level.) Remember that without any shelter even tough, tolerant plants may be smaller than normal if they are exposed to constant winds. Next time you are at the beach notice the Rosa rugosa that grow there. You will probably see that the ones closest to the water that have no shelter are smaller than the ones that grow in a place where they get a break from the wind.

Q. I don't have oceanfront property but it seems to me that the growing conditions here are different than where I used to live in southwestern Massachusetts. Does the ocean effect the growing conditions even though I am over a mile away?

A. Being surrounded by the ocean effects this area's growing conditions in two primary ways; the temperature of the ocean cools and warms the spring and fall air temperatures respectively, and the general level of humidity is increased. The long and the short of it is that we have cool springs, warm falls, and it's party time for the fungi practically all year long.

Someone once said to me "On Cape Cod we have January, February, March, March, March, June." This explains the spring weather in a nutshell, although many of those "March" days are really quite lovely. The cold ocean temperatures keep this area cool in the spring, so plants are sometimes slower to break dormancy here than in other areas of the Northeast. We have to wait longer for the soil to warm up, which is good to know if you are planting seeds that need warmth to germinate. It is also worth remembering that the cool air temperatures, that we will bless in July while Boston is sweltering, will keep our heat-loving tomato and basil plants from springing to life early in the summer. Some say that in this area plants act like true New Englanders...they get to where they need to be, but it takes them a bit longer to warm up.

In the fall the ocean, now warmed from the summer, keeps our temperatures above freezing after most areas in the Northeast have had several heavy frosts. So if we have three months of March early in the year we also have three months of September later on. Many cold-hardy annuals and perennials will look good into December, and our soil may not freeze until after New Year's! This is good news for those who buy bulbs in September but don't get around to planting them until after Thanksgiving.

A multitude of fungi thrive in both the cool moist air of spring, and the warm moist summer and fall air; some of these fungi cause assorted leaf spots and other problems for plants and the people trying to grow them. It is worthwhile, though, to remind ourselves that there are many *beneficial* fungi about as well. The fungi that we consider our garden allies attack or inhibit the growth of many harmful insects and other fungi. Because we want these beneficial fungi to thrive, it is wise not to over-use fungicides, since such products kill the good guys along with the bad. I would advise all gardeners in this area to encourage the "good fungi" by amending the soil with compost and other organic matter, and not treat leaf spots and other "bad fungi" with fungicides unless you really need to. More about controlling fungi in Chapter 7.

• • •

Q. I understand that the humid air contributes to plant diseases. Isn't there anything I can do to prevent them?

A. We are not completely helpless in our pursuit of healthy plants. Yes, the level of humidity helps fungus to thrive and plants in this area may be more prone to leaf spots and mildew than they are in other areas. Knowing how to best water your garden, however, can help keep such problems to a minimum.

Keep the leaves of your plants as dry as possible. This does not mean that you need to run outside with your hair dryer after it rains. It does mean that you should think about how and when you water your plants when it *doesn't* rain. Using soaker hoses to water your flowers, vegetables, and shrubs enables you to water the ground around your plants without getting the leaves wet. If you must use a sprinkler, or if you have an in-ground sprinkler system, be sure to water in the morning so that the sun and wind will dry the leaves quickly, and water deeply, but less often. Watering in the evening leaves moisture on the plants for an extended amount of time, giving fungi a longer period of time to get established, and most plants do not respond well to having their foliage hit with water on a frequent basis.

Most people find hand watering plants to be a restful activity, but for more than a plant or two it is really the worst way to water. Squirting the hose at a plant not only wets the leaves, but unless you are the most patient of individuals with lots of time to spend watering, you probably don't wet the soil very far down. Not only does the plant soak up this small amount of water quickly, but it also evaporates from the soil surface within a short amount of time. It then becomes necessary to water and wet the leaves again the next day. If you turn on a soaker hose or a sprinkler you can leave it on for a longer period of time, giving the plants enough water to satisfy them for a few days in normal weather, and for at least three or four days in hot, sunny weather. Those who miss being able to stand and stare at the garden while watering should give themselves permission to just stand and look at the garden. What has all this work been for if not your own pleasure? Perhaps a stroll through the garden while the soaker hoses are running will be just as relaxing as watering with the garden hose.

Q. Other than the watering, is there anything else I should be doing to discourage fungi?

A. The avoidance of fungal problems begins when a plant is purchased. Those wanting a low maintenance garden should select disease resistant cultivars whenever possible. A call to the Master Gardeners Hotline will help you determine if the plant being considered is prone to fungal problems, or is relatively impervious to diseases and pests.

Promptly cleaning up debris in the garden will be helpful as well. Leaves that are infected with a fungus fall to the ground, taking the fungus along for the ride. If left where it has fallen, the fungus will remain conveniently located (from the fungus' point of view), and ready to infect next year's plants. If you notice a plant that has leaf spot or mildew be sure to clean up all fallen leaves and dead plant material throughout the growing season. When cutting these plants down in the fall, destroy the cut stems and leaves. *Don't* put this infected plant material in your compost; throw it out, or put it in a separate brush pile. This is one time when recycling *isn't* a good idea!

Q. I have heard that the soil in this area is acidic. Is this true?

A. In general it is true that the soil on the Cape and Islands tends to be acidic. But it may or may *not* be true for your garden. Past additions of lime, or an alkaline water supply may have changed the pH level over time. The only way to know if your soil is acidic or not is to have it tested. Sometimes people assume that the soil is acidic and therefore needs lime, so they go ahead and add limestone every year. They may be doing it for nothing, however, if they don't know for sure that the soil is too acid for what they want to grow. Some plants, such as azaleas, holly, and blueberries like an acid soil. Others want to be growing in a more neutral environment.

The Cooperative Extension Service tests soil samples for a small fee. Be sure to provide them with samples from each distinctly different area you are planting in, such as the shrub border, perennial bed, or vegetable garden. Once you have decided which areas need to be tested, take a small amount of soil from three or four places in that area and mix them together. The samples should be taken from the dirt that is 4 to 6 inches under the surface since this is the area where the plant roots are growing. Mixing several of these samples together will give you an average reading for the entire bed. Be sure to note on each sample where the soil came from or what is growing in that area. Knowing what plants are being grown in the sampled area will enable those who test the soil to make the appropriate suggestion about needed treatment.

Q. What is wrong with having acidic soil? Do I *have* to add lime?

A. There is nothing wrong with acidic soil if the plants that you are growing in that soil like their soil on the acid side. Some plants, such as holly, azaleas, and blueberries, prefer acid soil; other plants will tolerate it. For many plants, however, acid soil means that the basic elements required for growth are less available to the plant when the soil is too acidic. This will mean that the plant will not grow as well, and any fertilizer that is put down won't be as beneficial to the plants as it could be. Acid soils are often deficient in calcium and magnesium as well. It's a good idea to have your soil tested every other year, and add lime only if needed, and according to the recommendations.

Q. What are planting zones and which one are we in?

A. Planting zones have been developed by mapping the country according to the average minimum temperature. Plants are classified as to which zone they will be hardy in. Most parts of Cape Cod and the Islands are in a cold zone 7, which is any area of the country that has an average minimum temperature of 0 to 10 degrees. Some are in zone 6, which is any area where the minimum temperature is between 10 degrees below zero and 0 degrees. A plant that will live through a winter when the temperature dips down to 0° could be a zone 6 or 7 plant. As a rule, plants that are hardy in colder zones will be hardy here. Gaura, for example, is a perennial that is hardy in zone 6, which is colder than zone 7, so I can grow gaura here on Cape Cod. (The lower the number of the planting zone, the lower the average minimum temperature.) I could not grow gaura where I used to live in the Berkshires (zone

5), or where I grew up in Wisconsin (zone 3...frigid).

Keep in mind that the minimum temperatures are *averages*. In a severely cold winter the temperature may dip below the average minimum, and some plants could die or suffer quite a bit of dieback. If the below average temperatures happen when there is no snow cover to insulate the plants it can be especially damaging. Individual plants may also be, for whatever reason, a bit more or less hardy than others of the same type. In an especially cold winter you might even lose zone 6 plants.

Keep in mind that just because a plant is rated as being hardy in a particular planting zone, it does not mean this plant won't die. Hardiness is not just a matter of surviving the cold; soil drainage, exposure to wind, and rapid variations in temperatures can also kill plants.

Should you ever gamble and plant a zone 8 plant? Perhaps, if it's a special plant. If it's something you love and you have a sheltered spot, why not give it a try? Just don't plant twenty of them, and know that come spring it may not return. If the perennial is one that blooms the first year, it can be grown as an annual. As gardeners we get used to having even hardy plants disappear for a variety of reasons. When this happens we replace the plants we love, or happily use the space to try something new.

Q. When is it safe to plant annuals outside in the spring?

A. You're going to hate this, I know, but the safest time to plant tender annuals on the Cape and Islands is after Memorial Day. We are all anxious to get into our gardens long before this. Warm days in early May call us outside, and we are further tempted by the annuals that are on display at garden centers and stores as early as mid-April. It may be possible to get away with planting things earlier, and for the past few years we have had warm temperatures in May, making early planting possible.

Planting a six-pack or two might be worth trying, if only for the pleasure of digging around in the garden on an especially warm spring day. If you want to be relatively sure that what you've planted won't have to be replaced, wait until close to May 30th. (I say *relatively sure* because it is possible, although not likely, to have a frost in early June ... it has happened.) Some annuals are more cold-hardy than others. Pansies and Johnny jump-ups will survive a few light frosts, as will snapdragons and alyssum. You can always put in your lettuce, peas, and spinach if you are dying to get into the vegetable garden. Console yourself with the knowledge that even if you plant them early, the annuals that want warmth to grow will only sit there shivering until after Memorial Day anyway, so what's the rush?

Q. What about shrubs and perennials; do they need to be planted after Memorial Day too?

A. The short answer to this question is no, you don't have to wait until after Memorial day to plant shrubs or perennials. But you *know* that it isn't as simple as that. The only complication in planting shrubs or perennials in April or May is that the place where you buy the plants may have gotten them from a grower that is in a warmer climate than ours. If that is the case it is likely that the plants are further along in their development than the plants in this region are. While it may be tempting to buy an azalea that is in full bloom a month ahead of time, if there is a hard frost the leaves and blossoms may be killed. The same is true for perennials. If the pots of plants at your garden center are further along than the same plants are in local gardens, be wary of planting them too early. If you want to go ahead and buy them, it might be wise to keep them outside, still in their pots, until mid-May. This way you can bring them into the garage if the forecast is for frost.

Q. Why is it a good idea to mulch my garden?

A. Mulch holds the moisture in the soil and keeps weed seeds from germinating; what could be better? Well, if you use an *organic* mulch it *does* get better. Mulch that is organic slowly breaks down, adding that organic matter to the soil. A garden that is mulched needs watering less often and grows fewer weeds. Mulching also provides a barrier between the dirt and the plants, making it just a bit more difficult for fungus to travel from dirt to plant when the rain splashes down. Mulching your vegetable bed is one way to slow the spread of fungi, such as early blight on tomatoes.

Q. I've heard that mulch robs plants of nitrogen and brings slugs. Is this true?

A. While it is true that organic mulches use nitrogen as they break down, studies show that mulches that lie on the surface of the soil get this nitrogen from the atmosphere. If large chunks of this organic matter are turned into the soil, however, then the nitrogen that is needed for decomposition is taken from the soil. So, if you are applying the mulch to the surface of your soil you don't have to worry. But if you are turning that mulch under the soil you can add an organic source of nitrogen such as blood meal, alfalfa, or cottonseed meal as you mix the mulch down into the dirt.

Mulching your garden does not bring slugs, but the mulch may provide places for the slugs to hide. This is especially true of mulch that may include larger pieces of the mulch material; this provides cool, damp places for slugs to escape the hot sun. Slugs will find places to sleep the day away even if you don't mulch. There is always a fallen leaf, bit of rock, or mossy flowerpot ready to shelter a slug or two. When you mulch your garden you aren't providing anything that the slugs can't find elsewhere. In fact, if you have a slug problem you can lay slug shelters (traps) for them to crawl under. Large leaves such as cabbage leaves, grapefruit rinds, or small smooth rocks and boards work well. You can pick up these traps during the day and dispose of the slugs. (Other methods of repelling slugs are discussed in Chapter 7.) Although slugs are often more of a problem on certain plants such as hostas, lupines, and ornamental kale, I wouldn't let the fear of slugs prevent you from mulching your garden.

Q. Do I need to buy wood chips to mulch?

A. There are several materials that make good mulch. The following is a list of some of the most common mulches used:

SHREDDED BARK OR WOOD CHIPS
Bark mulch can be bought by the cubic yard from most garden centers as well as purchased in large bags. Some towns provide mixed chipped wood at the local transfer station; check to see if your town

has this available. The finer shredded bark is most appropriate for flower beds and general around-the-house landscaping. Larger wood chips are also available but these are less effective at keeping the water in and weeds out. If you prefer the looks of larger wood chips it would be wise to lay newspapers or some shredded bark underneath the large sized chips.

NEWSPAPERS

This is a good mulch to use under a layer of wood chips or bark mulch. It is definitely the mulch of choice if you need to suppress weeds that are already growing. The wood or bark is necessary to hold the papers in place and to hide their less than attractive appearance. Some people wonder if the ink will add a toxic substance to the soil, but this is not a problem. Open several sheets to their full size and stack a bunch of them together. Wet them with a hose right away so that they don't blow away before you get them covered with bark. Lay down one wet stack after another (with their edges overlapping) until the area you want mulched is covered. If you are mulching a large area you will want to stop and add bark mulch every six packets of papers or so. That way if the phone rings and you get distracted, the piles that you have just laid down won't dry up and blow into your neighbor's yard.

HAY OR STRAW

Offered for sale and sometimes available for free, hay is great mulch for the vegetable garden. It can also be good for paths in the garden. Sheila Garry, a landscaper/garden designer in North Eastham used course yellow straw to mulch the paths in her country garden. The look of the brick edged flower beds with the yellow straw between the bricks was charming. Salt marsh hay is available in coastal areas; it is harvested and baled, then sold at garden centers. Salt marsh hay is more expensive than other types of baled straw or hay, and is best used as a protective, winter mulch. (More about this later.)

COCOA HULLS

This handsome mulch, available in large bags at garden centers, is fine in texture and a lovely dark brown color. The main disadvantage of cocoa hulls is the price, but if you are mulching a small bed and want something especially attractive, it may be worth the expense. Be sure to spread cocoa hulls on a calm day, and sprinkle them lightly with water to hold them down as they get settled. Because they are so lightweight, they can blow away if used in an exposed location. These hulls should also be spread thinly, as a thick layer tends to get moldy, and moldy cocoa hulls smell *TERRIBLE!* I used cocoa hulls over a bed of freshly planted tulip bulbs one damp October day and was delighted to discover that they smell like a cup of hot chocolate when first laid down. Cocoa hulls make a great mulch for window boxes and outdoor potted plants.

Buckwheat Hulls

Similar to cocoa hulls, but a bit less expensive, buckwheat hulls are small, lightweight, and an attractive gray/brown color. Best used in sheltered locations so that they are less likely to blow away.

Pine Needles

If you have many pine trees you have access to a great, free supply of mulch. Pine needles are lightweight and attractive. They will *not* cause the soil to become extremely acid. They make good mulch around plants such as strawberries because they quickly drain the water away from the berries that rest on top of the needles.

Seaweed

Those with easy access to seaweed or eel grass have a source of excellent mulch material. You need to be willing to haul it home in a large bucket or tub. The salt content is not a problem, but if it makes you feel better you can give it a quick squirt with the hose to rinse it off. It is also helpful if you think the various shells and driftwood bits that invariably come attached are charming ... perhaps mulching with seaweed put the "silver bells and cockle shells" in Mary Mary's garden. Most people find that although seaweed is an excellent soil amendment, it is a messy looking mulch.

Shredded Leaves and Grass Clippings

Most home gardeners have a ready supply of mulch in the form of leaves and grass clippings. The grass clippings must be dry before placing them on the garden, unless you are willing to spread them in a very thin layer so that the heat that is generated from thick layers won't harm your plants. If you have clover or weeds in your lawn you will transfer the seeds from these plants to your beds. Grass clippings are probably best used in vegetable gardens, or partially broken down in compost piles before used as a mulch.

Leaves can't be used right off the rake; whole leaves blow away when dry and pack down into a heavy mat when wet. It is best to chop them with a shredder or the lawn mower before using them as mulch. Letting them break down for a year in a compost pile will turn them into a good mulch or soil amendment.

PLASTIC

Black plastic is available in rolls to use as mulch in vegetable gardens. Stones, heavy branches, or wire pins must be used to keep the plastic from blowing away. The plastic will keep the rainwater from getting to the soil, just as it prevents moisture from evaporating out. Laying down soaker hoses before you put down the plastic becomes the most sensible way to water. The advantage to plastic is that it is effective, easily bought, and quickly laid down. Unfortunately it looks like, well, *plastic*. Additionally, it does not add organic matter to the soil, and it becomes just one more item to send to the landfill when you can no longer use it as mulch.

Q. I have some peat left over from planting my roses. Can I use that as mulch in the flower beds?

A. Peat is fine organic matter for amending the soil, but it does not make good mulch. When mixed with your soil and other compost, peat helps keep the soil moist; when spread by itself on the soil surface, however, peat actually repels water. It compacts to form a sheet that the rain slides off of, leaving the dirt underneath dry and the plants thirsty. If you have used peat for mulch, it may look damp after watering, but digging down an inch or so reveals soil that is bone dry. Peat that has already been spread on top of a bed can either be raked off or gently worked into the soil, taking care not to disturb the roots of established plants when turning it under.

• • •

Q. Is it true that I shouldn't put the mulch right up next to the stems of my plants?

A. Yes, this is true. I cringe when I see that some well-meaning soul has piled a mound of shredded bark eight inches up the stems of a shrub or the trunk of a tree. Not only is this "volcano mulching" ugly, but it isn't good for the plants. Piling the mulch so close to a plant invites diseases and insects, not to mention small rodents. Mulch around the stems keeps that area too damp; plants benefit from mulch, but they want a bit of breathing room. Leave a few inches of clear space between the mulch and the tree trunk or the shrub's stems. A smaller space will do around flowers and vegetables.

Q. I've read that you should remove your mulch in the spring, but also put mulch down for the growing season. Which is correct?

A. The type of mulch that you remove after winter has ended is a different type of mulch, put on gardens for a different purpose. The mulches that I've just discussed are left on permanently, and they are used for weed control, moisture retention, and soil amendment. A winter mulch is laid down after the ground freezes and its purpose is to protect the plants during the winter. Because this type of mulch is placed right on top of the plants, lightweight materials are advisable, pine boughs and saltmarsh hay being the two most commonly used. If heavier materials are placed over the garden it may cause the plants to rot or suppress the first spring growth. If you think about it, winter mulch would be unnecessary if we could depend on a deep layer of snow to blanket the garden all winter. Snow makes the best insulation for flower gardens; lacking a constant snow cover, however, branches and salt marsh hay will do.

Not all plants need to be mulched; most hardy perennials do not need covering. If you have a small garden you may want to cover the entire surface; if you have many beds you may choose to only cover plants that are a bit more tender or marginally hardy. In either case, the mulch should be put down *after* the ground freezes, which in this area is often around the end of December. (The time of year when you have nothing else to do but mulch your flowers, right?) The whole point of the winter mulch is not to keep the plants warm, but to keep them at a more constant temperature. Winter mulch helps the ground stay at a constant cold temperature, preventing occasional thaws and re-freezes that may push plants up out of the ground or trigger early growth.

Winter mulch can be removed when the weather seems to be warming and you notice that the ground in unmulched areas is beginning to thaw. This is usually in late February or sometime in March. (Since it varies so from year to year, gardeners have to rely on their good sense and a bit of luck when it comes to knowing the exact time to do it.) If you lift the mulch and notice that the plants underneath are growing, straining toward the light, it's time to remove the protection. Winter mulches can then be put over the paths in vegetable gardens, added to the compost pile, or used to cover other areas.

Q. Why can't I put the winter mulch down when I do the fall clean-up?

A. Since the purpose of winter mulch is to keep a constant temperature, it makes sense to insulate it *after* it has frozen. More importantly though, a thick but airy mulch put down in the fall is an open invitation to small critters like mice and voles to make your garden their winter home. Cozy coverings and tasty small plants or roots to munch on (without even leaving home) makes for prime rodent real-estate!

Q. Some of my shrubs died last winter and the winter wasn't very cold. How can I determine what could have killed them?

A. When trying to find out what has killed an established plant you need to think back and consider what may have happened to that plant the year before it died. Were the roots disturbed by any digging? Was the plant moved or pruned drastically just before winter? Was anything applied to the soil or inadvertently dumped onto the dirt around the plant? Try to remember if the plant looked healthy the previous year, or if it had been failing for some time.

Sometimes a drastic change in temperatures can be more of a problem for plants than the cold is. A long, warm fall followed by two weeks of sudden single degree-temperatures can kill plants because they have not gone into that cold period gradually.

Think about the previous growing season and remember if there were conditions such as drought that may have stressed the plant before the winter season even started. It's important to think about the amount of rainfall that was available to water the plant in the previous fall and winter. In our area the ground often does not freeze until after the New Year, but people usually forget to water their plants after the end of September or October. Remember that even though it is no longer hot outside the shrubs, trees, and perennials may still need watering. Even plants that have lost their leaves, or perennials that have died to the ground need to have their roots kept moist until the ground is frozen. Evergreen plants continue to lose water through their leaves all winter, so late fall watering is important to bring them through their dormant season in good health.

If you need help determining why your plants may have died, call your Cooperative Extension Service and ask for their help. They will ask you some of these same questions, however, so it will be helpful for you to review the plants' history before you call. And finally, frustrating as it is, we must remember that sometimes plants just die, and there may be no *obvious* reason.

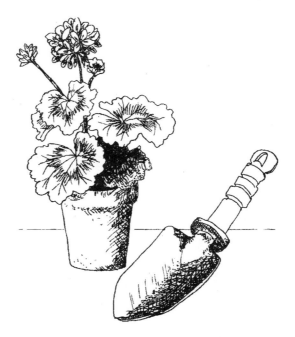

~2~

ANNUALS

ANNUALS

Annuals are plants that do not grow back each year from old root systems; they must be started every spring from seeds. This is good news for the gardener for several reasons. If a plant is depending on seeds to reproduce itself in the world, it needs to make lots and lots of these seeds in order to insure the continued survival of its offspring. Producing an abundance of seeds means first producing an abundance of flowers, and it is this profusion of flowers, usually blooming over a long period, that warms the hearts of gardeners everywhere.

The second advantage to growing something that must be replanted yearly, is that you are never stuck with one plant for longer than six months. A yard or garden can be a showcase of purple blossoms one year, and a riot of red and white blooms the next. If a particular annual is prone to disease, or attracts rabbits to your garden, it is easily dispensed with. There is no large root system to dig up and no guilt about nurturing a plant for two or three years only to throw it away; you simply don't plant it again the following season.

When growing annuals some garden maintenance is simplified because all old plant matter is removed at the end of the season. There is no doubt about whether a plant gets cut to the ground or grows back from old stems; all old annuals get cleared from the garden in the fall. Soil amendment is easier because there are no established root systems to carefully work around.

Annuals are useful to those who love perennials as well; they fill newly established flower beds with blossoms until the perennials mature enough to fill the garden. For all these reasons, annuals continue to be grown and valued by both novice and experienced gardeners. The following chapter celebrates these beautiful, useful plants, and addresses questions about choosing, growing, and maintaining them successfully.

Q. Should I buy annuals or start them from seeds?

A. When the seed catalogs arrive in the middle of winter I am always tempted to order seeds for every annual I love. I go through the catalogs turning pages down and marking everything that I want to plant. A week or two later, when the initial plant-lust has faded, I take a hard look at what I have marked and ask myself "How many of these plants do I have room for and which ones can I find at the garden centers?" If I only want a few plants, or if it is something that is commonly available, I will refrain from ordering the seeds. (Anyone who looks at seed catalogs in the coldest part of the year will know how difficult this is. Even sending for seeds is some *involvement with the garden*, an affirmation that it will once again be warm enough to plant!)

Whether annuals are purchased from the garden center or started from seed will depend on which plants are to be grown, how many of them are needed, and the amount of space and light available to grow them in. If you are planting only a few plants, the cost of the seeds will be about the same as the cost of the plants, so you may as well buy seedlings. If the plan is to plant many plants of the same color, buying seedlings makes it possible to get the exact number needed; starting them yourself may mean making do with the number that germinate, or the few that survive the cat's stroll on the windowsill come April. I would recommend buying those plants that are fairly common, unless you need large numbers of them and have the space and inclination to grow them. Some annuals, such as snapdragons, must be started very early in order to be large enough to transplant outside in late May. If you have a greenhouse this is feasible, but it gets more problematic on the average windowsill. If you are only planting annuals you may be interested in starting your own, but if you are also growing perennials and vegetables it would perhaps be better off to save your indoor growing space for these. Small perennial plants are usually sold singly, so a group of six gets fairly expensive. A pack of six annuals is fairly reasonable, however, especially if you're buying the most common varieties. For financial reasons alone, it makes sense to use the space and money available to start perennials or those varieties of annuals and vegetables unavailable elsewhere.

Q. Do I have to start annual seeds indoors, or can I plant them directly into the ground?

A. Look at your seed packets and see how long the annuals that you want to grow will take to germinate. Those that germinate quickly can be direct seeded into the ground. Most seed packets also give information about any special requirements needed for successful germination, such as heat or an overnight soaking. Follow these instructions! Success is possible even if this information is ignored, but good results are far more likely if the advice is followed.

Annuals that grow well from seeds planted directly in the ground include sweet peas, nasturtiums, zinnias, alyssum, California poppies, sunflowers, calendula, and nigella.

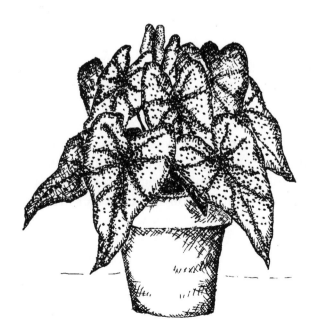

Q. I planted annual seeds in the ground last year and nothing grew. What happened?

A. The most likely answer is that they dried up. The trickiest part of direct seeding annuals in the garden is keeping the seeds and seedlings moist until their root systems are big enough to stand a few days without watering. If the seeds have just germinated (this starts with a tiny, tiny root), and you don't notice that the bed is dry, the tiny root will die; it will not rejuvenate even if you water that evening. This may mean that you need to water your seeds two or even three times a day in order to counter the effects of the warm sun. Don't go overboard in the other direction, though. Too much water can wash seeds out of the flower bed. It is also possible to have so much water that the seedlings rot.

In addition to being careful to keep the seedbed damp, it's also important not to plant them too early. Annuals that do well in the cool spring temperatures such as California poppies and Johnny jump-ups, will germinate even if the soil is not yet warm. Heat loving zinnias and asters want warmer soil to start in, however, so it is better to wait until the end of May before planting them. If in doubt, follow the directions on your packet of seeds, seek help from an online seed forum, or call the Extension Service for advice.

Q. I started some cleome and cosmos seeds indoors last year. They all germinated but they grew very tall and spindly so when I put them into the garden they flopped over. How can I prevent this next year?

A. It sounds as though the light wasn't strong enough. When young plants don't have enough light they strain upwards, toward the sun. If the natural light isn't strong enough consider starting your seedlings under artificial lights. Shop-light fixtures are inexpensive and ready to hang. Most hold two bulbs, and you can fill them with standard florescent bulbs or gro-lights. The key to growing sturdy seedlings under lights is to hang the lights only two or three inches above the seedlings. I put my fixtures on chains hung from hooks so they can be easily raised as the plants grow.

Once your annuals have grown three or four true leaves (the first set of leaves are the seed leaves, or cotyledons...any that form after these are the true leaves) it is advisable to pinch off the growing tip of the plant. This will make the plant branch out, producing a plant that is bushy and full.

Q. If I buy six packs of annuals early in the season, can I keep them in those little cartons for a few weeks until I plant them?

A. Many people like to purchase the annuals that they see early in the season because they know that if they wait they may find that their favorite variety has been sold. If you decide to take some of the small six packs home more than two weeks before the plants can be safely planted, I would recommend that you transplant the plants from the six pack holder into little pots. Not only will this provide more root space for the plant while it is waiting to go into the ground, but it will be easier for you to keep the plants from drying out. Place the repotted plants outside and watch the weather forecast so that the pots can be brought inside if frost is expected. Giving the plants some liquid or time-release fertilizer will help them continue to grow while they await their permanent home.

Q. I am looking for an annual to plant at the cemetery. The flowers there don't get watered very often; are there any annuals that are drought-resistant?

A. There are a few annuals that are able to stand being thirsty. You might want to try some of the drought tolerant annuals listed in Chapter 9. *Pelargoniums* (geraniums) have long been a popular choice for cemetery plantings because they will tolerate drying out now and again. Mulching the area around the flowers will help keep the moisture in the ground for as long as possible. The annuals most suited to very dry conditions are probably *Portulaca grandiflora* and *Gazania rigens*. They are available at most garden centers in several colors. Portulaca are low-growing and not especially bushy, so you should place the plants three to four inches apart if you want to get a lush look. Both plants like good drainage and have flowers that close at night.

Q. Which annuals will do well in my shady yard. My beds only get filtered sunlight.

A. There aren't as many annuals for shade as there are perennials, so you may want to consider a mix of the two. This is particularly appropriate because there are many lovely spring blooming perennials that do well in shade; they will be finished blooming by the time the annuals come into their own. The annual that first comes to mind for shade is, of course, *Impatiens walleriana,* our old friend impatiens. Many people tell me that they are tired of impatiens…a case of overload I'm afraid. But for a mound of constant bloom in shady areas, it can't be matched.

Wax begonias are shade annuals valued not only for their bloom but for their foliage. The contrast of the darker reddish leaves against white flowers is especially lovely, and the varieties that have bright green foliage brighten shady areas. Tuberous begonias have larger flowers in assorted bright colors, and Rex begonias have foliage that ranges from pink to purple and silver. Both thrive in good soil, but if the area around them is too moist they are prone to crown-rot.

Other plants that thrive in shade and are grown for colored foliage are *Coleus* hybrids and *Caladium hortulanum.* Coleus and caladiums come in such a variety of colors that it is almost difficult to describe them. Rest assured that the look you are striving for, be it understated or garish, can be achieved with these two plants; whether you have bold, forties style wallpaper in mind or pink and cream loveliness, you will find a caladium or coleus to fit the bill.

Caladiums aren't annuals, per se, but bulbs that are not hardy in this area. You can buy the bulbs and start them indoors in the early spring, or get plants at your local garden center. A word in your ear about starting them yourself, however: they absolutely need heat to break dormancy. And I mean *heat.* I learned this the hard way a few years ago when I ordered two dozen caladium bulbs from a catalog. I planted them according to the directions and put them in my sunroom along with all the other flats and pots of seedlings. They were in the sun and the daytime temperatures in that room are always over 68°, but there they sat, for *weeks.* When June arrived I put the pots outside, thinking that a breath of fresh air might be just what they needed. Nothing. By the end of June I decided that they had probably rotted so I threw the pots of soil, bulbs and all, into the compost. Two weeks later what should arise from the heat of the compost pile, but caladiums. Every day a new one would pop up and unfurl a leaf or two; I would promptly pot it back up and put it on my shady deck. By the first of August they were gorgeous. When I told this story to Provincetown's Master Gardener, Gordon Gaskill, he confirmed my experience. He remembered working for an estate gardener who would start caladiums by planting them in wooden flats that were placed on top of the steam pipes that brought heat to the greenhouse.

Lacking steam pipes to place your caladiums on, you are well advised to put them on heating mats or some other source of bottom heat. Be sure that they stay damp but not overly wet, and pot them into their permanent homes when they have grown three leaves.

Q. The annuals that I bought died a few weeks after I planted them. How can I tell if they were unhealthy when I bought them?

A. When a plant is dead, it is often difficult to know anything more than it is a dead plant; it is easier to diagnose problems as they are happening. Choosing healthy seedlings is important, however, and if you look for healthy plants when you buy them you will know that the plants got a good start and were ready to grow when planted. Buy plants that look green and sturdy. Unless the plant is bred to have yellowish foliage, be sure to pick stock that has dark green leaves. Pick plants that look healthy, not necessarily the ones that are in bloom.

In general, plants that are covered in mildew or leaf spots should be avoided, with the following exception: while working at garden centers I have noticed that some shrubs and perennial plants that spend two or more months being watered by overhead sprinkler systems often get leaf spots as a result of having frequently wet foliage. These are healthy plants, all in all, and will grow well the following season given good cultural practices. If you purchase such a plant just be sure to clean up all fallen foliage or dead plant material to lessen the likelihood of leafspot the following year.

When you get your plants home be sure to keep them well watered until you are ready to plant. Small pots and six-packs dry up quickly, so check their soil daily. When it is time to put them in the ground, slip them gently out of their container. If the root system is large it will have wrapped around and around the bottom of the flat or pot; gently loosen this root mass with your fingers to spread the roots apart a bit. If the plant is plunked into the soil as is, it will take longer to get its root system established, and the plant will be quicker to wilt. That little ball of congested roots will dry up faster than a root system that is spread out into the soil. Keeping the newly planted seedlings well watered as they are getting established is also very important; if the weather is hot and dry they may need daily watering for the first couple of weeks. As with all plants, morning watering is best, and once the plants are established, watering deeply less often is better than a daily squirt of the hose.

After your plants are growing well in the garden inspect them frequently to check for diseases, insects or other problems. It is easier to deal with problems before they become out of control. Stake any tall growers, such as Cosmos, *before* they need support. Once a plant flops onto the ground the stems start turning skyward in a matter of hours. If you straighten the plant after this happens, the stems do not straighten, but will bend up and continue growing, resulting in odd-looking, permanently curved stems. Water annuals before they get wilted. It is all right to let the soil get dry, but when a plant starts to wilt it is stressed; repeated wilting from thirst may cause the plant to drop its older leaves, leaving it alive but ugly.

Q. When I planted annuals last year I would go out every morning to find them dug up and lying wilted on the ground. The same thing happened with my bulbs last fall. Who, or what, could be doing such a thing?

A. I doubt that you have mischievous neighbors who spend their evenings pulling up plants, so the answer is most likely a "what." Squirrels and skunks are the most likely candidates, with squirrels being the most likely of the two. They aren't really interested in the plants per se, only in the fact that there is loosened earth around them. To the squirrels and skunks, loosened earth means that something wonderful *must* be buried there; a tasty grub, perhaps, or a nut that another squirrel has saved. They dig in the loosened dirt, pushing the young plant or bulb aside in their quest for treasure. You then find the bulb or plant on the ground, the plant wilted and crying for water. I had to re-plant my pansies several times one year for this very reason!

Usually this is a minor problem, and after replacing the plant and watering it well the seedling recovers and isn't bothered again. Watering well may in fact discourage the critters from digging it up in the first place, as the watering firms the soil so it is less obvious that it has ever been disturbed. If your treasure-seeking animals are particularly persistent you could cover the small plants with loose chicken wire or floating row cover for a week or so until the soil is compact and less appealing. I used cayenne pepper sprinkled around the plants; it's difficult to know if this was successful or if the squirrels just weren't interested in that particular area...the squirrels weren't talking. If you try this method be sure to water well before sprinkling on the pepper, and renew the pepper after the next watering.

Q. Do I need to deadhead all my annuals?

A. Aside from making the plants tidier, snipping off the spent flower heads encourages most annuals to produce new blooms. It also promotes compact and flower-filled growth. Most annuals do not die to the ground and then come back from the same root systems as perennials do. They have one season to perpetuate their species, and they do this by making seeds. For the annual plant, the flowers are a means of attracting pollinators in order to produce seeds. So if you cut the spent blossoms off, the plant will produce more flowers in an attempt to grow seedpods. Keep this in mind when you are removing the wilted petunia blossoms...many people just remove the old petals and leave the seedpod that is developing under the flower. In order for deadheading to be effective, the slightly swollen area just under the flower must be removed. Deadheading is especially important for petunias, geraniums, zinnias, dwarf ageratum, dahlias, snapdragons, and most other annuals that have sizable flowers. Deadheading is usually not necessary on very small flowering plants like alyssum or *Nierembergia*; impatiens need not be deadheaded unless they are looking leggy, in which case cutting off a good portion of stem *and* flowers will stimulate them to branch out. Picking bouquets of flowers to bring indoors can be an easy way to deadhead, although it is done while the flowers are still fresh. Aliveheading we might call it…well, probably not. Nevertheless, if you cut the flowers above the first set of leaves on the stem below the bloom, the plant will usually send two new flower stems out from the leaf nodes (where the leaf and stem meet) and you will have lovely cut flowers for your bedside table.

Q. If I don't deadhead, but let the plants go to seed, can I save the seeds, and plant them, growing my own annuals next year?

A. If the annuals that you planted are hybrids, the plants that you grow from seed may not be true to type; that is, you may not get the same type of plant from the seed of a hybrid. Hybrid plants usually develop seeds that will be genetically identical to the parent plants that were used to create the hybrid. Note that I say usually, because sometimes hybrids do come true from seed.

I had some tall blue *Ageratum* self seed in my garden a few years ago. I let the seedlings grow and by midsummer I had a great crop of ageratum plants, but I had four or five different *types* of *Ageratum,* all looking quite different from one another. One plant looked very much like what I had grown the year before. Others were taller, with thinner leaves, and pale, pale blue flowers. One plant had *huge* leaves and very few flowers at all.

Knowing that you might not get the same plant, you can certainly collect the seeds and grow them the following season. Many annuals will reseed (grow the following season from seeds scattered the previous season) with no help at all. Some will even cross pollinate and self-hybridize, giving new colors and growing habits in the next generation of plants. Pansies are perhaps best known for doing this in the home garden. Annuals that usually reseed are *Cleome, Calendula, Portulaca, Alyssum, Nicotiana alata, Violas,* and California poppies. Cosmos often self-seed but they may not be true to the same type that you planted the previous year; usually the self-seeded plants have lots of foliage and fewer flowers. You may find yourself weeding many of the seedlings out, particularly those of prolific re-seeders such as *Cleome.* I always figure that I will be weeding *something* out of my garden anyway, and it might as well be excess flowers as weeds.

Q. I am only in this area on weekends ... what annuals would be good for me to plant?

A. Annuals that are drought resistant, such as the ones mentioned as being appropriate for cemetery plantings, would be good choices for your situation as well. Plants that don't require a lot of dead-heading such as *Cleome, Cosmos, Nirembergia,* and *Impatiens,* would also be fine for weekend residents to plant. You don't want to spend your entire weekend maintaining the garden, after all. Planting a combination of easy-care perennials (see Chapter 3 as well as the plant lists in Chapter 9) and flowering shrubs along with a few annuals will provide you with a lovely garden without too much attention. This is assuming that you keep the size of your flower beds reasonable, and the numbers of plants at a minimum. Better to start small and see how long it takes you to tidy-up, weed, mulch and water. A garden should never be a *chore.*

Q. My house is rented and I can't dig flower or vegetable beds in the yard, but every year I long for a garden. How can I have a garden without digging more beds?

A. Container gardens are the perfect solution for both full year renters and those who rent for the summer only. Most annuals can be grown in large pots, and many vegetables as well. Larger pots allow for deeper root systems and can contain more plants. Individual annuals can be grown in smaller pots, as can most of the herbs. Pots of several sizes, filled with all manner of annuals, vegetables and herbs are beautiful and can satisfy the urge to garden.

Large tubs, half-barrels, and plastic or clay pots can be purchased at garden centers, discount stores, and larger hardware stores. Yard sales are often a source of inexpensive used pots and planters. Almost any container can be adapted for plants as long as some drainage holes are drilled in the bottom. Think about old toys, suitcases, and kitchen items; a nice collection of pots can always be enlivened by an unexpected container or two.

Plants in container gardens are usually placed closer to each other than they would normally be planted in a garden. It isn't unusual to establish plants three or four inches apart in a pot. Planting things closely gives a full look from the start; the season is short, after all, so your containers should be lovely right from the beginning. Because there are several plants growing in a small amount of soil it is necessary to fertilize the plants throughout the growing season. Time-release fertilizers are available that are mixed into the potting soil before the plants are put into the pots, and mixing in some organic, slow-release fertilizer at the same time will provide nutrients later in the summer when the time-release has been used up. Some gardeners prefer to mix their fertilizer with water...just be sure not to fertilize a thirsty plant. If the soil is very dry, water the container first, and then apply your liquid fertilizer after the plant has had some time to absorb the moisture. If you want to keep your fertilizer organic, pots can be watered with diluted fish and seaweed extracts. This are available at most garden centers.

Keeping your container garden watered is of prime importance. Because most pots are fairly small, the soil in the pot dries up quickly. Pots in sunny locations may need watering once a day. A light layer of mulch on top of the soil will help keep things moist, but may also prevent you from noticing that the soil surface is dry. If you are unsure if a pot needs watering, push a finger into the soil. If it feels dry up to two inches below the soil surface, you should water. Usually the look of the plants will tell you if they need watering long before your finger touches the soil. If the growing tips of the plant are drooping, it is thirsty. When the soil in a pot is really dry it may need to be watered twice. The potting soil pulls away from the container as it dries, leaving a space where the water runs down and out the drainage hole. Water an extremely dry pot once and wait a few minutes for that water to be absorbed; when the soil near the pot has expanded, it is ready to be watered again.

Be sure to notice how much sun shines on the area where the containers are going to go, so that the pots can be filled with plants appropriate to such conditions. If your pots will be shaded it won't work to fill them full of basil and zinnias. And if you pictured your sunny deck awash with pots of caladiums you will be in for a great disappointment when their shade-loving foliage gets sunburned. Picking the right plant for the location is as important in container gardens as it is when you grow a plant in the ground.

Q. Aside from very tall plants, can I grow *any* annuals in my window boxes?

A. Once again, the most important consideration is picking the right plant for the location. If the window-boxes don't get much sun they should be planted with shade-loving annuals such as *Impatiens* or plants that tolerate semi-shade such as *Browallia*. Geraniums (*Pelargoniums*) have long been popular choices for window boxes not only because of their large, colorful flowers, but because they do well when planted in hot, sunny locations.

Reliable watering is as important for window boxes as it is with other containers. Because there is little soil in boxes, and they are often filled with light-weight potting mix, it may be necessary to water twice a day in very sunny locations. Most garden centers carry a product that when added to the soil acts like little sponges, absorbing moisture when you water the container or window box, and releasing it to the plants as needed. If you can't check your boxes every day or if you don't remember to water, these crystals may give you the extra time between waterings that you need. (Be sure to follow the directions on the package.) If regular watering is the rule, however, don't use these crystals, as they will keep regularly watered containers too wet. Water-retentive crystals can also be a problem if it is a particularly rainy summer; too much rain will promote root and stem rot.

In addition to the location of your boxes, you will want to consider the bloom-time of the plant that you are interested in planting. Some annuals will bloom all summer regardless of temperatures; others are more picky. California poppies, for example, like to bloom when it's cool; they would look wonderful cascading over the edge of a window box in early June, but would most likely die when the heat of July hits them.

Lobelia is another plant that likes it cool. I am constantly puzzled that so many people choose lobelia to plant with their geraniums in a window box. Yes, the combination of the red or pink geraniums looks great with the vivid blue of the lobelia, but the geraniums love heat and sun and the lobelia wants it cool and shady. You *may* get away with it and have beautiful boxes all season long, but chances are the lobelia will be gone by the middle of

July. Although it is not as deep a blue as lobelia, a longer lasting cascading companion for geraniums is *Scaevola*. This annual loves the sun and, like geraniums, it tolerates a bit of drying out. Another annual to pair with the geraniums in boxes is *Nierembergia*, a frilly foliage plant (like lobelia) but with showier blossoms. It is available with white or purple flowers, and thrives in the sun.

No matter which plants are chosen for window boxes, be sure that they all like similar growing conditions, and be aware of their bloom period. Deadhead your plants as discussed above, and fertilize them as the season goes on, either with a time release fertilizer, or with a mild liquid feed every two weeks.

Q. My window boxes and containers got a mold in them last year. How can I stop this from happening?

A. Window boxes look best when planted fully, but these are the same conditions that foster molds, mildew, and fungus. The best you can do is to try to plant things that look full but allow for some air circulation. Plants with small, needle-like leaves, for example, will allow for more air circulation than a plant with large floppy leaves. Intersperse large-leafed plants (such as geraniums) with other plants that have smaller leaves. Use cascading plants to create a full look as well, and don't allow these to become so thick as to create a heavy mat. Selective thinning of stems may be necessary.

Water window boxes and container plantings by sticking the hose or watering can under the leaves so that the soil, not the plant, is being watered. Water early in the morning so that any moisture on the leaves has plenty of time to dry off. Be sure that you are not over-watering; although boxes and containers dry out quickly, it is possible to keep them too wet, especially if the skies are cloudy or there is fog. Always feel the soil with your finger to see if it really needs watering. Finally, inspect your containers regularly...if you see a spotted or moldy leaf, pick it off and throw it away. Fungal problems can often be kept under control by promptly removing the first foliage that shows symptoms.

• • •

Q. In the middle of the summer my impatiens suddenly looked as if they had frosted. They certainly didn't freeze; what could have happened?

A. They could have been cooked! Impatiens have very watery, tender foliage, that is very susceptible to heat and cold damage. Chances are your plants were watered with water from a hose that had been in the sun. The sun-warmed water in a garden hose can be almost scalding; if the water is sprayed onto the plants without letting it run until cold, it can cook the plants' foliage. If the plants get severely hurt by scalding water they may have to be replaced.

Q. By the end of summer my window boxes look ratty. Should I rip everything out and replant?

A. You certainly can rip the summer bloomers out and replant, but it doesn't have to be so all-or-nothing. Consider taking the worst-looking plants out, or removing those that are clearly done for the year. Cut back those that have gotten leggy but will continue to bloom into the fall. Petunias, for example can be cut back one half to two thirds of their length; give them some liquid fertilizer after their haircut, and they will fill out and begin to bloom again soon. Then take a good look at what is left and decide what is needed to fill in the gaps. At that point you would do well to fill in with plants thought of as fall bloomers. Mums, marigolds, pansies, or ornamental kale would be nice choices. More cold-hardy plants can be added later if needed.

Q. I'm tired of the usual annuals that I see. What can I plant that is different, and why don't I see more unusual varieties in the stores?

A. We often see the same tried and true plants in stores because they are just that ... tried and true. Most of us want what we know will be successful. When most people buy and plant annuals they expect a plant that will flower for them all summer. Some of the lesser-known annuals may be lovely, but they may only bloom toward the end of the season or stop blooming as soon as it gets hot. The plant-buying public is partly to blame for a limited selection because they usually will not buy a plant unless it has a bloom on it. This means that plants that take longer to set blossoms will not sell as well, and stores soon learn to avoid them.

That said, there has been an increasing interest in unusual annuals and tender perennials. More garden centers are stocking them, and several nurseries have opened that specialize in such plants. (see *Resources*) Keep in mind that the more unusual annuals are not usually for sale in the inexpensive six-packs.

Raising a few plants from seed may be a less expensive way for you to try unusual plants. Growing two or three every year is a good way to familiarize yourself with quite a number of plants in a few years time. I try to grow at least two plants every year that I haven't grown before. Often I decide that I won't grow them again, but some become my annual "must haves." Often a plant will be lovely, but not well suited for the area I am planting it in. *Mirabilis jalapa,* for instance, has the lovely common name of Four-O'clock for a very good reason. The flowers only open when no longer in the direct sun, or around four o'clock in the evening. This can be wonderful if they are planted next to a deck or patio where people sit for late afternoon tea or evening cocktails. They were less successful when I planted them by the entry I used only in the early part of the day. It wasn't the right plant for that location.

Some of the more unusual annuals were old favorites that are not as widely planted now. Chapter 9 contains a list of annuals that are lovely, but not seen as often as the usual impatiens, geraniums, and cosmos. In looking over the list I realize that most of them are plants that I don't want to do without!

When planting annuals that are perhaps less tried and true, remember as well that the growing conditions in that particular year may influence your success or failure. While this is true to some extent for all plants, those that are less well known may not be widely planted because they are less consistent in several types of growing conditions. *Nemophila* was a great success for me one year when, thanks to the eruption of Mount Pinatubo the year before, the weather was unusually cool all summer. Later attempts to grow it haven't gone as well since this plant does not like heat. Someone with a flower bed that is exposed to the morning sun but shaded from the afternoon heat may have better luck with this little charmer.

Other plants may also thrive in one location, but die in another; if you love a particular plant, experimenting with location could be the key to growing it successfully. It is also worthwhile to remember that whatever the weather is like in a particular year, there will be plants that love those conditions and those that do not. The year the *Nemophila* did well the tomatoes suffered terribly.

Q. My containers often look so lovely in the late fall ... is it possible to bring them indoors and keep them until next spring?

A. Success or failure, what have you got to lose? The plants will die in the frost anyway, so give it a try. I wintered over a pot of petunias and *Helichrysum petiolantum* (licorice plant) one year, and I always bring in my *Mandevilla* vines. I had to cut the *Helichrysum* way back in January because it had aphids, but the petunias bloomed all winter and the entire pot *exploded* with new growth and blooms when it was put outside again in late May. Many of the plants we grow as annuals in this climate are perennials in a warmer region, so they in particular would winter over well.

My experience with the aforementioned pot will tell you two things about keeping annuals indoors: 1) They are prone to insect infestations, and 2) You will most likely need to cut them back to rejuvenate growth. Leave them for a couple of weeks after they are brought in, so they can be enjoyed for awhile at their fullest. When they start to look straggly cut them back *hard*. They *will* start to get leggy because they won't have nearly the same amount of light indoors, even if placed in the sunniest window. Some plants, like geraniums, may continue to look pretty good, and you will be tempted not to cut them back. The result will be large plants in the spring and *huge,* leggy ones in midsummer! Keep in mind that in warmer climates geraniums are as large as shrubs. If you let them go early in the winter you will be left with a plant too large for its pot or window box in the early summer. Cutting the plant down at that time leaves you with stumpy stems just at the time you want a pretty outdoor display. Be ruthless in December or January, however, and you will thank yourself for it in May.

A sunny window in a cool room is probably best for keeping annuals over the winter. They will be resting, so don't feed them until

February or March, and only water when they are dry. (Don't let them wilt, but don't water unless the soil no longer feels damp. The plants won't dry out as quickly when they are resting in a cool space.) Keep an eye out for aphids, mealy bugs, scale, and white flies. If infested with any of these pests treat with insecticidal soap according to the directions. Trim off any leaves heavily infested with scale, and scratch what you can from stems and leaves before spraying.

When it is time to put the pots outdoors again be sure to put them in a shaded location after the nights have turned warm. The process of "hardening off" plants grown indoors usually involves gradually getting them used to the outside world by increasing the time spent outdoors each day. A large pot will be too heavy to put in and out so it is important to put it in the shade at first, and not to put it out too early. After the plants are toughened up the pot can be moved to its permanent location.

Q. What causes the leaf spots on the geranium leaves? They are dark areas ringed with yellow, and the leaves usually get sick looking and fall off the plant.

A. These leaf spots are a fungus and are usually a problem when geraniums are watered in such a way that their leaves get wet. When watering plants that are planted in the ground, use soaker hoses or try to stick a watering wand nearby at ground level. Water potted plants or those in window boxes by sticking a gently running hose under the leaves, trying as much as possible not to wet the leaves or to splash dirt up into the lower foliage. Remove any spotted leaves promptly and throw them away. Wash your hands after handling infected plants to avoid spreading the fungus to other plants.

Q. My annuals – including my impatiens - didn't do well last summer; all over town people have lovely flower beds and mine just sulked. What could be wrong?

A. Ask yourself the following questions:

Did I prepare the soil? Annuals (and other plants) won't do well if they are planted in compact or infertile soil. Turn even the best soil over to a depth of 12 to 18 inches, and dig organic matter (compost, peat, or composted cow manure) into areas of sand or clay.

Did I add some time-release or organic fertilizer when I planted? Annuals need more fertilizer during the summer than shrubs or perennials do...add some slow-release fertilizer even if you are going to use a liquid as the summer goes on.

Did I water regularly and deeply? A squirt with the hose every day isn't enough. I guarantee that if you hand water, you will be bored long before that flower bed has gotten a good, deep soaking. It is far better to set the sprinkler on a bed for a couple of hours once a week, than it is to water shallowly every day. Plants need a deep soaking in order to develop deep root systems.

Is the flower bed being hit by the automatic sprinkler system that is watering the lawn? Most annuals don't like having their foliage sprinkled frequently. Adjust your lawn sprinklers so that they miss the flower beds, or so that they water deeply but less often. This is better for your lawn as well.

Q. I love the cape daisies that have appeared in the garden centers in the past few years, but they always stop blooming in the middle of summer—what am I doing wrong? Do they need more fertilizer?

A. Osteospermum, commonly called Cape Daisies, are lovely flowers available in a variety of colors from white and yellow to all shades of purple and pink. Often, the daisy-like flowers have blue or purple centers, and they catch my eye and wallet in May as they do yours. These are cool weather annuals, however, so you can only expect the same bloom period with Cape Daisies as you can with pansies. These plants stop blooming when the weather gets hot.

Plant pansies and Osteospermum in boxes and containers where you have the space to add summer-bloomers like Scaevola, geraniums, or wax begonias. If the early bloomers are combined with annuals that will fill out and bloom later on, you will have the best of both worlds in your garden.

~3~

PERENNIALS

PERENNIALS

Most gardeners enjoy having some plants that can be counted on to grow in the same spot every year, gracing the garden with lovely foliage and flowers. Plants that grow each spring from established root systems are called perennials, and there are many of these wonderful plants to choose from.

Perennials come in a variety of sizes, from the tiny *Veronica repens* (creeping speedwell) to the large-leafed *Heracleum lanatum* (giant cow parsnip). Just as they differ in size, so too do they differ in the growing conditions that they require. Some perennials want to grow in full sun, others in shade. Many plants want the soil to be well drained, while others want their roots wet. There are even a few plants that want a little of this and a little of that…Iris, for example, are said to want "their feet wet but their ankles dry." There are plants that do best when allowed to grow undisturbed for years, and there are others that need to be dug up and divided on a regular schedule. Perennials also differ in the season that they bloom, and in the length of time that they are in flower. Clearly the gardener can't treat all perennials in the same manner and have them all grow well. This chapter includes information about the wide range of perennials that grow well on the Cape and Islands, and details the steps necessary to grow and maintain healthy plants.

Q. I'm tired of planting annuals every year; can I plant perennials so that I don't have to go to all that work each spring?

A. I would never discourage anyone from planting perennials, but I want to be sure that you go into this change with your eyes open.

Perennials are plants that come back from their roots every year, but this does not mean that they can be planted and forgotten. Some perennials, *Aconitum* for example, dislike being disturbed once they are planted. Others need dividing every three or four years to keep them looking their best. A perennial garden is never finished. Plants spread and must be weeded out, plants sometimes die, and there are always plants that grow too tall or too short for where they are placed.

Another difference between annual and perennial gardens is the speed at which they get established. If you plant annuals in May you have a garden full of blooms in late July. Many perennials don't bloom the first year they are planted, or if they do bloom they are often much smaller than they will be as mature plants. Perennial gardens are not for the impatient, and they are (surprise!) one of the most high-maintenance gardens you can grow.

You may want to start by planting a few clumps of perennials and filling the area around them with the annuals that you have always loved. The *Hemerocallis* hybrids (daylilies) would be good perennials to start with if you have a sunny or mostly sunny garden. Daylilies aren't too fussy and their foliage is attractive throughout the season. There are varieties of daylilies that bloom in early, mid or late-summer, and they combine beautifully with annuals and other perennials. Other perennials can be added each year, gradually filling in the bed back to front; continue to plant annuals to fill in any bare spaces. Some other low-maintenance perennials include: *Baptisia australis* (false indigo), *Chelone lyonii* (turtlehead), *Epimedium* species, *Geranium cantabrigiense* (a cranesbill geranium), *Hostas, Liatris spicata, Sedum* 'Autumn Joy' and *Persicaria* 'Firetail.'

Q. I want to put perennials in my flower bed instead of annuals. Which perennials will bloom all summer?

A. I must admit up front that this is a question that makes me cranky. I hope that you haven't fallen into the habit of thinking that the only beautiful plant is a blooming plant! At the risk of sounding peevish, I remind everyone that green is a color too. The *variety* of greens (not to mention purple, yellow, and silver foliage) in a garden is a small miracle in itself...one that is often overlooked. I plead with you to look at your plants with "new eyes." See the incredible beauty in their buds, leaves, and seed heads as well as their blossoms. Remember that the foliage is usually there for far longer then the flowers; if you can appreciate the form, color, and texture of the entire plant then the garden will be a year-long source of interest and delight.

And whether you are interested in foliage or flowers, there are hundreds of perennials to choose from. If variety is the spice of life, then perennials do provide a flavorful diet. Annuals may bloom all summer but they will never surprise you in August with a color or fragrance that wasn't there in July. The key to planting a perennial bed that is beautiful all summer is to plant a variety of plants that bloom at different times. That way there is always something in bloom to enjoy in *addition* to the pleasure you are getting from the variety of buds, leaves and seed-heads.

Few perennials bloom all summer, and many that do bloom for lengthy periods are often short-lived. (How long have *you* been able to keep *Scabiosa* 'Butterfly Blue' alive in your perennial bed?) Perennials that have a long period in bloom are probably best combined with others that put on a single impressive show, be it only for a couple of weeks. Chapter 9 includes a list of long-blooming perennials as well as a list of perennials organized according to their bloom period.

Q. Is it better to order perennials from a catalog or buy the plants locally?

A. Looking at plant catalogs is one of the pleasures of winter. It is tempting to order everything as soon as the catalogs arrive, but it may not always be wise to do so. Many perennials are available at local stores and garden centers, and the plants that you buy locally will be larger than the ones that you can get through the mail. Not only are they larger, but when picking them out yourself it is possible to choose the largest and healthiest ones. Anyone who has ordered plants through the mail has had the experience of receiving two large healthy plants and one small, spindly one. Before rushing off a mail order, check to see if the plant you want will be available locally. Those who like to garden get pleasure from visiting local garden centers often; this is a good way to become familiar with what can be purchased in your area. When the catalogs start arriving the following season, you will have a general idea about which plants are only available by mail.

Some catalogs offer perennials that aren't as well known as others but are plants that nevertheless deserve a home in your garden. Be careful, however, to take catalog descriptions with a grain of salt. The information is sometimes less than complete. A wise gardener will write down the names of plants that are of interest, and then spend some time reading about them. Be sure to find out if the plant is hardy in this planting zone, if it requires a special type of soil, (well-drained, acidic or alkaline, dry or damp) and if it prefers sun or shade. The length of time the plant is in bloom may also be of interest; you may want to know if it is long-lived, invasive or particularly fragile.

Knowing the "code" for plant descriptions is a bit like learning the lingo used in real estate ads. Just as a "garden apartment" means an apartment in the basement, a plant that is called a "vigorous grower" is probably an invasive thug! If the description says that "a good trim after blooming will regenerate new growth" it usually means that at the end of its bloom period the plant probably flops into a leggy, sprawling mess.

Q. Is it safe for me to order plants grown in North Carolina? Won't the plants be less hardy because it is warmer there?

A. Hardiness is a genetic characteristic, not a cultural one. A perennial raised in North Carolina has the same degree of hardiness as the same plant raised in Maine. If the hardiness of a plant was determined by the area the plant was raised, it would be possible for us to grow hardy banana trees in Massachusetts!

When ordering plants that were raised in warmer climates, you will be asked to specify a date when it is safe to ship that plant to you. This is generally the day that it will possible, baring an unusual cold snap, to ship the plants and not have them freeze en route. It does not mean that you have to be able to plant those plants outside at that time. It may be more prudent to put the plants in pots for awhile so they can get accustomed to the local air temperatures. If the forecast is for temperatures below freezing, the pots can be moved indoors. If the plants you've received are straight from a hothouse they will need to be planted into pots and put outside gradually, a few hours a day.

There are seed companies and nurseries that specialize in growing extremely hardy varieties of plants, and these businesses are often located in cold climates themselves. Their location may allow them to test the hardiness of plants firsthand, but it is not their location that creates the hardiness in the first place.

Q. Can I grow my own perennials from seed?

A. Many perennials are easy to start from seed, some less so. When I fall in love with a plant I usually want to place several in my garden, and growing them from seed is the best way to get large numbers of plants economically. Before looking for seeds, however, it's wise to go to some source books to do a bit of research. (If you don't own any books on perennials you can find some at your local library.) Many guides to perennials include propagation information about the plants that they list, and two books on propagation are included in the Bibliography section of this book. These guides can tell you if the plant is best propagated by seed, division, or cuttings. If you learn that it can be propagated by seed, the next step is to search for a supply of the variety that you want. Garden magazines list many seed suppliers, particularly in their winter and spring issues, and you can do an internet search for more unusual varieties. Local garden centers are also carrying a wider selection of unusual seeds than they have in the past, so be sure to check locally first.

Seed catalogs will often include a code by the description of each plant, telling how difficult it is to grow that particular plant from seed. I will always try growing something from seed at least once, despite the degree of difficulty. I figure that it is worth an investment of two or three dollars (seed and soilless starting mix) in hopes of getting a dozen or more plants started; those plants would cost between three to fifteen dollars apiece if I bought them through the mail or at the local garden center.

Perennial plants started from seed in February are usually still very small in June. It is better if they are not planted into the garden at this point, but are transplanted instead into larger pots, one per pot. Keep them outside in a sunny area while they grow, and water and fertilize regularly. This allows the gardener to watch them closely, protect them from insects if need be, and nurture them along until September. At this point they can be transplanted into their permanent places in the garden. Although most plants will bloom the following year, they won't have the size and full shapes of mature plants until their third summer.

PREPARING THE SOIL

Q. I have heard about "double digging" new perennial beds. Is this something that I have to do?

A. When planning a new perennial bed it is advisable to start with soil that is as rich and loose as possible. Double digging is the process of digging the soil out of a new bed, to the depth of double the shovel's blade, then replacing a third of it mixed with equal amounts of topsoil or compost, and manure or peat. Do you have to do this? No, but those who do are never sorry. Chances are you will never again have the opportunity to amend the soil in the entire bed. If you have very sandy soil the least I would do is remove some of the sand and turn in as much compost and manure as I could get my hands on. Adding topsoil is good too, although it's wise to actually see the topsoil you are buying before having it delivered. Some topsoils that are available in this area are nothing more than dark sand; for those of us who already garden in sand it is not worth spending money for more, even if it is a darker color! Those who have soil that is mostly clay may *want* this sandy topsoil, however. Adding sand and organic matter improves the drainage of clay soils.

Although it means putting off planting until the following season, starting to amend the soil a year in advance could prove less expensive than doing it quickly. As early in the year as possible, dig some of the soil out of the bed that you want to plant in. Begin to pile in as much organic matter as you can get your hands on. Spend the summer adding seaweed, grass clippings, and shredded leaves to the bed. Many stables welcome people who will haul away horse manure. It's usually free for the shoveling. Mix all this organic matter into the soil with a pitchfork or Rototiller and let it settle in over the winter.

I have visited many gardens since the first edition of this book was published, and one of the most common mistakes I have seen is the failure to amend the soil *well* over a large area. If the peat or manure is only dug in an area two feet in diameter, how will that perennial do well when its root system reaches beyond that two foot perimeter? Once the plant's roots hit the compact or poor soil it will begin to languish or die.

As a gardener I understand the desire to start putting plants in the ground as quickly as possible. Taking the time to amend the soil before planting will result in healthier plants and this means less work later.

LOCATION, LOCATION, LOCATION

Q. I would like to start a perennial bed. I'm thinking of just widening the beds around the front of the house in front of the foundation plants. Would this be a good place for perennials?

A. Plan your future perennial beds as carefully as you would an addition to your house. It is tempting to place it in front of the foundation plantings because a bed of sorts already exists there; that may be the best place for it, and it may not. Planning it carefully will be worth the effort; once you get all those plants put in and established you won't want to dig them all up and relocate.

Light is the most important factor to consider when planning a perennial garden. The amount of sunlight will determine what types of plants you can grow. Most full-of-flower perennials that we envision when we think of a perennial garden grow well in full sun; they need at least five hours of direct sun per day, including the hours around noon when the sun is strongest. Location in your yard is also important. If the sunniest area on your property is out in the backyard behind the kids' swing-set, it might be wise to opt for a location that is less sunny but one that you will see more often.

Many people want a garden that they can see from a window of their house. A woman that I spoke to said that she wanted a flower garden that she could see from the window of her bathroom, because she gazed out this window every day when she brushed her teeth.

When I planted my small cottage garden I tore up a third of our front lawn to put it in. I wanted to be able to walk through flowers on my way in and out of the front door. Those who spend time on a patio or deck might want their garden located near that area.

Your foundation plantings might provide a lovely background for your perennials, provided the light is right. Flowers often look good when framed by a shrub border, fence, or wall; these structures offer some protection from the wind as well. Consider other locations in terms of light and frequency of enjoyment. If you still think that the front of your foundation plantings is ideal, then go right ahead. Be careful of the shrubs' roots as you dig and amend the soil for the new bed. Consider too how to best plant the flowers and still have room to prune the shrubs.

Q. I have always planted annuals in formal rows. How can I achieve a less formal look in my new perennial beds?

A. In the beginning, achieving a less formal look takes as much planning as formal rows. As a garden matures it often develops a plan of its own, and the gardener becomes an editor, leaving what works and moving what doesn't. Plant perennials in groups of three or five ... odd numbers are more pleasing to the eye. Although it is tempting to buy one of each perennial that you see, a large group of plants always makes a more impressive display than one or two. Remember a time when you've seen wild flowers that looked especially gorgeous; chances are it was a big stand of a single type of flower that got your attention, not a group of several types of plants. Large groups have impact; for this reason it is advantageous to do a bit of research to discover which plants you absolutely *must* have, and plant several of those.

Plant groups of three in a triangle, and larger groups in "S" shaped curves. Although the taller plants are placed toward the back of the bed, don't be rigid about this. A clump or two of tall plants in the middle of the bed will make it more interesting visually, and keep it from looking too formal. Once your bed is established you will find that plants will occasionally self-seed apart from the original clump. Leaving some of these where they appear can contribute to a lush, full perennial bed.

Q. My garden is very shady. Is it possible for me to have a perennial bed?

A. Just as there are many shades of gray, there are many types of shade. (Many shades of shade?) There are gardens that have about four hours of sun that would be considered part shade gardens. Other gardens receive dappled light through high or lacy trees, with a few short periods of direct sunshine. This semi-shade is probably the easiest type of shade to garden in since shade-loving plants and some of those who do well in part shade will, in general, do well here. Then there are those gardens that are in shade practically all day. These are deep-shade gardens, and your choice of plants for these areas is more limited.

As you plan a garden for shade, try not to picture the same type of flower garden that you would be able to plant in sunny areas. Gardens in shade and semi-shade are usually not the knock-your-socks-off beds of bright colors that full sun gardens can be. This does not mean that they are any less beautiful...they are just different. In some ways, especially in the heat of the summer months, shade gardens can be more pleasant places to linger.

Refer to the lists in Chapter 9 for specific plants that do well in shady spots. When planning gardens in shady areas be sure to plant large enough groups of smaller plants to make an impact. Because the beauty of some shade-loving plants is subtle, you will need to grow more of them to achieve a unified look to your garden. The exception to this are large-leaved plants that have such presence that only one plant works as a focal point in the bed. Extremely large *Hostas* or the marvelous *Ligularia* are plants that are prized for their "architecture" in shade gardens.

Most gardeners who plant in shady beds include plants that have a variety of foliage colors. A combination of a dark-leafed *Ligularia*, some bright green *Hostas*, and a variegated *Polygonatum* (Solomon's-Seal), for example, provides interest and contrast even without their blooms. Including a few plants with variegated foliage always brightens shady gardens.

It has been my experience that young plants for the shade often do not look like much. The pots of small *Cimicifuga, Ligularia, and Aruncus* that I have seen in no way compare to how lovely these plants will be in the garden. Even the smaller shade lovers such as *Pulmonaria* and *Galium* (sweet woodruff) don't look like much when you see them in pots at the garden center. I think that this is the reason that many people are not as familiar with these and other plants for shady spots. When it comes to choosing a plant in the nursery, most people will opt for a full *Hosta* instead of the stick with two leaves that claims to be a *Cimicifuga*. After looking at a picture in a book about perennials, or even consulting a plant catalog to see what a mature plant will look like, have faith and be bold ... plant something less familiar!

SUMMER BLOOMERS

Q. I would like to have a perennial bed but I am only here in July and August. What plants can I put in that bloom in the summer and are relatively drought resistant?

A. There are many perennials that tolerate drought; an extensive list is included in Chapter 9. A few of the easiest summer bloomers are *Hemerocallis* hybrids (Daylilies), *Perovskia atriplicifolia* (Russian Sage), *Gaillardia grandiflora* (Blanket Flower), *Rudbeckia* hybrids (Blackeyed Susan) and *Aster novi-angliae* (New England Aster). You may want to put in a few *Yucca filamentosa* as well, since their foliage is always lovely and the tall white blooms are so striking. This combination of flowers will give you a garden full of yellows, oranges, blues and purples throughout the summer months. (If you must have some pink, add several *Echinacea purpurea* -purple coneflower.) Be sure to pick some daylilies that are late-season bloomers, so that you have some flowers opening throughout the summer. Remember too that a mulched garden will hold in the moisture and keep the weeds down when you aren't around. Even drought-tolerant plants like a bit of mulch.

GRASSES

Q. The ornamental grasses are very popular now. Should I consider these for my perennial bed?

A. Ornamental grasses are valued in perennial beds for several reasons. The taller varieties make a nice vertical background in the garden, providing structure in a space too small for a shrub or tree.

Ornamental grasses add late fall and winter interest, as most of them have lovely seed-heads at this time. Several of the *Miscanthus*, for example, have plumes that are lovely throughout the winter. Grasses are also valued for their drought tolerance. They are not only attractive, but are for the most part pest-free. I value grasses in the garden for their motion as well. We often think of perennial plants in terms of color of bloom, as well as the color and texture of the foliage; a plant that sways with the smallest breeze adds motion to the garden as well.

Choosing a grass for the perennial bed is the same as choosing any other plant. Information about the mature height, preferred growing conditions, and general adaptability should be researched before planting any plant. Most grasses grow to be a large clump, so don't put them too close to other perennials. Some grasses are invasive, and others prone to self-seeding in the garden. (A word to the wise ... stay away from the running ribbon grass – *Phalaris arundinacea*, and deadhead your sea-oat grass – *Chasmanthium latifolium* - to avoid rampant seeding!) Some grasses, such as purple fountain grass, should be treated as annuals, since they are not hardy in this climate.

Q. How do I take care of ornamental grasses?

A. Once established, ornamental grasses are very drought tolerant and need little care, but you will need to water newly placed plants about once a week through the first season. Fertilize them with a general organic fertilizer in early spring. You should leave the grasses standing through most of the winter for two reasons; the dried stalks of grass are attractive and add interest to the winter garden, and the clumps are more prone to crown-rot if they are cut in the fall. Remove the old stems in February or March, cutting down to 6".

Q. I bought a perennial that was labeled as growing four feet tall, but it is only two feet tall now that it is growing in my garden. It is planted at the rear of the bed where it doesn't show. Why was the size that was printed on the label so wrong?

A. It is possible, of course, that the label on this plant was mixed with another before you purchased it. Many people take plant labels out of the pots to read them, and although most people intend to place them back into the same pot, they are often stuck into a neighboring pot by mistake. Children often pull out the tags as well. I remember a visit I made to a garden center when my oldest child was two. He was being so patient and quiet that a friend and I spent some amount of time looking at all the plants on display. I turned around at one point to see that he was busily taking the labels out of dozens of pots and placing them in other containers! So it is possible that the size on the plant label was information intended for another plant.

If this is the first year that the plant is in your garden I would wait and see what happens next year. Most perennials don't achieve their full height the first year in a garden. In fact, it is a general rule that you won't see what a perennial is *really* like until its third year in the garden.

The sizes that are printed on information tags are approximate; the same plant will grow differently in different locations depending on the soil type, amount of light, and the growing conditions during each individual year. I had lovely *Lysimachia punctata* (yellow loosestrife) in my garden in the Berkshires for years. It always grew to three or three and a half feet tall in that location. When I moved to Cape Cod I brought some with me and sited it accordingly in my cottage garden. But year after year it has reached only two feet in height. It just does not get as high in my sandy soil as it did in the clay of Spencertown.

DEADHEADING

Q. Is it very important to cut off the perennials' spent flower heads?

A. Cutting off the wilted flowers from a plant (deadheading) is done for several reasons. In part, it prevents the plant from devoting its resources to making seeds. Cutting off the blooms enables the plant to devote all its energy to strengthening the plant, without the distraction of the seeds. For some perennials, prompt deadheading encourages continual or repeat blooming. Lady's mantle, for example, will bloom again if deadheaded, and most summer phlox will continue to blossom if the wilting flowers are quickly removed.

Don't worry though, that any failure to remove the spent blooms will result in the decline of an otherwise healthy plant; a plant is designed to grow and produce seeds. The failure to deadhead will not cause the plant to die. (This is not true of biennials. Plants that are biennials will die after producing seeds in their second year, and their life may sometimes be extended another year by prompt deadheading.)

Some people also feel that a deadheaded plant looks tidier, or they don't want the spent blooms to distract from the plants that are currently in flower. I urge you to make your own judgment about this on a plant-by-plant basis. I love how the seedheads of *Iris sibirica* look in the fall, and I think that the dried flower stalk of the *Filipendula rubra* is almost prettier than the blossom.

Deadheading also prevents a plant from self-seeding around the garden; although you may want the lupines to reseed, you may be less inclined to put up with the thousands of Queen Anne's lace that appear.

Q. I'm finding that maintaining a perennial bed is much more work than I anticipated. Is there any way to cut down on these chores?

A. Early in my gardening years I asked a friend if her large perennial garden was a lot of work. "Well..." she answered, "it ain't instant coffee!" There will always be jobs that need to be done in the garden; a little organization and a flexible attitude will keep them from becoming overwhelming.

Maintenance will be less if you plan your garden with care. Anyone who loves flowers will be tempted to buy whatever catches their attention at the plant shop. If your goal is less maintenance, restrain yourself! Knowing in advance what type of care the plant requires will help you avoid those plants that need a lot of fussing to keep them alive and looking good.

Before buying or growing a new plant do a bit of investigation about its growing habits. Many perennials are more carefree than others. Avoid plants that spread very rapidly; they have to be divided quite often to keep them in bounds. Some plants, silver mound *Artemisia*, for example, sprawl and get leggy as they grow; they require a good haircut to keep them looking neat. Find out if the plant you are considering needs such attention, and decide if you are willing to provide it. Plants that need staking should also be avoided.

Why put in flowers that need to be supported when you can plant ones that will hold themselves up? Consider plants that are carefree and disease resistant. Hybrid tea roses, for example, require quite a bit of spraying and feeding in order to keep them looking their best. With so many lovely flowers to choose from, why put up with a Prima Donna that has to be spoon fed? If you have already planted something that you regret, dig it up and give it to someone else. A rose by any other name may smell as sweet, but one person's hybrid tea is another's skunk cabbage.

Laying down soaker hoses under a layer of mulch will go a long way toward cutting down on perennial bed maintenance. If the watering system is in place you won't have to lug the hose and sprinklers around. Watering the soil, not the leaves, will also help prevent fungus growth as discussed in Chapter 1. At the risk of boring you by repeating it again, mulch keeps the moisture in and the weeds out.

Save all your moving of plants for the spring or the fall. April or late September are ideal. As the summer passes and you notice plants that are too tall or too short for their location, make a list or tag them with a piece of yarn. Put stakes in the places where you want them to end up, reserving that spot at the time when you can clearly visualize how the plant will look in that location. Mark any plants that have self-seeded into an awkward location, as well as any that will need dividing to keep the clump vigorous. In the fall or the spring spend a day or two moving all these plants. It is much more efficient to do it all at once than to drag out the shovels, wheelbarrow, and bonemeal several times. Consolidate other tasks as well. Spend an evening deadheading rather than feeling that you have to snip each flower head off as soon as it goes by.

Finally, never expect that all the work will be done, and don't be afraid to bring in some hired help once in awhile. If you expect a garden to stay "finished," or to always look its best, you will have no peace.

Q. My lupines were lovely for four years but this year they just disappeared. What could have happened?

A. There are a number of reasons why plants suddenly disappear from a perennial garden. Sometimes they die in an especially cold or dry winter, particularly if they went into such a winter already stressed from a long summer drought. If the winter or spring is abnormally wet, and the soil isn't well drained, it is always possible for plants to rot. Another possibility is animal damage. Perhaps rabbits have moved into your garden for the first time. Rabbits love lupines! (Woodchucks are worse...they love *everything*.) If animals were responsible, it is likely that you would have noticed the lupines as they were being munched. Here yesterday, bitten today, gone tomorrow.

It may also just be a case of the plants having lived out their natural life-span. To paraphrase George Orwell, all perennials are perennial but some are more perennial than others. There are some perennials, like peonies, that live and thrive undisturbed for years. There are others, like your lupines, that spend two years as small young plants and another two or three as glorious mature specimens. After making and dropping their seeds for this period they consider their duty done and say good-bye. Usually a few of the seeds that they dropped will have sprouted, giving you a continuing supply of lupines.

Other plants that are considered short-lived perennials are *Delphiniums, Digitalis x mertonensis* (foxglove), *Geum, Gaura* and *Lychnis coronaria* (rose campion). Don't let the short life-span of these plants discourage you! If you love a plant it is worth starting a few from seed every year, buying a couple of plants, or watching for self-seeded young ones to relocate and nurture. I say relocate because healthy seedlings will undoubtedly spring up directly under or in the middle of another plant; they will need to be moved when young so that they have enough light and room to grow. If you buy or transplant a few new plants each year or two you will insure your *perennial* enjoyment of these short-lived plants.

DIVIDING PERENNIALS

Q. I had a clump of shasta daisies that were beautiful for five years. The past two years there have been fewer and fewer blossoms. What is the problem?

A. Just as some perennials have a short life span, others need rejuvenating every so often. Shasta daisies (are they now renamed *Chrysanthemum* x *superbum*?) require regular dividing in order to keep them looking fresh as...well, you know. Many perennials lose vigor in the center of an established clump and new growth only occurs on the perimeter. When you see this happening, you know that it is time to divide. Other plants need to be divided when they start to outgrow their allotted space in the garden. Dividing an established perennial is the quickest way to get several clumps of the same plant; divisions of older plants grow much more quickly than new plants started from cuttings or seed.

Perennials that bloom in the spring should be divided in late August or early September. Other perennials can be split in April or in the fall. The easiest way to divide an established clump is to dig it all up, set it aside and cut the clump with a sharp knife or your spade. Divide the plant into clumps that are roughly 10 or 12 inches in diameter. Place one of those clumps in the spot where the original plant was growing, and distribute the rest elsewhere...maybe into your neighbors yard!

It is difficult to contemplate digging up an established plant, especially since it hasn't been *that* long since it was a small, young perennial that you thought would *never* look lush and gorgeous. Be ruthless. It is easy to dig up a clump that is eighteen inches in diameter...it will be impossible once that clump reaches three feet across. The pieces that get planted back into the garden will revive and fill out quickly. Given some TLC, mature plants usually recover from the uprooting very nicely.

Go ahead and pop the entire plant out of the soil using your shovel, and then using the same shovel, chop off a large chunk of the newest from the outside edge of the plant. Ignore any illustration you may have seen in books or magazines that shows perennials being divided using two garden forks...this method does not work.

When replanting your divided plant, throw a handful of bone meal or some super-phosphate fertilizer into the hole and mix it into the soil underneath where the plant is to go. Water the plant well after it is placed in the ground, and be sure to keep it watered if it doesn't rain.

Divide your Shasta daisies every three or four years. Other plants should be split as you notice them increasing in size, or looking less vigorous. It is easier on the gardener to divide a clump a year too early than to wait a year too late.

Q. I divided my peonies last year and they didn't bloom this year. Did I make a mistake by dividing them?

A. *Paeonia* are the couch potatoes of the plant world...they are content if they *never* move. This does not mean that you can't divide them, however, just be prepared for them to grumble a bit. If they are planted according to their liking, your peonies will bloom again. Be patient while they stretch their roots and get settled in.

Peonies are picky about how deeply they are buried. The crown of the plant (the place where the new shoots are formed and start to grow) should be no more than two inches below the soil surface. Placing the plant so that the red shoot nubs are an inch to an inch and a half below the surface should be fine.

Be sure that peonies are planted in an area where they will get at least five hours of strong sunlight...they won't bloom well if they are in the shade. If you are going to provide support for those heavy peony blossoms, put it in place before you need it. Grow-though supports are available at garden centers.

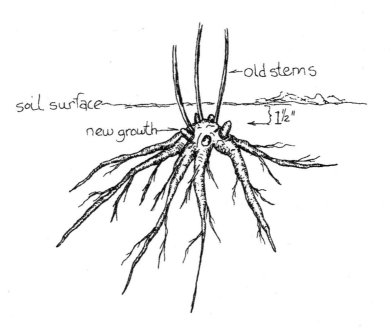

Q. I love delphiniums but I can't seem to keep them alive in my garden. What am I doing wrong?

A. You probably aren't doing anything wrong. Delphiniums are plants that will break your heart twice...first because of how lovely they are, and then again when they disappear from your garden. And they *will* disappear. Not only are delphiniums one of the short-lived perennials that we discussed, but they are pretty darn fussy during that short life! Many are top-heavy and need to be staked or they topple over in the first stiff breeze. Since stiff breezes are the order of the day near the ocean, delphiniums aren't well suited to this area. (Stake them before you need to. No sooner will it pass through your mind that the blossom is getting top-heavy and should be staked soon, when a gust of wind will come along and blow it over.) This plant is also a favorite of woodchucks, and deer; if you have critters, your plants may be their salad bar. Water splashed on the foliage encourages fungus growth on delphinium leaves; if the leaves of your plants have yellow, brown, or black spots on them, or black edges, fungi are at fault.

Delphiniums like the weather cool but not cold; they want their soil high in humus, deeply amended beds that are well drained but moist. They like to grow in soil that is on the sweet side; lime the soil and test for pH regularly. Delphiniums don't want their garden to be too moist, however, because they are also prone to crown and root rots. Getting the picture? Picky, picky, picky. If you love them and have to have them, plant several and be prepared to replace a few every year. Like unlacquered solid brass, delphiniums need constant attention to keep them looking their best...and their best is gorgeous.

INVASIVE PLANTS

Q. I planted goutweed in my flower bed and now it is taking over. Help!

A. Anyone with *Aegopodium* in their garden has my sincere sympathy. Also called Bishop's weed, it has handsome dark green or variegated white and pale green foliage, a lovely Queen Anne's lace type of flower, and it's very invasive. It is one of the plants that will give a gardener headaches and panic attacks. Others of this ilk are

Houttuynia cordata (chameleon plant), *Lysimachia clethroides* (gooseneck loosestrife), *Macleaya cordata* (plume poppy), and *Oenothera speciosa* (evening primrose).

There are several other perennials that walk the line between fast-spreaders and out and out thugs. For those of you that have large spaces to fill I have included a list of fast-spreading perennials in chapter 9. Many of these plants are lovely, and deserve a spot in your garden. The problem is, if you give them one spot they will soon take ten feet. One possibility is to put these enthusiastic growers into pots. I love *Phalaris arundinacea* (ribbon grass) but I don't have a place that it can spread, so I have it in two large pots on my deck. It's lovely ... and contained.

Anyone with a flower bed that is bounded on all sides by concrete or large buildings might want to plant some of these "vigorous growers" in such a location. (If you plant the *Houttuynia* however, I'd lock my doors and windows at night...this plant knows no boundaries!)

What to do if you already have such a plant in your garden? Persistence is the name of the game. Dig as much up by hand as possible. You may have to resort to an application of an herbicide that is sold at garden centers. I don't ordinarily encourage such products, but in some cases such as goutweed or poison ivy, they are necessary. Use such products according to directions. You will need to cover any plants that you don't want killed since the herbicides will kill any plant that they land on. Several applications may be necessary for some plants, and you may find small new ones sprouting up for years.

Some very invasive plants will undoubtedly require multiple efforts to get them out of your garden. Dig all of them up, spray any newly emerging foliage with herbicide, lay several layers of newspapers and bark mulch on the area to smother it, and pray a lot.

I battled *Aegopodium* in my garden in the Berkshires for years. It came into my flower bed along with a peony that was taken from a friend's garden. At first I thought nothing of it...I had a thirty by fifty foot slope to fill with perennials. I was young and inexperienced.

I really *should* have noticed what this plant can do; for years I passed by a woods near Lenox that was *carpeted* with goutweed. I drove by these woods on a daily basis and saw that only the goutweed grew on the forest floor; it was really quite lovely. But did the sight of that one little plant in my garden set off any alarm bells? I ignored it the first year and paid for my oversight for twelve years afterward.

I wish I could tell you that because of my efforts the garden was finally free of this scourge, but the truth is after twelve years we moved. There were many perennials in that garden that I didn't move to Cape Cod for fear of bringing a piece of *Aegopodium* with them. Despite my resolve to avoid it, one of the Iris plants I did relocate must have had a small goutweed root in it. When I saw a small *Aegopodium* sprout in the middle of the Iris foliage, I dug it up and threw it in the garbage...Iris and all.

FERTILIZING PERENNIALS

Q. Do I fertilize perennials differently from other plants?

A. Before I get into details about fertilizer and perennials, I want to stress that it is better for perennials and shrubs to be fertilized on the light side. Studies continue to show that although fertilizer makes a plant grow larger and faster it does not make it more healthy. That large growth is tender growth, and therefore more prone to insect and disease attack. For most plants, a moderate amount of fertilizer applied in the spring is sufficient. Apply organic fertilizers any time after the ground thaws, or apply chemical fertilizers in May. Exceptions to the once-a-year rule are daylilies, oriental lilies, and roses. These plants benefit from at least one liquid feed in midsummer in addition to the application in the spring. A general balanced fertilizer is fine for a perennial bed early in the spring. A light application of 10-10-10 or a similar organic fertilizer can be applied in late March. Fertilizers with a higher middle number, meant for a blooming plant, are also fine. Although perennials need nitrogen, too much encourages leaf growth. It is preferable to strengthen the root system of perennials by using a fertilizer higher in phosphorus and potassium. When in doubt, use a fertilizer such as 5-10-10, or similar ratio. This would also be the preferable type to use if manure is also added to the garden.

A general guideline for the amount of fertilizer necessary is to allow 50 pounds of complete fertilizer per 1,000 feet. If manure has also been added decrease the amount of fertilizer to 30 to 40 pounds per 1,000 square feet. This is a standard application; your own garden may not need as much. If your plants seem to be thriving, it is better to use less fertilizer. Always take care to apply fertilizers around the base of the perennials, not on top of the plants. Work it into the soil a bit if possible, and water it in well.

When I plant any perennial I throw a small handful of super phosphate or bone meal into the bottom of the hole and dig it in well. Research shows that phosphorus doesn't leach out of the soil like nitrogen does, so it will be available to the plant as its roots grow.

Adding fertilizer, be it organic or chemical, should be viewed as just one small step in the maintenance of healthy growing conditions for your perennials. The regular addition of compost to your perennial bed is, in my opinion, more important than the fertilization.

Q. No matter how carefully I plan things out, there are always times when I have "holes" in my perennial bed. This is especially true in August when I have cut many of the earlier bloomers back. What can I do about this?

A. This is an ongoing problem for most perennial gardeners, partly because a garden is always changing. Just as you figure out a way to fill one bare spot, the death of a plant creates a new one!

Many gardeners grow or buy older annuals to fill in those mid-summer spaces. If you start several annuals in attractive clay pots early in the season, you can place these pots around the garden in those places that need a quick filler. Perennials can be grown in pots for the same purpose. You can enjoy these plants on a deck or patio, then move them into the garden as needed.

The other possibility is to note what month your garden needs some areas filled in, and find plants that will be in bloom at that time. Plant them as you need them, or put them in the following spring. With some planning you will be able to hide the "holes," or perhaps plant something nearby that will look so spectacular that no one will notice a bare spot.

Q. I bought some perennials last August that were blooming when I bought them. I selected them because I wanted something in my garden that would bloom in late summer. This year, however, they bloomed in July. Are plants always this changeable? When should I expect them to bloom next year?

A. Buying plants that are currently in bloom can be deceiving. Plants often come from the grower in bud, since the majority of the plant-buying public wants to see a bloom on a plant when they buy it. This does not mean that the plants *normally* bloom at that time of year. In the early spring plants shipped to garden centers usually are coming out of greenhouses, and are well ahead of those grown in the local gardens. Later in the year you can find plants that growers have kept chilled or started later in the year in order to have spring blooms on the plant in August. Regardless of how they are grown, immature plants often bloom later than they will once they are established; it is very possible that a young plant will bloom up to a month later the first year than it will in the future.

Variations in growing conditions from year to year can also affect the time when a plant blossoms. Just when you think that you know when something will come into bloom in your garden, a change in temperature or rainfall will alter its normal pattern. One year some friends asked me to provide the flowers for their daughter's Bat Mitzvah. Since the occasion was planned for mid-June in the Berkshires, I envisioned bouquets of iris, peonies, yellow loosestrife, and lupines. That spring the temperatures were especially hot starting in May, so all the June bloomers were finished blooming by June first! The arrangements were made using flowers that normally bloomed in July, with the help of several wildflowers that were also blooming ahead of schedule.

Most books about perennials give approximate times that the plants will be in flower. For a general guide to plants that are in bloom month by month, see Chapter 9.

Q. I have quite a few areas around the shrubs that would look better if they had plants growing in them. Which plants make good ground covers?

A. When most people think of ground covers they usually think first of pachysandra, ivy, or vinca. These plants certainly have their place; *Vinca minor*, for example, is one of the few plants that grows well in the deep shade and dense roots under maple trees. But many other low growing perennials, shrubs, and vines make good ground covers. There are two lists of ground covers in chapter 9; one list is of ground covers for sunny areas, and the other is of plants that make good groundcover in shade and part-shade.

Plants that I am especially fond of for groundcovers in shade and part-shade are: *Aster divaricatus* (white wood aster), *Lamium maculatum* 'White Nancy', *Epimedium* species, *Carex* 'Ice Dance', and *Geranium macrorrhizum*.

In sunny areas I like *Ajuga reptans* (bugleweed), *Geranium macrorrhizum* (perennial geranium), and *Arctostaphylos uva-ursi* (bearberry). Bearberry is really a shrub, but so low-growing and handsome, as well as pest and disease free, that I have to mention it here. *Thymus ssp.* (creeping thymes), *Erica ssp.* and *Calluna ssp.* (heaths and heathers) are also good ground covers that are drought tolerant as well.

Most people think that a ground cover has to be low to the ground, but if the purpose is to choke out weeds, look attractive, and be low-maintenance, than any plant that can be so described could be a groundcover regardless of height. For example, Goldstrum *Rudbeckia* (black-eyed Susans) makes a wonderful ground cover in sun or part-shade. Perennials like the black-eyed Susan or hostas are especially good choices for gardens that are near trees; when the leaves fall, it is easy to rake these areas when the plants have died to the ground.

Q. I never am sure if I am dividing or cutting my perennials back at the right time. Is there a general rule of thumb about perennial garden maintenance?

A. Truth be told, many jobs in the perennial garden can be done whenever you get around to them. I have divided perennials in the heat of mid-summer and gotten away with it because I watered well afterwards. You can put new plants in the garden anytime from spring through fall if you pay attention to the watering after they are in the ground. Remember that a newly planted perennial (or shrub or tree) has a root system only as big as the pot it came in, and this small root-ball dries out quickly. As for clearing the garden out and cutting things back, it can be done in the fall or spring, according to the gardeners preference. The general rule of thumb for cutting plants back is that if the foliage still looks good leave it in the garden. Good looking foliage is still capable of photosynthesis, and is feeding the root system. Many perennials, such as *Epimedium* and *Aurinia*, keep their foliage through the winter. All that is needed for such plants is to clean up dead or damaged leaves in the spring. So keeping in mind that your maintenance routine is completely up to you, the following schedule makes sense and works with the natural rhythms of nature.

Spring
Transplant, divide, prune, fertilize with organics, plant new perennials, mulch. (Best done in this order...don't mulch before plants are divided or new plants put in place.) Weed.

Early Summer
If using chemical fertilizers, wait until early May before applying. Shear tall asters, Nippon (Montock) daisies, tall balloon flowers, chrysanthemums, *Boltonia*, and *Eupatorium* to keep them shorter and more bushy. Mid-to late May is a good time to do this, although it can be done anytime before July 1st. Cut between a third to one half off of the growing stems. Weed.

All Summer
Water deeply if needed; in all but the hottest weather, a good deep soaking equivalent to an inch of rain, once a week is all that is needed if your soil is amended and the garden is mulched. Deadhead, monitor for insect infestation or disease; remove any diseased or odd-looking foliage promptly. Weed.

Fall
Cut stalks when dead, label or transplant and divide, being sure to water newly divided plants through November. Amend soil by adding a layer of compost, or composted manure on top of established beds. Lime if needed (test soil first) and wait until after the ground freezes to place winter mulch over tender plants.

Organic fertilizer may be put down before the soil amendments now instead of in the spring. Weed.

Winter
Dream, plan, pray for snow. Weed...yes, you will find weeds growing throughout the winter; pull them out whenever you notice them.

Q. When do I cut back woody perennials such as lavender and Russian sage?

A. Cut woody perennials (many, such as lavender are almost "subshrubs.") in the early spring just as they start to break dormancy. Do not cut lavender down to the ground, but prune a third to one half of the live wood off. Remove any dead wood. Cut Russian sage to between six inches to two feet depending on the shape and fullness of the plant. If the plant is full and has a nice shape, leave it higher. If it is thin and scrawny, cut it shorter because this will stimulate more growth. Most Russian sage will come back if cut completely to the ground. You should also cut Nippon daisies down low, pruning old stalks to the ground or up to six inches high. Buddleia and Caryopteris, which are true shrubs but are often grown in the perennial garden, can be cut to between six inches and two feet from the ground as well. With all woody plants, removing deadwood is the first step.

Q. When is the best time to transplant perennials?

A. Although I will admit that I have moved perennials in just about every month of the year, I do believe that whether you are moving a shrub, tree, or perennial, the early spring is the ideal time to transplant. At that time, everything about that plant is primed to grow, so it is best equipped to recover. In addition, you are more likely to remember to keep a recently moved plant watered in the spring than you are in the fall. No matter when you move a plant, however, regular watering after the move and throughout the next growing season is essential.

~4~

SHRUBS AND TREES

SHRUBS AND TREES

Shrubs and trees may be the most widely grown plants; even those who wish to keep their gardening activities to a minimum like to have shrubs and trees on the property. Because these plants are larger than the smaller flowering annuals and perennials, the initial planting of a shrub or tree becomes very important. Although it is usually easy to dig up a perennial that is not planted in the most appropriate place, moving a large shrub or tree is more problematic.

In addition to proper placement, the methods used when planting a woody ornamental, and the way it is cared for as it grows, will effect its future growth and health. In this chapter I answer questions about the type of shrubs and trees that thrive in various locations, and the care required to maintain them. The chapter concludes with answers to questions about pests, diseases, and problems that are particular to woody landscape plants.

Q. I ordered a shrub from a catalog and was surprised to get a little stick in the mail. Will it ever grow to be a big bush, or should I go out and buy one at a nursery?

A. If the plant-by-mail companies were scrupulously honest they would include a picture of the way the plant will look when it arrives on your doorstep, along with the picture of a mature bush or tree. (Some of my favorite catalogs don't have any pictures at all, just written descriptions. I'm not sure if this is better...my imagination creates images far more beautiful than any picture could.) If it is healthy, your plant will surely develop into a lovely shrub; give it some TLC in the form of amended soil, mulch, and regular watering. Sometimes it is better to plant such young plants into pots and baby them along in containers over the summer, planting them into their permanent locations in the fall.

Buying shrubs and trees through the mail is fine if you can't find that particular variety in an area nursery, but if what you want to plant is available locally you are better off buying it in person. Not only do you get a larger plant this way, but you can inspect what is being sold and choose the healthiest plant that is the right size and shape.

Q. Is better to buy shrubs and trees that have been grown in containers, or are field grown plants that have been balled and burlapped better?

A. Field grown plants are usually larger, which is the reason that many people prefer buying balled and burlapped plants. In ideal situations, field grown plants are regularly root-pruned to keep their root systems contained. When done properly, such plants suffer minimal shock when dug up and wrapped with burlap. Unfortunately not all growers are so conscientious, and when some fairly large bushes and trees get dug up, their unpruned roots get cut off in the process. This leaves a fair size bush or tree with only a few roots to support it. Such a plant will have to struggle the first few years of its life in order to stay alive, and there may be considerable die-back of branches over the first two winters.

It is impossible to tell from looking at a balled and burlapped plant if it has a good root system or not. If it *does* have a healthy root system you wouldn't want to disturb it by washing away the soil, but exposing what roots are there is the only way to tell. When you buy a "B & B" plant it is best to assume that the root system is good, and to plant it undisturbed. (See the next question for information about planting shrubs and trees.) If the root system is sparse, the plant will not flourish the first year or so, and may even lose leaves, show die back of twigs and branches, or stop leaf and flower development mid-season.

Container grown plants are the answer for anyone who does not desire to take a chance on a B & B plant. Shrubs and trees grown in containers never have their roots disturbed, so they are less likely to suffer from the same planting shock as a field grown plant. Many sizes of plants are now available in containers, so home landscapers have a choice of all but the largest sizes of trees and bushes.

The root system of a container grown plant should be examined as well, however; if a plant has grown in a pot for too long the roots may have started to girdle (choke) each other, or the plant's main stem. Although many plants grown in pots have some roots circling the bottom of the container, these are usually easily loosened and pulled away from the dirt ball. If the plant that you are considering has roots wound so tightly around each other that it seems difficult to free them from each other, then another plant should be chosen.

Container grown plants are usually of a manageable size for the average gardener and homeowner as well, which is important because a plant that is easily handled is more likely to be planted correctly. If all your strength and attention is going into merely maneuvering the plant into its hole, you are less likely to want to move the plant out of, or around in the hole if it isn't right the first time!

Don't get me wrong; balled and burlapped plants can be healthy, large, beautiful plants. If you are replacing a mature shrub or tree that has died, and a small one would look funny in with other plantings, or if you want instant screening or shade, then only a larger field grown plant will do.

Container grown plants are not without their possible problems as well. If a plant is grown for too many years in the same-sized pot, the root system will be so pot-bound and congested that it becomes nearly impossible to loosen it before planting. Roots that have grown in such a confined space can curl around other roots or stems, eventually choking those roots and stems and killing the plant. It may better to buy a smaller container grown plant if it is more likely to be planted correctly, or if you are not willing to gamble that you may have to baby along a plant that has too few roots, but it is always wise to look carefully at the roots of a container grown plant before putting it in the ground.

In general, balled and burlapped plants need more frequent watering; put the hose next to the stem of the plant and let it dribble for about an hour in order to soak the root ball well. Do this twice a week throughout the first summer, and once a week in cooler spring or fall temperatures. Keep *all* newly planted shrubs and trees well watered through the first year, stopping only when the ground is frozen.

Q. How do I plant a new tree or shrub?

A. For years it was taught that the proper way to plant a shrub or tree was to dig a BIG hole, amend the soil with manure and peat moss, and put some of that amended soil back into the bottom of the hole before setting the plant in. Recent research shows that this may not be the best method after all. When comparing trees that were planted in this manner with those that were planted in a hole dug wide, not deep, and filled with the original soil, the latter plantings did better by far.

The thinking is that the growing roots are more likely to spread out, not down, so it is important that this soil be loosened by digging a wide hole. If the hole is dug too deep and filled with amended soil, that area will settle over time, sinking the tree or shrub until it is in a depressed area or is planted too deeply.

Researchers also speculated that the decomposition of the peat was taking some of the nitrogen away from the plant, and that the plant eventually did better if the soil that the roots first grew in was the same as the soil that the roots encountered later. If the textural difference of the amended soil near the root ball is vastly different from the soil native to the area, the roots won't cross the transition zone. Would you leave a five star restaurant to go to the diner next door?

PLANTING TREES

When planting a young tree that will eventually have a wide root system, start by digging a hole that is as deep as the root mass of the tree that is to be planted. You want the surface of the soil where you are planting the tree to be the same level of the surface of the soil in the container that holds the tree. It is easy to see the surface of the soil in a container grown plant, but where the soil surface should be on a balled and burlapped plant is not as obvious. When planting a balled and burlapped tree, untie the burlap ball and move a bit of the dirt away from the trunk of the tree, looking for the place where the trunk flares out into the roots. Sometimes soil is inadvertently mounded up the sides of the trunk when the tree is wrapped in the burlap, leading you to believe that the natural soil line is higher than it really is. THIS IS IMPORTANT. A tree or shrub that is planted too deeply will not do well, and in fact may die.

The hole should be three or four times wider than the size of the ball or container. Digging such a wide hole loosens the soil, allows you to remove any large stones that may be buried there, and gives space to spread out the roots if they are long enough to need spreading. The old adage "dig a five dollar hole for a fifty cent tree" still applies to the width if not the depth. After the hole is completely dug, fill it full of water and let it drain out.

If the tree is in a container, tip it out or slit the container carefully (so as not to cut the roots) and remove the tree with care. If the roots have gotten long enough to curl around the bottom of the container, or if a mound of roots has pressed against the sides of the container, gently loosen these roots with your fingers and pull as many of them away from each other as you can. If you plunk the tree into the hole with the roots curling in the shape of the pot, the roots may continue to grow in that same shape, around and around, eventually choking each other or the stem of the tree. When they are pulled free and spread into the soil a bit, they will grow out and create a strong root system more quickly. If you are unable to separate the roots out with your fingers, slit the bottom of the root mass, making an x with a knife; spread the four sections apart to encourage new roots to grow away from the old ball.

Place the tree in the hole, spreading out any roots. Check the level of the base of the tree again to make sure that the base of the tree will be even with the soil line around it.

TRUNK FLARE→   ←SOIL SURFACE→

B&B PLANT IN HOLE SHOWING CORRECT PLACEMENT AND SOIL LEVEL.

Fill in the hole with the dirt you have taken out. If the soil is pure sand, dig the hole as wide as possible, mix in some composted cow manure, and add the mix back into the hole. Amend the soil in the entire planting area rather than just around the root ball. Press the soil down with your hands or feet *gently*. Pressing with too much force causes the dirt to become compacted, making it hard for the growing roots to penetrate the soil.

When planting a balled and burlapped plant you do pretty much the same, but it is usually easier to place the ball into the hole before removing the wire and burlap. After putting the tree into the hole check to see that the root flare of the tree will be at the soil line when the hole is filled. If the ball is wrapped with a wire basket, cut it away with wire snips. Cut any ropes or twine that hold the ball together as well, and remove all strings and wires from the hole. Carefully cut the burlap away from the dirt, and remove it from the hole as well.

People are sometimes mistakenly advised to leave the burlap around the root ball and let the tree's roots grow through it. It is unwise to do this because growers will sometimes use a synthetic fabric burlap that does not break down. Even burlap made of natural fibers can bind the roots up for far too long. The tree should have as few impediments as possible to stretching its roots. DO NOT LET ANYONE TELL YOU IT IS OK TO LEAVE ALL THE BURLAP ON. If any of the roots need to be stretched out into the hole after removing the burlap, do so, and fill the hole as previously described.

After filling the hole to restore a level soil line, you may want to mound a bit of soil up into a small berm in a ring around the tree's roots. This berm will hold the water in the area as you water the tree, insuring that the water will soak into the soil and not run off. Do not plant the tree lower than the soil line; do not create a small depression instead of a level area with a berm. The water-holding berm is just to help hold the water as the tree is getting established. After the tree has been in place for a year or two it is not necessary to maintain the berm.

Water the tree well with a gently dripping hose or sprinkler. You may want to give the tree a "root stimulating" fertilizer at this point, making sure to mix it according to directions, and only adding it to the soil after the tree has been well-watered first. The tree should

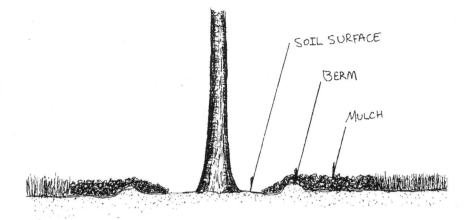

not be fertilized any more for the first year or two until it is well established. Be sure to keep the tree well-watered for the first year after you plant it, particularly in the fall before the ground freezes.

Mulch the area around the tree, keeping the mulch six inches to a foot away from the trunk of the tree. A layer of mulch two to three inches thick is adequate. Small trees do not need to be staked. If the tree has a large crown that makes it top-heavy, the tree may be staked using three ropes running from the tree to three stakes placed equal distances around the tree. Run the rope or cord through a small section of old garden hose or rubber tubing (available at garden centers) to protect the trunk of the tree from chafing, and don't tie it around the trunk too tightly. The ropes should not be tied too tightly to the stakes either; allowing the trunk to sway back and forth a bit triggers the production of hormones that signal the roots to grow strong. For this reason it is also wise not to leave the ropes on a tree for longer than one growing season. If the tree does not blow in the wind the root system may not grow as extensively. Once again it seems that nature knows best, and our attempts to "help," by staking a tree, may actually be making things worse.

PLANTING SHRUBS

Shrubs are planted using the same methods as described for trees. I do think it wise to amend the sandy soil with composted cow manure and topsoil. It is possible to dig a wide enough hole for a shrub so that you are amending most of the soil that the plant will be sending roots into, and it is unlikely that the area will be dug up again to add organic matter to the sand there. Because sandy soil does not hold nutrients, (as discussed in Chapter 1) organic matter will benefit the area where the shrubs are planted.

Follow the same procedure for spreading the roots, filling the hole, watering, and mulching that is described for planting trees.

Q. If I don't amend the soil when I plant shrubs or trees, how does the organic material that you say is so necessary get in the soil?

A. Amend the soil around shrubs and trees the same way nature does it—from the top down. You can put your woody plants on the same schedule as the perennial garden. Once a year spread a two-inch layer of compost, composted manure, or half-rotted leaves around the plants. A good schedule would be to spread these amendments in the late fall, and then fertilize and cover the area with a two-inch layer of mulch in the spring. This continual application of both organic materials will keep the soil amended.

Q. Do roses get planted the same way as other shrubs?

A. Roses like to grow in well-drained soil that is rich in organic matter, so it is important to dig a wide hole (at *least* three feet in diameter) and amend the soil with compost, peat moss or composted manure. Roses need good soil, so don't skimp on the organic matter! Mixing in two or three handfuls of bone meal or super-phosphate, and a couple of handfuls of wood ashes or lime will help as well.

Remove container grown plants from their pots and spread the roots out if necessary. If the plants are bare-root, dormant stock, build a cone of soil in the center of the planting hole and fan the roots over and around it. Adjust the height of the bush if necessary so that the base of the shrub is at surface level. In this planting zone, the graft of the plant (the knob at the bottom where the new canes grow from) can be planted above or below the soil line. In colder areas this graft is always planted below the surface to help protect it during the winter.

Pat the soil around the roots gently, building a small berm to retain the water around the plant for the first growing season. Water well and mulch the surface, keeping the mulch a few inches from the stem of the plant.

Q. There are two shrubs in my yard that aren't too large, and are planted in the wrong place. When is the best time to move them to another location?

A. Early spring is the best time to transplant shrubs and small trees. The plant is poised to break dormancy and grow, and the weather is usually cool and wet. The plant will lose less water through its leaves when the weather is cool, and the rain will help ensure that the plant gets an adequate supply of water. Dig as large of a root ball as you can carry, so that the root system is disturbed as little as possible. Sometimes it is possible to work a tarp under the severed roots so that the plant can be dragged to its new location; this allows you to dig a larger and heavier root ball than you otherwise could.

Shrubs and trees can also be transplanted in the early fall, provided that the plant was kept well watered throughout the summer, and will continue to be watered up until the time when the ground freezes. Moving a plant that has already been stressed by a condition such as drought is risky; if the summer has been dry and the shrub has not been consistently watered, it is better to wait until early spring for transplanting. Keep such a plant well watered until the ground freezes in late December, so that it will be as healthy as possible when it is transplanted. Shrubs that are moved in September should be watered deeply once a week if it does not rain, with regular soaking through November. If you are not likely to haul the hose around in forty degree weather, or if you drain your faucets for the winter, wait until spring to transplant. Root systems that will support the tree throughout the winter are growing all fall, even though the tree is otherwise dormant, so adequate moisture is especially important.

Q. Should I prune a shrub after planting it?

A. Before planting a new shrub or tree, prune off any dead branches or twigs. Leave all growing tips on the plant, delaying any other pruning until the following year. If there is a branch that crosses and rubs against another branch, one of them can be removed; other than that, hold off on the cutting. Waiting to prune a plant until it is established is wise because the growing tips are signaling the roots to grow in order to supply the top growth with the water and nutrients that it needs. Leaving all areas of new growth creates a stronger root system. If the plant cannot support all its leaves after having its roots disturbed, it will jettison what it can't maintain.

Q. When should I prune an established flowering shrub?

A. It would be easier if I could just answer "prune all shrubs in the spring," or "the fall," or "under the light of the full moon," but it isn't as simple as that. It can generally be said, however, that shrubs that bloom in the summer (on new growth) should be pruned in the early spring. Usually sometime in mid-to late March, just when the plant is gearing up to break dormancy. Plants that bloom in the spring are usually pruned just after they blossom. There are exceptions to this general rule, of course; some summer-blooming shrubs such as hydrangeas set their buds just after blooming, and these buds bloom the following summer. If this type of plant is pruned in early spring the bush will not flower that summer because all of the buds, formed the previous summer, will have been removed. Noticing if a shrub blooms on new growth or last year's growth will help you to know when to prune it.

It is important to note that not all shrubs need pruning every year, and pruning is not the same as shearing. **Pruning should be done to improve growth and appearance, not control size.** If plants have been chosen with care and planted in an appropriate place they can be allowed to grow to their full size. Shrubs that are naturally full do not need help staying dense, and often all that is needed to maintain a shrub's natural form is to periodically remove dead wood or some of the oldest growth. Pruning is the selective removal of some of the branches or buds.

We have all become accustomed to seeing shrubs that have been sheared into stiff-looking balls and cubes. I am not sure if this practice started because people had to keep foundation plantings from growing up over the windows, or if it evolved out of our misguided attempts to feel on top of things by controlling even the shapes of the plants in our yards. In any case, it is time that we reeducate our eyes, if for no other reason than to conserve time. Who wants to spend their time carving shrubs into shapes that look like they came from a child's toy train set-up?

The following is a list of some of the most commonly planted shrubs in this area with pruning guidelines given.

PRUNING DECIDUOUS SHRUBS

Abelia x *grandiflora* (abelia): This shrub is semi-evergreen in milder climates, but usually loses its leaves in the Northeast. Prune in late winter by removing deadwood, branches growing into the center of the plant, or anything odd or funky. Larger, older plants with several main stems can be renewed by removing a third of the oldest growth every year, cutting these branches to six to twelve inches above the ground. Although Abelia continues to bloom over the entire summer, minor clean-up pruning to maintain its natural form can be done throughout the season.

Berberis thunbergii (Barberry): In the early spring prune out oldest stems at the base of the plant to thin the bush and stimulate new growth. Prune growing shoots at various lengths to maintain natural shape. Touch-up pruning can be done throughout the growing season.

Buddleia (butterfly bush): Prune this shrub in late winter/early spring. Cut all growth down to a foot high or to ground level. This shrub flowers on new growth, and it will grow up to six feet in a single summer, so if you don't cut it down hard you will end up with all of the flowers (and butterflies) up high where you can't see them. Be ruthless.

Caryopteris (bluebeard): Late winter/early spring is the time to cut this shrub down to 6 to 12 inches from ground level. Go ahead...cut it down hard.

Clethra alnifolia (summersweet or sweet pepper bush): Removal of dead wood, oldest stems, suckers and general pruning can be done in the late winter/early spring as Clethra blooms in the summer on new growth. Do not shear.

Cornus alba and *Cornus sericea* (tartarian dogwood and redtwig dogwood): Late in its dormant season prune out a third of the oldest stems at the base of the plant. This will encourage the plant to sprout new stems, which have the brightest colored bark. Do not shear.

Cotoneaster: Prune in late winter/early spring. Remove all dead branches and thin oldest wood at the ground. Maintain the natural shape by pruning at the base and cutting branches to emphasize its natural shape.

Cytisus (broom): Prune right after flowering, cutting back the newest branches that have leaves by a half to a third of their length. Cut only green whips. Don't cut into old, leafless stems since they don't sprout new growth from old wood. You can shear this plant or cut by hand, but start doing it when the plant is young...once it is tall, old and woody there is no renewal pruning that can be done.

Euonymus alata (Burning Bush): Prune (or shear hedges) in late winter/early spring. Compact form need only be thinned at base to take out excess or dead branches. Large bushes can be pruned near the ground and selective branches shortened to maintain natural shape.

Forsythia: Prune either in the winter (and force the pruned branches in a vase indoors) or after flowering. Oldest wood, excess suckers, and dead branches can be cut out at base in the late winter/early spring. Selective tall branches can be thinned and pruned back to reduce size while maintaining natural shape. Shearing forsythia or chopping it off at the top should be against the law.

Hibiscus syriacus (Rose-of-Sharon): Late winter/early spring is the time to prune this shrub by cutting branches back a third. Taking out a third of the oldest branches each year will promote vigorous growth.

Hydrangea macrophylla (bigleaf hydrangeas): Prune in the early spring when the plant is breaking dormancy and you can clearly see what is living and what is dead. Remove deadwood first. If the plant is over four years old take out a third of the oldest canes right at the ground. (If there are six old canes remove two, for example. If there are twelve old canes remove four.) This stimulates the plant to grow new canes that will be more productive. After removing older growth, trim the tops of the plants down to just above the first or the second pair of buds you come to. On some canes these buds will be near the top of the plant; on others, the first live pair of buds may be further down the stem. Cut about 3/4 of an inch above the buds, making a slanted cut. Remove any flower heads from last year at this time. Note: if you cut the canes of hydrangeas down short in the fall or the spring you will be cutting off the buds that turn into flowers. Newer varieties such as "Endless Summer" bloom on new and old wood, so for maximum bloom, they're pruned in the same way.

Hydrangea paniculata (peegee hydrangea): Late winter/early spring is the time to prune this fast growing shrub that blooms on new wood. Overgrown multi-stemmed shrubs can be rejuvenated by cutting a third of the stems down to two feet from the ground. Cut another third the following year, and the remaining stems the year after that. For tree form peegees, thin lateral branches (branches that come off of another stem) and remove suckers from the base.

Hydrangea quercifolia (oakleaf hydrangeas): Flower buds are formed on this plant the year previous to blooming so it should be pruned right after flowering if at all. The best approach with this plant is to prune out deadwood and anything odd or weak in the spring; leave the rest alone.

Kerria japonica: Prune after flowering and thin excess canes by cutting oldest stems at the ground. Prune the many new shoots (often called "suckers") off at the ground anytime you notice them.

Kolkwitzia amabilis (beautybush): For plants with many trunks or main stems, prune oldest stems at the ground, removing a third of the stems each year right after the bush has flowered. Otherwise just clean up dead or odd branches in the spring. Do not shear.

Lespedeza thunbergii (bush clover): Prune this late bloomer in late winter or early spring, cutting it down by half or to as low as 6 to 12 inches tall.

Ligustrum (privet): Late winter/early spring is the time to prune or shear this shrub, although you can clean it up just about anytime. Thin oldest stems at ground level to maintain natural shape. Clip branches throughout the summer if needed.

Lonicera (honeysuckle): Prune in the early spring. Cut out a third of the stems each year to rejuvenate older shrubs. Hand prune; do not shear.

Prunus x cisten (sand cherry) Cut out oldest stems at the ground each year. Prune after flowering. Cut out deadwood and anything odd or weak-looking. Do not shear.

Rhododendron (deciduous azaleas): Late winter/early spring is the time to prune if it is needed, and stems pruned can be forced indoors. (Note that this applies to **deciduous** azaleas; for pruning times for other rhodys, see evergreen section.) Thin out a third of old stems each year by cutting back to half of their length.

Rosa species (Roses): Prune most roses in late winter/early spring, and begin by removing all dead wood. A good guide is to prune your roses when the forsythia blooms. Canes can be either cut to a foot to eighteen inches above ground level, or half the previous year's growth can be removed. Cut above an *outward* facing bud, making cuts at a 45-degree angle. (This bud will become a new branch, and you want that branch to grow out away from the center of the plant so that the rose has an attractive shape.) Prune out any thin, spindly canes and any that cross and rub against each other. Prune ramblers and climbers that bloom on second-year growth after flowering. The shorter you cut your rose bush down, the fewer flowers it will have that summer.

Spiraea: Prune spring blooming varieties such as the white flowered bridal wreath right after flowering. (Spring-blooming varieties bloom on last year's growth.) Remove deadwood and any odd branches that don't contribute to a good shape. Cut such branches into the inside center of the plant so the cut does not show. Do not shear this plant. Summer-flowering plants such as the pink *Spiraea japonica* are pruned in early spring, and these can be sheared or cut back by about a third with scissors. Another light shearing right after bloom will stimulate new growth and more flowers.

Syringa vulgaris (lilac): Lilacs should be pruned in the spring immediately after they bloom. Cutting main stems back will result in the loss of blossoms from those stems in the next year; lilacs form their flower buds the year previous to blooming. Young plants can be left to grow for a few years without pruning. Older plants should have a third of the oldest stems cut each year, and some of the suckers thinned out. Old shrubs that are blooming at the top of the plant can only be rejuvenated by cutting a third of the old stems back each year. These older stems can be cut to the ground, or down by a third of their size as the gardener prefers. Prune out most new shoots (suckers), leaving one or two for new growth.

Viburnum species: Most viburnums can be pruned in early spring, although they don't always need it. Old wood can be trimmed to the ground to revitalize the shrub. Remove deadwood.

Weigela hybrids: Prune these shrubs after blooming. Mature shrubs may need a thinning of old wood annually. Prune to desired size. Weigelas bloom on year-old wood. Do not shear this plant...they have a wild and woolly shape and should be enjoyed as such.

PRUNING EVERGREEN SHRUBS AND TREES

Buxus species (boxwood): Major pruning or shearing is done in the late winter/early spring, with touch-up pruning to maintain shapes done throughout the summer as needed.

Chamaecyparis (false cypress including Hinoki) Prune out dead branches and prune in early spring if needed. (Rarely needs much pruning.) Do not shear!

Euonymus fortunei (wintercreeper): Prune the many cultivars of Wintercreeper in the late winter/early spring. Climbing vines can be pruned throughout the season to maintain shape if needed.

Euonymus japonica (evergreen euonymus): Thin branches and prune in late winter/early spring. Light pruning to improve shape can be done until midsummer. Do not shear!

Ilex species (holly): Prune in late dormant season, although spot pruning to maintain shape is all right just about anytime. Light pruning of selected branches provides holiday decorations at Christmas time. Inkberry holly (*Ilex glabra*) can be thinned in late winter. Japanese holly (*Ilex crenata*) can be thinned or sheared into formal shapes at the same time.

Juniperus (junipers): Large trees such as *Juniperus virginiana* (Red Cedar) seldom need pruning except to remove deadwood. Plant such trees where they can attain their full height. Shrubs can be pruned in late winter/early spring if needed. Prune low -growing junipers by lifting top branches and cutting the older, lower branches inside the plant; when you drop the top growth back down, those branches hide your cut. Always prune to maintain the natural shape of the plant. Don't just chop the ends off in an effort to keep the plant smaller; malpruned junipers are ugly.

Kalmia latifolia (mountain laurel): Prune this broadleaf evergreen right after it flowers. Old branches may be thinned out and faded flowers pinched off to encourage bushier growth. Don't shear this plant.

Mahonia aquifolium (Oregon grape): New growth can be pinched after flowering to promote bushiness. Older stems that have lost lower leaves can be cut to the ground in late winter/early spring.

Picea species (spruce): In general, little pruning is needed except to remove dead branches. If bushier growth is desired the growing tips can be cut by a third to one half in the spring when new growth first emerges.

Pieris japonica (andromeda): Any pruning necessary is best done after flowering. Old growth can be cut back to rejuvenate old, leggy plants. Plant Pieris where it can attain its full height so that little pruning is needed. Plants bloom on old wood, so plants that are sheared to control size seldom bloom.

Pinus species (pines, including White pine): Little pruning is needed but a dense habit can be encouraged by cutting the new growth tips (called "candles") by one third to one half. Candles are cut in the spring when they have grown to about six inches long, but before the needles start to expand. Remove deadwood whenever necessary.

Prunus laurocerasus (cherry laurel): Prune this broad-leaved evergreen in late winter or just after it has bloomed in the spring. When planted in a location where it can attain its full size, little pruning is needed.

Pyracantha coccinea (firethorn): The Pyracantha is a vigorous grower that bears flowers and berries along the stem of last years growth. Prune out a quarter to a third of the oldest stems each year in early spring, and prune other stems right after flowering to maintain size.

Rhododendron species (rhododendrons and azaleas): Pinching the new growth of these plants results in more blossoms and bushier shrubs. When the new growth is still soft and the leaves immature, pinch off about one inch just above a set of leaves. If large-growing Rhododendrons have been planted next to the house, pinching new growth should be begun as soon as possible to keep these plants from overgrowing the space allowed. (The need for this continued maintenance can of course be avoided if only low-growing varieties are chosen for foundation plantings.)

Larger plants can be shortened by cutting branches back to a side branch or dormant bud. This can be done all at once or by thinning a third of the oldest branches back, every year for three years. A similar approach can be taken with plants that have multiple stems growing from the ground; thin out old branches by cutting a few of them at the base of the plant. Although healthy plants may come back if cut to the ground in one fell swoop, it is risky to rejuvenate an old bush this way. Weak or stressed plants may give up completely when given such a drastic pruning.

Azaleas should not be sheared. Their natural shapes are much more lovely than any that a human might sculpt, and shearing prevents flowering since the flower buds are formed on old wood. Do any light hand-pruning right after they bloom or as new growth is emerging.

Rhododendrons can be pruned either after they flower or in the early spring. (Pruning in early spring will remove flower buds formed the previous year.)

Taxus species (yew): These evergreens are most often sheared, especially when planted as foundation shrubs. Although they take shearing well, this results in foliage growth only on the outside of the plants, with the inside branches remaining bare. To maintain a more natural shape for individual shrubs or an informal hedge, thin out about a quarter of the old growth by cutting selected stems back to the lateral (side) branches. This pruning can be done in the early spring. Yews have at least two growth spurts during the summer so they often need either another shearing or light pruning later in the summer to tidy them up. Older shrubs can be rejuvenated by cutting stems down to twelve inches from the ground in late winter/early spring. Follow such renewal pruning with a light application of fertilizer and regular watering through the summer.

Thuja occidentalis (arborvitae): Only occasional touch-up pruning is needed for these plants. Remove dead wood anytime, and thin if needed in late winter/early spring. You can shear an inch or two off arborvitae in the spring, but don't cut them back by much; they will not grow back from bare wood.

Tsuga species (hemlock): Trees need little pruning, but hemlocks grown as hedges need shearing or pruning in the spring. Sheared hedges can be encouraged to grow more dense by thinning selected branches in early spring.

PRUNING VINES

Actinidia chinensis (kiwi berry): This vine blooms on old wood and needs heavy pruning to keep it of reasonable size. Prune in the spring, removing half of the old wood. Cut down to just above a healthy bud.

Akebia quinata: The Akebia is a vigorous grower that can be pruned in early spring or after flowering. Thin oldest growth out every spring and rejuvenate old vines by cutting to the ground.

Campsis radicans (trumpet vine or creeper): Prune heavily in early spring, cutting out growth that held flowers the previous year. Prune out suckers from the base of the plant and pinch growing tips to encourage branching. Trumpet creeper blooms in the summer on the end of the new growth, so don't hesitate to hack it back.

Clematis species: In order to know when to prune the Clematis it is important to know when the variety that you have blooms. Those that bloom in spring on old wood, such as *C. montana*, get pruned right after flowering. Varieties that bloom later on new growth, such as the Jackmanii hybrids, get pruned in early spring; cut them down to a foot or two from the ground, leaving three or four buds on the remaining stem. Clematis that bloom twice in the summer such as "Nelly Moser" and "Ramona" get pruned right after the first blossoms fade. Pruning these varieties after the first flowering encourages the second blooming.

Hedera helix (English ivy): Heavy pruning should be done in late winter/early spring, but clean-up trimming can be done throughout the growing season. Ground cover ivy can be rejuvenated by high mowing or cutting with pruning shears.

Hydrangea anomala (climbing hydrangea): Prune in the late winter/early spring, removing old wood to control size and keep growth strong. Flowers on new growth.

Lonicera japonica (honeysuckle vine): Prune in early spring and throughout the summer if needed. Many of the newer hybrids continue to bloom on new growth, so a mid-summer removal of old vines will stimulate the vine to continue to flower.

Parthenocissus quinquefolia (Virginia creeper): and

Parthenocissus tricuspidata (Boston ivy): The vigorous growth of both of these vines must be controlled to prevent them from taking over where they are planted. Prune unwanted growth and dead or diseased vines in early spring. Other pruning to keep the vine within bounds can be done throughout the summer. Old vines can be rejuvenated by cutting them to the ground.

Polygonum aubertii (silver lace vine): Blossoming on new growth in late summer, this vine should be pruned in the spring when danger of frost is past. Rapid growth renews the vine even if heavily pruned.

Wisteria floribunda and W. sinensis: Both the Japanese and Chinese Wisterias are rapid growers that can be pruned throughout the summer. Hard pruning can help encourage young vines to blossom. As young plants reach the desired size, begin thinning new growth, leaving one or two buds. Prune back leafless shoots as they grow. All side branches can be shortened by half in the spring. Watch for and leave the short stems, called spurs, which are loaded with flowering buds.

Q. I have a new house to landscape. How do I begin to put in foundation plantings?

A. Begin your landscaping with careful consideration. Faced with a new house sitting on what seems to be a vast expanse of bare earth, many people rush to plant shrubs around the foundation just to get *something* green growing there. At this stage, it seems impossible that the cute little rhododendron and the lovely blue spruce will ever get large enough to even look established. It doesn't take long however, for those small plants to go beyond established to become enormous trees and bushes; those cute, little plantings soon grow large enough to block windows and knock against the house in any strong wind. Careful consideration will save you from spending hours on pruning, or worse, having to remove a lovely tree or shrub simply because it is too large for that location.

Your first decision should be whether any plantings are necessary around your house at all. We have all become very quick to surround our foundations with an unbroken line of greenery. Our eyes have come to expect round balls under the windows and pointy cones at the corners. Yet with foundation plantings, as with much else in design, less is often more. Planting a few well-chosen shrubs is preferable to putting in many surrounding the entire house. More plants can always be added later if necessary.

The plantings around your house and in your yard should be planned for *your* maximum enjoyment. What good is a line of blooming Azaleas around your foundation if you can't see them when you look out of your windows? Perhaps it would be wiser to plant those Azaleas in a shrub border around the patio so you can see them from the dining room windows. If a sidewalk is the usual route into your house, plant the shrubs that will give the most pleasure there, where they will elicit a smile every time you come in and out of your home. Two or three shrubs that have fragrant summer flowers will send their scent into your bedroom if you plant them near the window. How *you* use your house should determine what gets planted next to it.

Choosing the right plant for the location is the next consideration. Pay a visit to a local nursery and see what is available. Note those plants that you like and begin looking for fully grown examples of these plants in other peoples' yards. Spend some time researching the ultimate size a mature shrub or tree will be so that you will avoid the rhododendron-blocking-the-picture-window syndrome. Remember that the sizes given for the height and width of a mature plant are approximate; final sizes vary according to growing conditions and the individual plant. Many popular shrubs are available in dwarf or small-growing cultivars.

Knowing what the light is like in an area to be planted will also determine what plant is appropriate for that location. A plant that will thrive in moist dappled shade will probably not do well in a dry southern exposure. Once you have a list of the growing conditions in each location that is to be landscaped, you can begin selecting the right plant for each of these areas. Some suggestions for lower-growing shrubs suitable for foundation plantings can be found in Chapter 9.

• • •

Q. I don't have much time to spend maintaining a garden, but I love plants and flowers. What can I do that is fairly low maintenance?

A. Mixed shrub borders are an ideal way to have flowers around your property and keep the hours that you spend on maintenance to a minimum. The key is to choose the shrubs wisely. Considering the ultimate size that a bush will attain is as important in a low-maintenance garden as it is for foundation plantings. Choosing shrubs that will thrive in the area that they are planted is also important; a plant that is not happy with its location will be under stress, and stressed plants are more subject to attack from insects and diseases. Plants should also be chosen for pest and disease resistance. A plant that needs to be monitored for fungal leaf spots or insect infestation takes more time and may mean heavier use of chemicals to control problems. Choosing a plant that is disease and insect resistant is part of an approach to gardening called Integrated Pest Management (IPM). See Chapter 9 for a list of carefree shrubs.

Q. I would like to plant some of the beach roses in an area where I have already planted some ornamental grasses. I added topsoil and organic matter to the soil before the grasses were put in; will the beach roses do all right if the soil isn't pure sand?

A. Your *Rosa rugosa* will think they have died and gone to heaven. Although the beach rose will live in the sand at the seashore, it does not need such conditions to thrive. In fact, I think you will see that your roses look better than any you have ever seen at the beach!

Q. How, and when, do I prune my *Rosa rugosa*?

A. *Rosa rugosa* can get pruned in the late winter or early spring. As with all shrubs, remove dead wood first. Cut any canes that are shooting up where you do not want them to be...if left alone, *Rosa rugosa* will take over your yard. After that, cut the canes down by at least half. This encourages the plant to stay bushy. You can run a lawnmower over this plant and it will come back like gangbusters.

Q. I would like to plant a shrub border that blooms in the summer. Which shrubs are in bloom in July and August?

A. There are several lovely shrubs that bloom in the summertime. Before buying any plant make sure that the light and moisture available will suit the plants that you have chosen. Some shrubs that bloom in the summer include: *Buddleia davidii* (butterfly bush), *Caryopteris* x *clandonensis* (bluebeard), *Clethra alnifolia* (summersweet), *Hibiscus syriacus* (rose-of-sharon), *Hydrangea macrophylla* (bigleaf hydrangea), *Hydrangea paniculata* (Peegee Hydrangea), *Hydrangea quercifolia* (Oakleaf Hydrangea), *Potentilla fruticosa* (cinquefoil), *Spirea japonica &* x *bumalda,* and *Vitex agnus-castus* (chaste tree). I am particularly fond of the *Spirea* x *bumalda* (bumald spirea), and *Spirea japonica* varieties that have lime-green or golden foliage. Cultivars such as 'Goldmound' and 'Magic Carpet' have bright foliage in addition to their pink flowers.

Another summer-blooming shrub that grows well on the Cape and Islands is *Abelia* x *grandiflora*. Abelia grows well in sun or half-shade, is well-sized for most home landscapes, is relatively pest and disease free. Although the flowers are not very showy, it blooms most of the summer. Besides abelia, the hydrangeas and clethera are the best for areas that are partly shaded.

Q. Are there any shrubs that bloom in the fall?

A. Although it has yet to achieve great popularity, *Lespedeza thunbergii* (bush clover) is a late-blooming shrub with flowing, graceful foliage. The pea-like flowers are in shades of pink, pink-purple or white. This shrub grows between four and eight feet high, depending on the variety, and about as wide as it is high.

If you are looking for a low plant, there are heath and heather varieties that bloom well into the fall. If you want a high shrub (almost a small tree), the *Heptacodium miconioides* (seven-son flower) is in full flower in September. This multi-stemmed plant has beautiful foliage and fragrant, white flowers followed by pink sepals that last for two or three weeks after the flowers have fallen.

• • •

Q. When I bought my buddleia the person at the nursery told me to deadhead the blossoms after they have wilted if I want to encourage more blooms. Do I need to do this to other flowering shrubs as well?

A. The spent flowers of *Buddleia davidii* are removed because this summer-flowering shrub blooms on new growth. When you regularly cut off the wilted flowers, the butterfly bush will bloom all summer. Deadheading the flowers won't create more blossoms on shrubs that form their flower buds in the previous year, or those that grow slowly. Other than the buddleia, shrubs that will continue to bloom if deadheaded are the two summer-blooming spireas, *Spirea* x *bumalda* and *Spirea japonica* and *Vitex agnus-castus* (chaste tree).

Q. I love rhododendrons and would like to plant a few near my house. Are there some that stay small?

A. There are a few rhodys that stay under five feet tall. Local nurseries usually carry a selection, and smaller plants are available from catalogs as well. The *Rhododendron yakusimanum* (shortened by most to "the Yaks") have gotten a lot of press lately because of their handsome foliage and maximum three-foot size. The lower growing azaleas would mix well with the other rhodys that you plant; your local nursery can point you toward the compact varieties.

Q. I am usually on the Cape for part of the summer and I love the blue flowered Hydrangeas. Can I take some back to my home up north?

A. The bushes you see on the Cape and Islands are hardy to zone 6, but even these may die to the ground in an especially cold winter. Because the flower buds form the previous summer, a cold winter can freeze the buds and prevent the bush from flowering even though the shrub itself lives through the winter. There are several blue hydrangea cultivars that are hardy to zone 4, however and bloom on both old and new wood. 'Endless Summer' is the most well known of these, but others such as 'All Summer Beauty' and

'Penny Mac' are also available and worth trying.

I have also heard of people in zone 5 and zone 6 constructing wire cages around their plants and filling these cages with dry leaves that insulate the stems and buds during the coldest months. If you are game for such treatment you could try planting a shrub that was purchased on Cape Cod in your most sheltered location and using this cage-and-leaf method to protect it. I personally cannot stand looking at caged plants. I don't even stake them in my perennial garden. This is most likely a result of living with a dozen caged fruit trees for several years.

Our home in the Berkshires was right on the deer's route from a field to a stream, and the deer would munch on the baby apple and pear trees as they passed through. In order to save the trees we constructed cages that were wide enough and high enough to keep the deer away from the trees while they grew. It worked. The trees are eight feet high today and bearing fruit, but I had my fill of looking out the window at what appeared to be a tree zoo.

Bear in mind that even if a plant is hardy in your area it may also grow differently because the soil is different as well. These plants obviously like the well-drained, acid soils of the Cape and Islands. Given the uncertainty of temperatures and soil in your area, it may be easier if you forgo the Hydrangea planting at your home; it's much easier to plan on vacationing in this area at the beginning of every August!

Q. I see such beautiful roses around the Cape and Islands. Which roses do the best here?

A. Visitors to the Cape and Islands in the summer often come to associate this area with blue Hydrangeas and both shrub and climbing roses. There are several varieties that are popular for their disease resistance and long periods of bloom. They include:
Aloha: Medium pink climbing rose that is very sturdy but not too large. Repeat bloom if deadheaded promptly.

Betty Prior: A floribunda rose with single pink flowers that bloom in clusters. 5 to 6 feet tall.

Blanc Double de Coubert: Shrub rose with fragrant, white semi-double blossoms. Yellow foliage in the fall.

Bonica: Medium pink, double flowers with a long midseason and repeat bloom. Flowers in clusters on bushes that get 3 to 5 feet tall.

Carefree Beauty: Clusters of fragrant, pink, semi-double flowers in midseason and again in late summer/fall. Orange rose-hips add winter interest. 5-6 foot-tall bush.

Carefree Wonder: Bushy, vigorous rose growing to 4-5 feet. Flowers have pink petals with white eye, singly and in clusters.

Climbing America: A strong repeat blooming climber with coral flowers. Deadheading helps keep this plant blooming all summer.

Dublin Bay: Climbing rose with red flowers and good repeat bloom.

Flower Carpet: The Flower Carpet roses are available in red, pinks, yellow and white. Low growing, and good disease resistance. Deadhead for continual bloom.

Graham Thomas: Yellow flowers in mid-to late summer. Prune after flowering for repeat bloom. Fragrant flowers on bush 5-7 feet tall.

Meidiland Roses: Several colors available, the most popular being the Pink Meidiland and Scarlet Meidiland. Midseason clusters of flowers and repeat fall bloom. Bushes 3 to 6 feet tall.

New Dawn: Climbing rose to 15 feet. Light pink flowers, mildly fragrant. Beautiful in June, but not as reliable for repeat bloom as the tags claim.

Sally Holmes: White blossoms in sprays over a long period. Large shrub or small climber, 6 to 10 feet tall. Long period of bloom.

The Fairy: Compact shrub to 2 or 3 feet tall. Clusters of small, pink, double flowers in July and fall repeat. Deadheading encourages repeat bloom.

Q. What do I need to know about successfully planting and growing roses?

A. If your soil is sandy, amend it with a good amount of compost, composted cow manure, and peat. Be sure to mix these in over a wide area, keeping in mind that the roots of your plant will extend around three feet away from the stem. After your roses are planted, fertilize them every spring and summer, and have the soil tested for pH every other year; lime if needed. Water roses deeply once a week in a drought, and always in the morning so that the foliage dries quickly. Keep them away from automatic sprinkler heads that come on frequently.

Q. Other than Rhododendrons, which shrubs grow well in shade and part shade?

A. A list of shade tolerant shrubs is included in chapter 9, but I will list some of my favorites here as well. The Meserve Hybrid Hollies (blue holly) will do well in partly-shaded areas, as will the lower growing *Ilex crenata* (Japanese holly).

Skimmia japponica (Japanese Skimmia) has gotten quite popular in this area over the last few years. It is evergreen, low-growing (3 to 4 feet high with similar spread) and the male plant has attractive flower buds in the winter. Female plants have bright red berries that are colorful from mid-fall through the winter. Be sure to plant skimmia in a place that is sheltered from direct sun in the winter, and cold winds.

One of my favorite deciduous shrubs for shade is *Clethra alnifolia* (summersweet), that blooms in August with fragrant flowers of white or pink. *Rhodotypos scandens* (jetbead) isn't seen much, but it is a fairly rapid growing shrub for shade that has white flowers in the spring and tiny black berries that remain on the plant in fall and winter. Both Clethra and jetbead have lovely golden foliage in the fall. I was also delighted to discover that the goldfinches eat the Clethra seeds in the spring; I looked out into my yard one day to see the Clethra so covered with the small yellow birds that it looked like it was in blossom.

Itea virginica "Henry's Garnet" is a shade-tolerant, fairly low-growing shrub with lovely flowers in June, and bright red foliage in the fall. *Kerria japonica* is a deciduous shrub, but its stems remain green throughout the winter, and it is covered with bright yellow flowers in the spring. (It continues to flower sporadically throughout the summer.) Kerria tolerates quite a bit of shade and the somewhat smaller, variegated variety, "Picta," brightens up dark corners even when not in bloom. Kerria produces many side shoots, however, that will need to be clipped on a regular basis. *Abelia* x *grandiflora*, mentioned previously, will do well in half-shade and it blooms throughout the summer. Several of the newer cultivars stay under four feet, making it a nice choice for smaller properties. And finally, *Forsythia* x *intermedia* (Forsythia) does very well in dappled sun or part shade.

Q. We have a newer house with little landscaping in between our yard and our neighbor's property. Are there some shrubs or trees that will grow quickly and give us some privacy?

A. Starting out with a "blank slate" to landscape is exciting in that you can plant just what you want. It is also distressing that so much is needed and it may be some time until your yard has the lush greenery, and the privacy, that mature shrubs and trees provide. Spend some time now developing a master plan to guide you. This will help determine what you need to plant now for rapid growth, and what you can plant now, as well as over the next few years, for long-term enjoyment. It might be worthwhile to hire a landscape designer to walk your property with you and either develop an overall plan, or give you a few ideas about possible directions.

In the rush for privacy many people buy several of the same type of shrub or tree, and plant them close together in a straight line. By choosing several types and sizes of plants, and planting them in a staggered placement, the shrubs are given more room to grow, and the landscape is much softer, and more natural in appearance. And with a variety of plants in place, if one of them dies you will be able to replace it with just about any new plant and the screening will still look attractive. If you have used only one type of plant, you could lose it all if an insect or disease comes along that your selection is susceptible to.

Once you determine the areas where you need quick growth for privacy, any of the following plants are known for a fast growth rate. Remember that to attain the most growth each year, shrubs should be planted in soil that is well amended with organic matter, and they should be watered regularly.

x *Cupressocyparis leylandii* (Leyland cypress) A tree not a shrub, but a very fast-growing evergreen, growing about three feet each year. Several cultivars available. It may be advisable to plant container grown plants since the fibrous root system is difficult to transplant by ball and burlap. If B&B plants are used, keep the root balls well watered while the trees are getting established. Can be pruned to contain size and shape if desired.

Elaeagnus umbellata (autumn olive) Although some people consider this shrub to be a real weed, it grows up and out to beat the band and has pleasing gray-green foliage. Ultimately reaching 12 to 18 feet tall and an equal or greater width, it is tolerant of poor soil, salt-spray, and drought. The bush in my partly shaded yard went from two feet tall to seven feet tall in two seasons.

Forsythia x *intermedia* (forsythia) Our old favorite in early spring when we are all starved for color. Fast growing and lovely in a mixed shrub border or planted in groups. Eight to ten feet high and of slightly greater width.

Ligustrum species (privet) Upright, multi-stemmed, deciduous shrub that grows 12 to 15 feet high. Can be pruned to encourage bushiness, or sheared if you like the look of rectangular bushes. (My prejudice shows here.)

Philadelphus coronarius (sweet mockorange) Fast growing to 10 to 12 feet and equal width, mockorange is an old-fashioned favorite with sweetly scented flowers. Perhaps best in a mixed shrub border. Fastest growth seen if planted in soil high in organic content and watered regularly.

Q. I don't have much time for yard and garden chores. Which shrubs are relatively care-free?

A. Although there is no shrub that you can plant and ignore forever, there are some that are not usually bothered by insects and diseases, and that require little pruning. Attention to choosing the plant best suited for the site, and planting it well, will result in a healthier shrub; healthy plants require less maintenance. Letting plants grow to their natural forms means less work with the pruning shears. Remember that once you start to shear a plant into tidy shapes it becomes much more difficult to let the plant grow naturally again. Pruning can be just a spring clean-up of dead branches and a thinning of older wood. Many of the shrubs I have mentioned earlier are great, relatively trouble-free plants. In addition to those, consider the following:

Chamaecyparis species (falsecypress) Several cultivars of this evergreen are available in a variety of sizes, and foliage colors ranging from yellow to gray-blue, to dark green. Most prefer full sun although some cultivars will tolerate a little shade.

Hibiscus syriacus (rose-of-sharon) a popular plant for the late summer flowers and, for most varieties, upright growth. Although in other areas of the country this shrub may succumb to leaf spot and canker, it seems to do well here.

Hydrangea quercifolia (oakleaf hydrangea) A United States native that is often overlooked, the Oakleaf Hydrangea grows to about 6 feet in height with an equal or greater width. White flowers in mid-summer, lovely fall color, and interesting exfoliating bark in winter are some of this shrub's attributes. *H. quercifolia* tolerates full sun but is happier when planted in moist semi-shade.

Ilex glabra (inkberry) Slower growing evergreen with small, somewhat shiny green leaves. The species is native to North America and several cultivars are available including compact varieties that grow 3 to 4 feet tall. Shade tolerant but best in more sun.

Ilex verticillata (winterberry holly) This deciduous shrub is especially good in areas with moist or even wet soil. Growing to 6 feet or more, the female plant is most striking in early winter when covered in bright red berries. A male plant is required for berry set.

Itea virginica "Henry's Garnet" (Virginia sweetspire) Itea is also native to the U.S. (are we starting to see a pattern here?) and although it prefers moist soil it will tolerate a dryer location as well. Adapts to sun or shade. The cultivar "Henry's Garnet" grows to 3 or 4 feet high. Prune in early spring to remove dead foliage and unwanted suckers.

Myrica pensylvanica (northern bayberry) An adaptable, salt tolerant plant for sun or half-shade. Deciduous to semi-evergreen, (depending on the winter temperatures) Bayberry grows from 6 to 10 feet tall. With a name like *M. pensylvania* you know that this is another North American plant.

Rhodotypos scandens (jetbead) A rapid grower to 4 to 6 feet high, jetbead tolerates sun, shade, crowding and pollution. Small clusters of black berries stay on the plant throughout the winter. I fell in love with this shrub in Margo Goodwin's garden where I first saw it covered with its black berries and leaves in golden-yellow fall color.

The clusters of black seeds were still on the plant the following spring when it was covered with emerging green leaves and small white flowers.

Viburnums There are many species of this large shrub, and they are relatively trouble-free. Especially nice are the Doublefile, Sargent, and American Cranberry.

Q. Which shrubs would live on a small island in the middle of a street? No one is able to water it, so any flowers we have planted usually die.

A. A grouping of one type of drought-tolerant shrub would probably be most attractive. *Yucca filamentosa* (Adam's-needle Yucca) grows well in dry soils, and the variegated varieties provide bright yellow and gray-green foliage twelve months a year. *Comptonia peregrina,* (sweet fern) is not a fern at all, but a low-growing shrub that is extremely drought tolerant. It is a plant that does not get as much attention as it deserves, most likely because it is a native plant that grows with abandon in the wild. Large native plants do not transplant well, however, so purchase this plant from a nursery. It would be nice under-planted with a low-growing drought tolerant plant such as thyme or *Sedum* 'Autumn Joy'.

Ornamental grasses are all drought tolerant and look great from early summer well into the winter months. Avoid grasses that run such as blue lyme and ribbon grass. Plants that stay in a clump, such as *Miscanthus, Panicum*, and *Pennisetum* are all lovely.

Heaths and heather would also be lovely planted on a triangle. Plant several varieties for contrasts in size, foliage color and bloom time. Because heaths and heather have a wind-swept look naturally, they are best planted in loose, staggered layouts, instead of in rows. Both should be sheared right after bloom to keep them looking their best.

Plan to put the plants in the ground in early spring, or in the fall, when there is a greater likelihood that there will be some rain to water them; even drought-tolerant plants need some watering when they are newly planted. Mulch the area around the shrubs to help hold soil moisture and prevent the germination of weed seeds.

Q. I am interested in planting heath or heather on a slope near my driveway. What is the difference between the two and how do I take care of them?

A. Heath and heather make a beautiful planting, especially on slopes. Be sure to dig amendments into sandy soils; compost or peat or a combination of the two would be perfect. Heath and heather are drought tolerant once established, but you will need to water them once a week over the first summer if it hasn't rained. Both grow well in acidic soil, and they don't like to be fertilized! Mulching around your plants with compost or bark will keep weeds down and provide the slight amount of fertility that these plants require.

Many heaths are winter blooming; select an assortment of plants from both the heath (*Erica*) and heather (*Calluna*) families, choosing a variety of foliage colors and bloom times. Prune your plants right after they bloom. It is especially important to shear off the old flower heads as your heather finishes blooming; as the flowers drop off they leave bear stems that will contribute to a ratty looking shrub if the plant is not pruned.

How can you tell them apart? Remember the phrase "Heaths have teeth and heathers have feathers." This rhyme refers to the foliage shape; the tiny needle-like leaves on a heath look like tiny sharp teeth. The leaves on a heather look like minuscule feathers coming off of the main stem.

Q. We have two sloped areas in need of ground covers. One is in the bright sun and one is in shade. What would be good to plant in each area?

A. Ground covers can either be shrubs, perennial plants, or low growing vines. If the sunny slope is dry, pick drought-tolerant plants. A lovely, low-growing evergreen that hasn't been planted as much as it should be is Bearberry, *Arctostaphylos uva-ursi*. This is the dark green plant with the small, shiny leaves that you see both along Route 6 and the lower part of Route 3. (Don't try to stop and dig some up from the wild. It does not transplant well or root well from cuttings.) Bearberry is attractive all year, pest free, and drought-tolerant, but it dislikes being hit frequently with water from an automatic sprinkler system.

Heath and heather can be used as a ground cover in sunny areas, and 'Goldstrum' Rudbeckia makes an excellent perennial groundcover that will be covered with hundreds of 'black-eyed-Susans' in mid-to late summer.

The shady area will need to be planted with a different choice of plants. *Vinca minor* (periwinkle) grows well in the shade as does *Epimedium* and *P. tricuspidata* (Boston ivy). The climbing hydrangea, *Hydrangea petiolaris,* makes a lovely ground cover for shade. It takes a few years to get its root system established, but it grows vigorously after that. If the area that you plant these in also contains trees, be aware that Boston ivy will climb trees as readily as English ivy. If you don't want ivy-covered trees you will either need to attentively prune the shoots away from the trunks, or plant another groundcover. A complete list of groundcovers for sun or shade are included in Chapter 9.

Q. I would like to plant a shrub between a flower border and the neighbors lawn, but it can't get too high; it must also remain quite narrow in order to fit in the space available. Because the flower border is already established I would want plants that are large enough to show above the perennials. Is there a shrub that would meet these requirements?

A. While I agree that a shrub would provide a nice backdrop for the perennial border, I'm afraid that you are asking the shrub to do the impossible. In wanting a plant to start out about the same size it will end up, you are asking it not to grow! Perhaps a fence would better serve the purpose. A fence or even a series of posts can be covered with annual or perennial vines, giving you a background of green in a small space.

Q. I have a large arbor in my backyard that I would like to cover with a vine. I would plant a Wisteria, but this arbor does not get enough sun. Which other vines will grow quickly and do well in part shade?

A. If a dense covering of large leaves is desired, *Aristolochia durior* (Duchman's pipe) would grow well in part shade. This rapidly growing vine is most often seen covering a front porch of an older home with its large, overlapping leaves usually hiding the unusual pipe-shaped blossoms. If your arbor gets more use in the later summer, the *Polygonum aubertii* (silver lace vine) might be the vine of choice as it blooms in July/August. silver lace vine is a very vigorous plant that grows well in either sun or shade, and is tolerant of dry soils. *Ampelopsis brevipedunculata* (porcelain berry) and *Lonicera* species (honeysuckle) also do very well in part shade. Climbing hydrangea grows well in shade and is a lovely plant, but it will take three or four years before it really takes off.

Q. Which vines would quickly cover an arbor in full sun?

A. If the arbor is large and strong, either *Wisteria* or *Campsis radicans* (trumpet vine) are good for fast growth. The *Clematis maximowicziana* (sweet autumn clematis) or *C. montana* (anemone clematis) are also vigorous growing vines. Many of the Honeysuckles (*Lonicera* species) continue to bloom throughout the season on new growth (you must continue to cut off spent flower stems) and most are vigorous to the point of being weeds. If your arbor is small (such as the white arched entries that have enjoyed renewed popularity) another clematis or a climbing rose would be a better choice, perhaps combined with an annual vine such as morning glory for late-summer bloom.

Q. We have a small property but we would still like to plant some trees in our yard. Can you suggest some trees that won't overwhelm our yard and house?

A. There are many trees that grow to between 15 and 40 feet. It is wise to not only choose trees that will be the right size for a small property but ones that will be relatively carefree as well; a low-maintenance tree is not prone to any serious insect or disease problems. I have included a list of such trees in Chapter 9. It is largely drawn from a listing of low-maintenance trees written by Roberta Clark and Deborah Swanson of the Massachusetts Cooperative Extension System. This excellent listing is available from the Extension office (See Chapter 8) and it contains information about the size, growth rate, required growing conditions, and unique features of each tree.

Q. Which trees are rapid growers?

A. I refer you, once again, to Chapter 9 for a list of trees that have the reputation for growing rapidly. Keep in mind that many trees that grow quickly don't *stop* growing; they will get huge. If a rapid grower is desired because you want huge trees as quickly as possible then one of these may be what you are looking for. Most rapid growth in trees is seen when they are planted in good soil and kept watered during their first few years of growth. In fact the sweetbay magnolia and the white willow listed prefer growing in a damp location.

If a large-sized tree is not what will ultimately work well on your property the best choices would be the Amur Maple, Carolina Silverbell, River Birch, or Japanese Snowbell. It is better to buy the largest one of these that you can afford, plant it well and water it regularly, and not have an overwhelmingly large tree to deal with thirty years down the line.

Most evergreens are not rapid growers, the most notable exception being the leyland cypress. Given regular watering, these trees can put on three feet of growth per year when planted in a sunny location. Be advised that they too can get quite large, as can the other evergreens listed in Chapter 9, the Norway spruce. Leyland cypress are amenable to pruning; Norway spruce are not.

Q. I don't water in my yard when there is a period of drought. Don't the trees' roots go deep enough to keep them moist?

A. Like most people, I grew up thinking that the roots trees sent into the soil went down as deeply as the top went high. In truth, very few trees have a tap root (the Pitch Pine being one of them) and although the roots may spread out to a width equal to the spread of the tree, the roots of most trees are in the upper two feet of soil. If you think about it this makes sense; the soil near the top has all the organic matter and nutrients, as well as being the place were the rain hits first. A tree that sent its roots *down* would be last in line for these essentials, while all the under-story plants gobbled them up. The feeder roots of a tree stay near the soil surface where the action is. This being the case, you will help your trees and shrubs to stay healthy if you can water them during a drought.

It was pointed out to me recently that although a tree may survive a period of no rain and be seemingly fine, the repercussions of drought may be felt a year or more later. Not only is that tree less able to stand a hard winter, but because its root system has dried out and been diminished it is more likely to be blown over in strong winds. If there are water restrictions in your area it is wise to let the lawn go dormant, let the perennials struggle along under a blanket of mulch, but give the trees a weekly watering whenever possible.

DISEASES, PESTS, AND PROBLEMS OF TREES, SHRUBS & VINES

Q. How can I encourage my Wisteria to bloom?

A. Much to most gardener's dismay, newly planted wisteria can take up to 12 years to bloom. Besides having patience I offer you the following advice:

Don't give your wisteria any extra nitrogen, and make sure that it is far from a lawn that is being fertilized. Dig some bone meal or super phosphate around the base of the vine. Prune the new growth back *hard*, once in early spring and again in mid-summer as it starts to send out new tendrils. Some people also root-prune the plant by cutting with a spade in two places eighteen inches or so from the stalk of the plant. (Don't root-prune all the way around the plant for fear of cutting too many roots off...you want to jump-start it, not scare it to **death.**) The idea is to convince the plant that the end of the world is near, and it needs to hurry and bloom so that its seeds will perpetuate its kind for the future. I have even heard of some people whacking the stem of the plant with a rolled up newspaper! Aside from such plant-abuse, just make sure that the plant is in a location that receives at least five hours of full sun, and have patience.

Q. My blue hydrangeas were lovely for several years but they no longer bloom very well. How can I revive them?

A. Prune out the older stems of the plant, a few every year, by cutting them to the ground. Add some compost around the plants to renew the organic matter, taking care not to dig too close to the plant if you are turning the compost into the soil. Bone meal or super phosphate applied before the compost is spread will help stimulate flowering. Another application of weak liquid plant food can be given in early June and July. Let the plant grow to its natural size without pruning if possible; if your Hydrangeas are being pruned in the spring, the flower buds are being cut off; these shrubs form their flower buds the previous year.

There are several reasons that a blue or pink hydrangea might not bloom. Ask yourself if any of the following might be responsible for your lack of flowers:

1. Too much shade. Hydrangeas bloom well in part shade but won't flower in dense shade.
2. Too much nitrogen; the most likely source of this is from lawn fertilizers. Separate hydrangeas from the grass and keep the fertilizer spreader well away from the edge of this area.
3. Pruning the plant too far down after the buds have formed in the late summer. If the canes of your plant are all cut down in the fall or spring, you will have cut off the tiny buds that would have gone on to produce flowers in the summer.
4. Too cold. There is a point where hydrangeas are stem hardy but not bud hardy. If they are in a location that is too exposed to cold winds, this can be enough to kill the buds over the winter or in the early spring. If you suspect that this might be your problem, try moving the shrub to a more sheltered location.

Q. How can I keep my hydrangeas blue? Can I turn the white ones blue too?

A. Aluminum in the soil turns the hydrangeas blue, and the soil pH largely determines the availability of aluminum to the plants. To keep the Hydrangeas blue be sure not to add lime or wood ashes to the area around the plants. Use a fertilizer for acid-loving plants. An application of garden sulfur or aluminum sulfate, available at garden centers, will also help to keep that outrageous blue color. Apply aluminum sulfate sparingly; too much can be toxic to plants. Hydrangeas with the colored blooms are Hydrangea macrophylla, or big leaf hydrangeas, but the white flowering type is Hydrangea paniculata, or peegee hydrangeas. (Oakleaf hydrangeas also have white flowers.) The only way to turn the flowers on these plants blue is with a can of spray paint; the blossoms will not change color no matter what you do to the pH of the soil.

Most people don't have to work to keep hydrangeas blue in this area; our soil is naturally acidic and people usually have more trouble keeping their hydrangeas pink. (To keep them pink, spread lime around the plant twice a year.) If you are using an acidifying fertilizer such as Hollytone, this is usually all that you need to do to maintain a healthy shrub with blue blossoms.

Q. How do people get that deep purple color on a hydrangea?

A. These are plants that would have deep pink flowers in alkaline soils. Plant a variety such as 'Glowing Embers' and fertilize with an acidifying fertilizer, and you will have purple flowers. There is no way to turn light blue varieties, such as Nikko Blue or Blue Prince dark purple.

Q. Every summer my hydrangeas get dark spots on their leaves. They are very ugly. Is this a fungus? Do I need a fungicide?

A. Yes, it is a leaf spot fungus, but you don't necessarily need a fungicide. My guess is that your plants are in the path of an automatic sprinkler system. Hydrangeas don't respond well to having their foliage frequently hit with water. Adjust the sprinklers so that they are not hitting the shrubs, or change the timer so that your sprinkler is on for a longer period of time but less frequently. Always water in the morning so that the sun dries the leaves quickly. Hydrangeas do need to be watered if it doesn't rain, but it is better to water them deeply less often, or use a soaker-hose that won't sprinkle the leaves.

Q. My lilacs don't bloom. What can I do to get flowers?

A. Check to see if the shrub is getting full sun. If the bushes were planted in a shady area, or if trees have grown up to shade them since they were planted, they aren't receiving enough light to bloom. The pH of the soil can also effect blossoming; lilacs like an alkaline soil, so if the soil is too acidic they will not be happy. Dig some lime into the soil around the base of the plant or dig some wood ashes into the dirt to sweeten the soil. Be sure that they are not getting too much nitrogen either in the fertilizer that you apply directly on the shrub, or from fertilizer applied to grass around the base of the lilac plant. Large, older bushes may need some rejuvenating pruning. Finally, be sure that you are not pruning them in the springtime. lilacs form their flower buds the season before they blossom; if they are pruned later in the fall or in the early spring these buds will be cut off before they have a chance to open into flowers.

Q. Should I wrap the trunks of my young trees to protect them?

A. It depends on what you are protecting them from. If the trees are very young and the bark is tender, small animals such as mice or voles may find the bark a handy food supply in the winter. If this is the case, wrapping some wire mesh or using the expandable hard-plastic tree protection could keep such small rodents away from the tree. Similar protection of may be necessary if a weed-eater is routinely used to cut weeds around the base of the tree. Wrapping the trunk in this manner should *always* be viewed as a short-term solution however; it is very easy to grow used to seeing this material around the trunk of the tree, and to forget that it was put there temporarily. The danger is that the wire will be left in place as the tree grows, and even if it has been wrapped loosely when it was first installed, as the tree grows it will eventually become too tight. This will kill the tree if it is left there for too many years. The hard plastic protection usually is made so that it will expand to accommodate growth, but it will also provide protection to insects hiding underneath it. For this reason it should be removed at the end of winter as well. Mulch is a better long-term solution to the problem of weeds around a tree. If the area is well weeded and then mulched, the use of a weed-eater can be avoided. The few weeds that might sprout between the trunk of the tree and the mulch can be pulled by hand.

Q. A limb broke off of a large tree in our yard. I trimmed it off the best I could; do I need to paint the wound with tar or paint?

A. Painting the wound of a tree is another example of thinking of a tree as we would a person. We want a bandage or salve on our wounds, so a tree must also, right? Well, not exactly. Trees are best left to heal their own wounds. Trimming off the broken limb was a good idea, but now the tree should be left alone. An open area on a tree or shrub does provide both insects and diseases with greater access to the tree. Painting the wound, however, not only does not prevent problems, but may be sealing problems inside instead of keeping them out. The best approach is to keep the wounded tree or shrub well-watered. If you have fertilized your trees and shrubs in the spring, and kept them watered in periods of drought, they will be better able to cope with an injury and any problems secondary to that injury.

Q. The large pitch pines on my property are not doing well. The ends of their branches are brown. I've noticed this on other trees around the Cape. What is the problem?

A. The larvae of the Nantucket Pine Tipmoth is to blame. In August, if you snap the dead branch tips off at the place where it starts to turn brown, you will most likely see a small orange-brown or reddish worm-like larvae. By the time you see the damage it's too late to spray with insecticides. It is impractical to spray large trees anyway, and such chemicals also kill any beneficial insects in the area. It is distressing to see so many trees either die or decline because of this pest, but our efforts should be put to planting a wide variety of trees that are pest-resistant.

The pitch pine, although not native to this area, has flourished around Cape Cod because it grows well in the poorest of acid, sandy soils. There is a problem with having an area were only a few types of plants are growing though; if any insect or disease comes along that attacks such a plant, it is able to sweep through the entire community, damaging or killing all of the plants. Plant a variety of young trees in your yard, and encourage planting of other species of trees in your town as well.

Q. I had some orange, jelly-like masses hanging from my red cedar trees last year. What are they and are they hurting the trees?

A. Those odd jelly-like growths are cedar apple galls. The red cedar trees (*Juniperus virginiana*) are the alternate host of this fungus that causes a rust disease called Cedar Apple Rust. As the name states, it effects both cedars and apples, although the effect is most strongly seen on the Apple trees. Those planting new trees should avoid planting both of those susceptible to the disease on the same property. Choose disease-resistant cultivars when planting apples, and choose another tree that is not an alternate host if planting evergreens on property where apples are already growing.
If possible, snip the orange galls off of the red cedar with pruners; if apple trees are growing near the junipers you may want to protect them by spraying with wettable sulfur. Spray every seven days for four weeks, beginning when you see the growths on the junipers.

Q. The leaves of my holly plants have gotten quite yellow. What could be wrong with these shrubs?

A. If the veins of the leaves are still green but the rest of the leaves are yellow, chances are that it is an iron deficiency. This sometimes happens because the roots of the plant have been damaged and cannot absorb the iron that they need, or because the soil is sandy with insufficient organic matter. A pH that is too high can also cause an inability to absorb the proper nutrients. Iron chelate can be applied to the ground around the shrub or sprayed onto the leaves to help correct the problem. Your plant may need fertilizing as well, and would benefit from some added compost if the soil is especially sandy. Have your soil's pH tested to determine if the acidity needs to be adjusted. Yellowing of the leaves (chlorosis) due to an iron deficiency is also commonly seen in rhododendrons and azaleas.

Yellowing of older holly leaves occurs in May; this is a natural drop of foliage and not a cause for concern. Check to see if the most recent growth and the new foliage is green, and the yellowing leaves are older ones. Fertilize holly in the early spring; apply organic matter and mulch yearly to keep trees healthy.

Q. Some of the leaves on my azaleas become puckered and are an odd color. What should I do about this?

A. This is azalea gall, a growth of abnormal leaf tissue caused by a fungus. It occurs on members of the rhododendron family including azaleas. Cut these galls off and destroy them. With most cases, hand removal of the galls is all the control that is needed.

Q. My euonymus shrub is looking quite sick and is covered with small, white stuff. What is it?

A. This is a common problem on euonymus, with the exception of the burning bush euonymus. It is euonymus scale, an insect that sucks the juices from the plant, damaging, or even killing the shrub. Spray the plant well with horticultural oil, used according to directions. (Repeat applications may be necessary.) If necessary, prune plant back to the ground and destroy the clippings.

Q. There are black, bumpy growths on and around the twigs of my plum tree. What should I do about this?

A. This sounds like Black Knot, a fungal disease common to plum and cherry trees. (Take a sample of the growth to the Extension or your local garden center for confirmation.) Black Knot is controlled by hand pruning all swelling growths off the branches, cutting six to twelve inches below the growth, and disinfecting pruners in a bleach solution. (One part bleach mixed to ten parts water) Destroy what you prune off. Persistent cases may need spraying in the early spring, before the buds break dormancy. Use a fungicide such as lime-sulfur according to directions.

● ● ●

Q. My pyracantha suddenly had several branches that turned dark brown. Will the whole plant die like this?

A. If the rest of the plant looks healthy, it is likely that fire blight is what caused some branches to die on your firethorn. Pyracantha is prone to this bacterial disease that is spread by insects. Shoots or branches die suddenly and quickly, turning brown or black as if burned. The best treatment is to cut the dead branches six to twelve inches below the first sign of brown leaves. Dip the pruners in a bleach/water solution (one part bleach to ten parts water) in between every cut. Antibiotic sprays used according to directions may help with persistent cases. Be sure to remove any neglected fruit trees effected with this disease as well. When planting new Firethorn plants be sure to look for varieties that are resistant to fireblight.

Q. My holly tree's leaves have brown curvy lines all over the surface. What causes this?

A. The Holly Leafminer is a fly maggot that feeds in the holly leaves beginning in June, but the damage is most noticeable from mid-August on. The brown lines that appear are the result of this maggot's feeding. Because the damage shows up after the insect has been feeding for some time, at that point it is too late to do anything about it. If there aren't many damaged leaves, removing them and throwing them away will get rid of much of next year's flies.

The flies emerge from the holly leaves in April or May. Placing yellow, sticky cardboard "trap cards" in the trees in the early spring will allow you to monitor for the adult flies. When the small, black flies are present on the cards, a chemical spray may be used. Several applications of insecticidal soap (3x a day every other day) is said to repel the adult flies as well. If the leaf-minor population is heavy in a particular year, the holly may lose its leaves, but new leaves will replace those lost.

Holly trees grown in part-shade seem to be more resistant to leaf-miner than those grown in full sun. Cleaning up dropped leaves, and keeping the holly healthy and vigorous with the proper amounts of fertilizer, organic matter, and water, will all help the trees to re-cover quickly from leafminer infestations. The "Blue" holly, (*Ilex* x *meservae*) are resistant to leafminer, and are hardy, handsome plants as well. When planting the Meserve Holly, be sure to plant a male plant somewhere on your property, so that you will have bright ber-ries on the female plants through the winter.

Q. I have been told that I shouldn't plant a dogwood tree. My neighbor's tree looks so lovely...why shouldn't I plant one?

and

Q. My dogwood seems to be dying. Every year fewer and fewer leaves come out on the tree in the spring, and the lower branches are com-pletely bare. Is there any way to save it?

A. Flowering dogwood (*Cornus florida*) is a lovely tree that is native to the U.S., but it is prone to a variety of disease and in-sect problems. Currently, the most damaging disease is Dogwood Anthracnose, a fungal leaf spot that usually causes defoliation and die-back of branches. Symptoms of this disease are leaf spots that are usually tan with dark rims. Large dead blotches or "shot holes" may appear, and leaves on the lower part of the crown are affected first. This disease may not be noticed until the leaves have started to drop from the tree, or the twigs and branches start dying.

Once anthracnose is firmly established on a tree there is little that you can do except to prune off dead and dying branches, rake up and dispose of fallen leaves, and keep the tree well wa-tered and fertilized. Dogwoods, like most shrubs and trees, are more susceptible to insect and disease damage when under stress, so keeping the tree healthy will help prevent such prob-lems. Be sure to water the tree roots deeply during a drought, using soaker hoses or another method of watering that does not wet the leaves.

Those who want to plant dogwoods should plant anthracnose-resistant cultivars such as the "Rutgers" or "Stellar" hybrids, or the Kousa Dogwood (*Cornus kousa*). Kousa dogwoods are lovely small trees that bloom a bit later in the summer than the traditional flowering dogwood. The late-season fruits and exfoliating bark give this handsome tree year-round appeal, and it is not prone to anthracnose.

Q. My *Pieris japonica* looks sick—the leaves are yellow instead of dark green. What is wrong with it?

A. *Pieris* and *Rhododendrons* are shrubs that are often victims of lace bugs. Plants that are growing in full sunlight are attacked more often than those growing in part shade. If the leaves of a *Pieris, Rhododendron*, or azalea look stippled or splotched, examine the undersides for signs of blackish-brown excrement. The lace bugs themselves are small (1/8") dark insects with silvery white wings. Lace bugs are most active in the spring and early summer, although they may reappear in late summer as well. Insecticidal soap or horticultural oil sprays are the most effective treatment for lace bugs; spray shrubs two times, one to two weeks apart. Pay particular attention to applying the spray to the underside of the leaves, since this is where the lace bugs are feeding. Severe infestations can also be treated with pyrethrum.

Q. Last spring the leaves of my rhododendron were brown and black, especially at the tips. Do they need spraying?

A. It sounds like you are describing winter damage. Many broadleaf evergreens get sun-scald or wind-burn in the winter months. Often, the deciduous trees that normally shade these plants have lost their leaves, making the evergreens underneath vulnerable to the winter sun. Broadleaf plants continue to lose moisture through their leaves in the winter, and if the ground is frozen they cannot absorb water to replace what has been lost. Snowfall often compounds this problem by reflecting the rays of the sun so that the plant is getting hit from above and below. Rhododendrons and cherry laurel are particularly prone to such damage. If you are bothered by the appearance of these damaged leaves you can hand-pick them off. The plant will jettison them later in the season, however; as the new season's growth comes in, plants will shed any leaves that are not capable of photosynthesis.

~5~

FRUITS AND VEGETABLES

VEGETABLES AND FRUIT

There is something very fulfilling about picking homegrown fruits or vegetables, and either eating them on the spot or carrying them to the kitchen to prepare something wonderful. Watching as our fruits or vegetables are destroyed by animals, insects, or diseases is as frustrating as the eating is satisfying. Fortunately, we are not completely at the mercy of the elements, pests, or diseases. There are many things gardeners can do to ensure a plentiful and healthy crop of fruits and vegetables, and the following chapter addresses the best ways to raise produce successfully.

Q. I would like to put in a vegetable garden—are raised beds a good idea?

A. Let me start by saying that paying attention to the soil is the most important thing you can do when you are starting or maintaining a vegetable garden. Whether the beds are raised or not, the regular addition of organic materials such as compost, composted manure, or other plant matter that has been tilled into the soil is of utmost importance.

That said, raised beds are a great idea for anyone gardening in soil that has poor drainage because of clay or large rocks in the planting area. People who garden in such situations can fill their raised beds with topsoil, compost, and even some sand, mix it with some of the underlying clay, and come up with a well-drained planting bed, eighteen inches deep. Most gardeners on the Cape and

Islands, however, have good drainage to beat the band. Are raised beds a good idea if you already feel like you are gardening in a sandbox? Other than providing good drainage, what is the reason to make raised beds?

First of all, raised beds don't have to be raised. In fact, if you are gardening in sandy soils it may work against you to raise them. The principle behind raised beds is to create a bed of enriched soil that is not walked on. Period. If you marked out a bed four feet wide that runs the width of your garden, amended the soil with organic matter that is dug in deeply, and never walked on that four foot bed, you would have a "raised bed." The area is made about four feet wide in order to have a bed that can be maintained without stepping inside, which would compact the soil. The whole idea is to keep the soil as loose as possible so that it is easy for the plants to send their roots down deep. Organic matter is added on top of the bed, or worked into the soil in the fall and early spring.

If that's all there is to it, why do people go to the trouble of actually raising the beds? For those gardening in clay it is easier to build a bed on top of the clay than it is to dig out the clay and add amended soil to a pit dug out of the clay. I know this firsthand ... I used to garden in the Berkshires where in order to plant a shrub you needed a pickax, a strong back, and a neighbor with a backhoe.

Some people like how beds made of lumber or stones look; there is something satisfyingly neat about a group of squares or rectangles. This is especially true if a small garden is being placed in the middle of a small back yard; the look of the rectangular beds visually ties the garden to the rectangular house and (in all likelihood) the rectangular yard. Those who place the beds in the middle of a lawn use the raised beds as a way of keeping the grass from growing into their vegetable patch. If the beds are built using boards or rocks, it becomes obvious when weeds are starting to encroach; it also becomes very clear where a person is meant to walk and where only earthworms are allowed to tread. It is less clear why gardeners who are growing in an open area of sandy soil go to the trouble of mounding the dirt up a foot or more in height.

Some gardeners decide not to use the raised method at all, opting instead to turn the soil yearly either by hand or with a plow or tiller. Those who favor raised beds don't want to disturb the soil structure by mechanical means. Others want to keep a layer of mulch on their garden at all times, a method made popular by Ruth Stout. Those who till their soil at least once a year like the chance to turn organic matter (be it mulch, compost, or weeds) deep into the soil and start with a clean slate. Each method has its advantages and I leave it to you to decide which one suits your needs.

Q. I don't have much space but I would like to grow vegetables in a small plot. How can I get the most produce from a small area?

A. Careful planning will yield quite a bit of produce from a small space. Begin by deciding which vegetables you *must* grow. If home-grown tomatoes are your favorite, for example, start by allowing space for two or three tomato plants. Plan to stake or cage the tomatoes, and grow any plant that vines, such as cucumbers or climbing string beans, up a trellis or fence. Many plants are also available in bush form as well. Plan to make several plantings as different crops go by. A late crop of carrots can be planted when the green beans are done bearing, for example. Lettuce can always be planted in between taller growing plants such as broccoli or Brussels sprouts. Plant small, rapid-growing vegetables such as radishes in between larger plants such as peppers; the radishes will have come and gone by the time the peppers get large. In late August plan to plant spinach in the areas where other crops have finished. The spinach will get started in the fall, producing a wonderful early spring crop.

If you plant your garden using the raised bed method described, you can fill the entire bed with vegetables so that no space is wasted. Be aware that when an area is planted intensely it will require a good amount of organic matter and regular addition of fertilizer. Mix slow-release organic fertilizers into the soil in the fall after clean-up, or in the early spring. Keep this small space cleared of all plant material that has gone by in order to reduce the risk of letting fungus over-winter in the soil. Water using a soaker hose so that leaves are not constantly getting damp—when the plants are growing so close together there will be less air circulation, so proper watering and clean-up become even more important in order to avoid disease.

Q. Should I have the soil in my vegetable plot tested?

A. It would be a good idea for you to have the soil tested for pH. This will tell you how acid or alkaline your soil is. Vegetables grow best in soil that has a pH of about 6.5. Cole crops like a soil that is even more alkaline, and adding lime to the area where you plant these vegetables (broccoli, Brussels sprouts, and cabbage) inhibits the bacteria that cause root knot. Improper pH makes it difficult for plants to use the available nutrients; you might have a rich, fertile soil, and still have struggling plants if the pH is either very high or very low. Without having your soil tested, however, you will not know if the garden needs an adjustment in pH or not.

The Master Gardeners at the Cooperative Extension will test soil for pH and give information about recommended amounts of lime if it is needed. Soil can be sent to Amherst, Massachusetts to be tested for nutrients and toxic substances. (Information about how to do this is included in Chapter 8) If things are growing well in your garden you will probably not need the more complete testing. But if there have been "unsolved mysteries" in the vegetable patch, or you have reason to think that your soil might be tainted in some way, it is worth the time and money to send samples off to Amherst.

Most people have their soil tested in the spring because this is when gardening is most on their minds. Testing can be done anytime the soil sample can be taken, however, and if it is tested in the fall and found to be too acidic, lime can be added that will benefit the garden the following season. Because it takes some time for the lime to have an effect on the soil's pH, the fall is the ideal time to lime a vegetable bed.

Q. Can I leave the mulch on my vegetable garden throughout the year?

A. My mother always used the "Ruth Stout method" of mulching in her garden in Wisconsin, and very successfully so. This style of mulching involves laying a thick layer of hay or other organic mulch on the garden and leaving it in place all year, replacing it as it breaks down. Kitchen waste and garden clippings are tucked under the mulch and left to compost in the garden. This method is timesaving in that you don't make a compost pile, never turn the soil, and seldom have weeds. The disadvantages are that the garden takes up a bit more space (since there are mulched areas between rows) and the soil takes longer to warm up in the spring. Cool soil is already an issue in this area, since the spring temperatures tend to be cooler here for a longer period of time. For those who are not in a hurry, or for people who are only in this area in the summer, this may not be a drawback.

Gardeners who are interested in planting as early as possible will do better if they wait to mulch their gardens until the temperatures are warm enough to plant the "hot weather crops" such as tomatoes and squash. Cool weather crops can be planted early, but left without mulch until sometime around Memorial Day. I have found that delaying the application of mulch also means fewer places for slugs to hide; this can help small seedlings and lettuce plants get established before those slimy beasts can devour them.

Any mulch left on the garden after the late fall clean-up can either be left or turned into the soil. This leaves the garden clean and prepared for planting in the spring. If fall plantings of spinach or garlic have been put in for spring harvest, these should be left as is, of course. These crops can be grouped near any left in the ground into winter, such as carrots, or late plantings of broccoli and Brussels sprouts. Areas filled with such late-bearing crops can remain mulched through the winter.

Q. Which vegetables can I plant early in the spring?

A. There are several vegetables that like to grow in cool weather; they can be planted in April as soon as the ground can be worked. Small plants of cabbage, Brussels sprouts, broccoli, and cauliflower can all be planted early, as can the seeds of beets, carrots, chard, kohlrabi, lettuce, onions, peas, spinach, mustard greens and parsley. These vegetables can also be planted in July and August for a fall crop, particularly successful in this area where the warm days/cool nights of fall often last into December.

Q. Which vegetables need to be planted when it is warm?

A. Warm weather crops can be planted outside on or after Memorial Day, although over the past few years it has been warm enough to plant them the third week in May. Tomatoes, basil, peppers, and eggplant seedlings can go in at this time. Seeds of such crops as beans, cucumbers, melons, pumpkins, and both summer and winter squash can be planted from around the third week in May on. These crops need warm soil to germinate, so if the nighttime temperatures have been warmer than usual then they may do well if planted a bit earlier. If the weather has been cool and cloudy in April and May then it will be better to wait until Memorial Day to plant these crops as well. Corn can be planted in early May.

Q. Which vegetables can I plant in the summer to get a fall crop?

A. Planting fall crops makes a lot of sense in this area since the autumn temperatures tend to be warm and the season often stretches into December. The following planting dates and crops are recommended by the Cooperative Extension Service in Massachusetts:

Plant by August 1st:	Beets
	Carrots
	Chinese Cabbage
	Kohlrabi
Plant by August 15th:	Kale
	Turnips
	Swiss Chard
Plant up until Aug. 30:	Leaf Lettuce
	Spinach
	Radishes
	Garlic (for next year's harvest)

Q. How do I fertilize my vegetable garden?

A. Because most vegetables are annuals they need fairly high fertility and good soil to do well. As I have stated earlier, the regular addition of amendments such as compost and manure are really more important than fertilizer. If you are using one of the many fine organic fertilizers on the market, you can apply them in the late winter or early spring. If you are using a chemical fertilizer such as a 10-10-10 or 5-10-5, wait until late May. Use any fertilizer at the rate recommended on the package. In late June or early July apply a soil drench of diluted fish and seaweed emulsion, which can be repeated in late July or early August.

Q. Why are cucumbers planted on hills?

A. A "hill" of vegetables isn't a raised area, but merely a group of plants. Cucumbers and squash are traditionally planted in groups because they grow on vines that travel away from where they were seeded. Planting them in a small circle lets you mulch all around this area, and contain the traveling vines in somewhat of an orderly way. (Plants such as pumpkins vine their way throughout the garden in spite of the best laid plans...this is why they make good neighbors with corn, which doesn't mind vines traveling around the stalks.)

It is smart to plant squash, cucumbers, and melons in small depressions instead of on raised hills, particularly in sandy soils. A wide, shallow bowl collects water, making it easier to keep young seedlings from drying out. In addition, a piece of floating row cover can be placed loosely over this depression, weighting it down on all sides with earth, rocks, logs or pinning it in place with garden pins. (These are long "U" shaped pins available for sale where row cover is sold, or easily fashioned out of heavy wire or wire coat hangers.) The row cover keeps seedlings warm and protects them from early infestations of squash bugs, cucumber beetles and other insects. Remove the cover when the plants get large and start to flower.

Q. If I plant several kinds of tomatoes next to each other will they cross pollinate and give me a different kind of tomato than what I planted?

A. The seed that you plant has the genetic characteristics of the "parent" plant or plants. The seed came from a mother fruit, and that was pollinated by another plant, so the seed will produce a plant with the characteristics of these parent plants, no matter which other plants grow around it. When you buy seed of a particular variety you can count on the produce coming true to type that year. (Baring any unusual labeling mistakes, of course.) The seeds in the tomatoes that you grow, however, can be formed from a pollination with another variety, and for this reason you will not want to save seeds from a patch of several different kinds of tomatoes. This is also true for squashes, cucumbers, peppers, melons, and eggplant. Many gardeners have had the experience of watching plants grow from the seeds of garden produce tossed in the compost...halfway into the summer they realize that they are growing Mystery Melons or Squmpkins! Corn is the only vegetable that is influenced the same year by the plant that pollinates it. Don't plant the ornamental Indian Corn or popcorn next to your patch of sweet corn.

Q. We don't need scads of produce...can I just plant one short row of each vegetable? I heard that they need to be planted in big blocks to be pollinated.

A. The only vegetable that needs to be planted in blocks for good pollination is corn. If you plan on planting corn you should plant in blocks of at least four rows, although the rows don't have to be long. Corn also requires quite a bit of spacing—about ten inches between plants and thirty inches between rows. Corn is one of the plants that does not like to be crowded in the garden, although it does not mind having a low vine such as winter squash or pumpkins growing around its feet. Other plants that like their "elbow room" are tomatoes, peppers, and eggplants.

Q. I can usually find tomatoes, broccoli and squash plants in my garden center, but I have a hard time finding other vegetables such as peas, beans, and carrots. Why don't garden centers have a greater variety of vegetable plants?

A. Traditionally, garden centers have sold the varieties of vegetables that take longer to grow, such as tomatoes, eggplant and peppers.

It is to your advantage to buy young plants so that your garden has somewhat of a head start. People who are especially interested in earlier harvests usually start their own seed indoors under lights or in a hoop house. They may also erect tunnels of floating row cover in the vegetable garden that will protect young plants and enable earlier planting and harvest.

But some plants are best planted from seed. Some, such as beans, peas, lettuce, spinach and chard because they are easy to grow from seed and, if you want to grow more than six plants, it is much less expensive to purchase seeds. Root crops such as carrots, beets, and turnips start forming their roots so early that the small six-pack that seedlings are grown in would impede their development. Don't be afraid of growing vegetables from seed! Just keep the seed bed damp (but not swampy) while the seeds are germinating and while the seedlings are small.

Peas, lettuce, squash, beets, carrots, beans, spinach, chard, turnips, kohlrabi, and radishes can all be direct seeded. Squash and melon plants are usually offered for sale or can be started at home indoors as well, but root crops are always seeded where they are to grow. Tiny seedlings are more vulnerable to insect and slug attacks; for this reason it may be desirable to give many plants a head start inside, transplanting them out when the weather permits. Cole crops such as broccoli, cabbage, and cauliflower are usually planted as seedlings in the spring, but direct seeded into the ground in the summer for a fall crop.

Q. Can I start my seeds indoors in recycled containers? Will old yogurt containers or milk cartons work as well as store-bought six-packs?

A. Many people buy plastic six packs because they are neat, clean and convenient, but recycled containers work just as well. If you have grown seedlings in your container before, soak it in a water/ bleach solution to kill any fungi or other pathogens before you plant it again. Be sure to make holes in the bottom of any plastic container such as yogurt cartons, so that the excess water can drain out of the pot. Small containers that will hold one plant per container are better than planting several plants together; when the root systems of grouped plants are separated they suffer more shock in the transplanting than do those that have been planted one per carton.

You might also like to try Master Gardener Harry Walker's method of growing seedlings. Harry makes tubes out of a half sheet of newspaper that is rolled to make a tube approximately two inches in diameter and four inches long. (I have rolled my newspapers around my rolling pin. Any straight tube of a smooth material, such as a glass bottle, would work just as well.) The edges are secured into the tube shape by either running a line of glue down the edge and sealing it shut, or stapling the end in place. Tubes are stacked next to each other in a tray or plastic planting flat, and each tube is filled with soil or soilless starting mix. (If the tubes seem unstable in the tray, a narrow band of newsprint can be run around the entire group of them and stapled to hold them securely upright.) Seeds are planted so that one seedling will grow in each tube. When it is time to plant, the entire tube is placed in the ground and buried. The roots come out the bottom, creating a deep root system from the very start, and the plants suffer no shock from having their root systems disturbed. The newsprint breaks down in the garden, adding its organic matter to the soil.

Q. What do the letters after the tomato names mean, and what is meant by the terms "determinate" and "indeterminate" that I see on the packets of tomato seeds?

A. The letters after a tomato's name indicate that it is a hybrid that has been bred to be resistant to various diseases that tomatoes are commonly prone to. The following is a list of the letters you may see on a package of tomato seeds, or on the label that comes with seedlings: V-Verticillium Wilt; F-Fusarium Wilt; FF-Fusarium, Races 1 & 2; N-Nematodes; T-Tobacco Mosaic Virus; A-Alternaria alternata; St-Stemphylium. Of these, it is most common to see varieties listed VF, which means that the plant is resistant to two of the most common fungi that attack tomatoes.

Other tomato plants may also be resistant to other fungi that are not letter designated, such as early blight and gray leaf mold. If a hybrid is especially resistant to other problems it will most likely be included in the description of that variety in a seed catalog if not on a plant label.

The terms determinate or indeterminate apply to how the tomato plants grow. Determinate plants will grow to a certain height and then stop. All the fruit on a determinate plant will be produced in a period that is about a month long. Tomatoes that are bred so that the bush stays small are determinate; an example is the variety called Patio. Indeterminate types will continue growing and making new blossoms and fruit until the weather gets cold. These are the types of tomato plants that can grow over the tops of the cages you have so carefully built for them and continue growing until frost. If you start your tomatoes indoors with an eye on early production, it is wise to get indeterminate types that will continue to bear fruit for a long time. Indeterminate varieties are good for those who want a constant supply of homegrown tomatoes for the table. Determinate types are good for people who want to can or freeze tomatoes, since these gardeners will want lots of fruit, all at the same time.

Q. How about heirloom varieties of tomatoes—are they better then the usual varieties that I see in the garden center?

A. There is not a clear yes or no answer to this question. I have enjoyed growing heirloom tomatoes because they are fun (Green Zebra!) or better tasting (Brandywine) or because they are unusual. But that does not make them better for the average gardener. Brandywine may have better flavor then most modern varieties, but the vines are not disease resistant, and many people find the fruit to be ugly and hard to cut into neat, attractive slices. (Brandywine fruits are irregular, bumpy, and pink.) If you have space for more than three tomato plants by all means experiment with several varieties. But if you only have space for two or three plants I would stick with some of the tried and true varieties such as Celebrity, Better Boy, or Supersonic.

Q. Someone told me to bury the tomato stem when I plant my seedlings. Why is this done, and should I bury the stems of other plants as well?

A. Tomato seedlings are planted with a portion of the stem buried because they have the ability to develop roots from the entire length of their stems. Most other plants don't do this, or it is not as necessary to take advantage of this ability. Burying the tomato stem insures that the plant has a deep root system from the start. A deep root system is advantageous in order to support the plant's growth, and to keep the roots where they are less likely to dry out. When planting the young tomatoes, remove the bottom set of leaves, and plant the entire section of bare stem in the ground. Keep the lowest tomato leaves from touching the ground, which will help with disease prevention. When the leaves are near the ground, splashing water will carry various fungal spores that are in the dirt up to the plant.

Q. Should I remove the suckers from the tomato plants as they grow?

A. There are many gardeners who religiously remove the suckers, which are the small shoots that look like mini-tomato plants that grow between the main stem and the side branches. Taking them off the plant insures that all of the plant's energy will be directed to the tomatoes forming on the main stems. The thought is that removing the suckers tends to make the fruits on the main branches larger. Do you have to take them off? No. I never have bothered, not because I have any strong opinions about it one way or another, but simply because there are so many other things in the garden that capture my time and attention before the tomato suckers do. There are many gardeners who feel that they get fewer tomatoes if the suckers are removed. The suckers do produce flowers and fruits in time, although those fruits are smaller than those produced by the main stems. Because the growing suckers add the weight of their foliage to the plant, indeterminate varieties of tomatoes get heavy if the suckers are not removed. Taking the suckers off of this type of tomato will keep staked or trellised plants from falling over.

Q. Is it possible to grow vegetables in containers?

A. Containers filled with vegetables are not only practical, but can be extremely ornamental as well. Those living in condominiums can grow their favorites in boxes or pots on a terrace, and containers enable people with limited areas of sun to place their growing produce where the most light is. Large pots or barrels filled with potting soil are an excellent way to give small children their own vegetable garden. (The size is manageable for them, there is little or no weeding to do, and once the harvest is in or they tire of the project, the pots can be filled with flowering annuals from the garden center.) Any large container, usually deeper than 18 inches will do. Five-gallon tubs are ideal.

Use a good quality potting soil, and be sure to start with fresh soil every year. Plants grown in containers will also need to be fertilized when planted and every three weeks while they are growing. You can use any fertilizer made for vegetables, a liquid 20-20-20 (all-purpose garden fertilizer) or fish/seaweed emulsion. Compost tea, brewed from your homemade compost and water, is also beneficial for vegetables in pots and boxes.

Most vegetables can be grown in containers, although the most suitable ones are smaller-growing varieties and plants that grow in bush form. Bush cucumbers, for example, are better suited for pots than vining cukes are, unless a trellis is supplied. Any plant that grows more than about 18 inches high will most likely need a stake, particularly when the produce starts getting heavy.

Smaller plants can grow under and around larger ones in containers, taking advantage of all the space available. Planting lettuce around eggplants or Brussels sprouts is just one example. Low growing flowers such as alyssum, portulaca, or pansies could be planted around the vegetables as could herbs such as parsley and coriander. There are several smaller, ornamental and edible basil that would be lovely planted with cherry or patio tomatoes.

Follow the same good cultural practices as you would in a larger garden. (see next page)

Q. I planted my first vegetable garden last year and I think that I had every pest and disease in the book! As much as possible, I want to have an organic garden; how can I have a healthier garden this year?

A. Do not despair...there are many things you can do to have a healthy, productive garden short of hauling in the DDT. (That may have resulted in productive gardens, but far from healthy ones!) More and more gardeners are interested in a practice called Integrated Pest Management, or IPM, both in the vegetable garden and throughout their home landscaping. Those interested in using IPM choose plants that will need the least amount of pesticides and fungicides to maintain their good health. Physical means of controlling pests are used as a first line of defense. This means that instead of reaching automatically for the bug spray, methods such as handpicking, or hosing pests away with a strong stream of water are used. Good cultural practices maintain the health of the right plant in the right location.

Paying attention to the following basic guidelines each year will go a long way toward healthy plants, in your vegetable gardens as well as in the rest of your yard:

1. Grow only disease-resistant strains of vegetables. This may mean buying seed every year, since most disease-resistant varieties are hybrids that won't come true from seed that you have saved. It's worth buying new seed or plants. Notice in catalogs, seed packets, and plant labels which varieties are resistant to problems.
2. Rotate crops if space permits. Planting the tomatoes in a different section of the garden each year prevents any diseases that winter over in the soil from having immediate access to the plants the following year.
3. Keep the plants happy as they grow. Regular water, amended soil, proper nutrients and pH, and the right amount of sunlight all keep the plants from being under stress. Remember that too much fertilizer or water can stress a plant as much as too little.

A stressed plant is more likely to be severely effected by pests or disease. Add as much compost as you can get your hands on; dig it into the soil, use it as mulch, and mix it in water for compost tea.

(Compost tea may be used to water your plants or sprayed on the leaves as a foliar-feed.) Studies continue to show that applications of compost inhibit disease organisms.

4. Water with soaker hoses so that the leaves are not kept damp. Soaker hoses under a layer of mulch keep water, and the pathogens that are in the soil, from being splattered up onto leaves from the dirt. Because fungi over-winter in the soil, anything that prevents them from traveling from the dirt to the plant will slow the spread of disease. A layer of mulch will help conserve moisture. If you water with a sprinkler, do so in the morning, and water deeply but less often.

5. Plant a variety of flowers in among your vegetables. Flowers attract beneficial insects, which prey on the bad guys. Open-faced or flat flowers in particular, such as cosmos, yarrow, Queen Anne's lace, or goldenrod, attract many beneficial insects.

6. Consider the use of floating row covers if insect problems can't be managed any other way. Growing your squash under this lightweight cover means that you will have to hand-pollinate the flowers. The bees won't be able to get into the plants, but neither will the squash vine borers!

7. Remove all plants from the garden as soon as they have stopped producing. If any fungus had infected the leaves be sure that the plant is thrown out or burned, not put into the compost.

8. Inspect all plants regularly. Removing any diseased leaves right away will slow the progress of the disease. Hand picking any insects, or trapping slugs, is easier when done on a daily basis. If you do choose to use any of the biological insecticides they will be most effective when used at the very start of a problem, not when an infestation is already out of hand.

9. Have a sense of humor. There will always be a vegetable or two that doesn't do well, just as there will be years when you have such a bumper crop that you are tempted to throw squash or tomatoes through the open windows of all cars parked along Main Street. As Gilda Radner's character Rosanne Rosannadanna used to say "It's always *something!*"

Q. Something ate my bean plants last year. The leaves looked like lace before the plants finished bearing their crop. How can I prevent that from happening this year?

A. Without seeing your bean plants it's difficult to be certain what ate the leaves, but in all likelihood it was the Mexican Bean Beetle. These beetles eat the underside of bean leaves, skeletonizing them. You can kill them with one of the botanical pesticides such as pyrethrum, sabadilla, or neem. Use any of these products according to the directions on the label. If you don't want to use even a botanically derived pesticide on the beans you can hand pick bean beetles from the plants.

Start looking for bean beetles in late June. Look at the bean plants carefully, especially the undersides of the leaves. If you notice any holes on the leaves examine these plants especially well; chances are you will find a beetle feasting nearby. Mexican bean beetles look sort of like fat, drab yellow ladybugs. They are slow and are easy to pick off a plant. I crush them with my fingers (I wear garden gloves so that it's not *too* gross) but you could also knock them onto the ground and smash them with your trowel. Look carefully at the undersides of all leaves for egg clusters. Bean beetle eggs are small and yellow or orange, laid in clusters under the leaves. Once the eggs hatch the spiny, yellow larvae eat their way to adulthood on your plants. Any group of eggs that you find and smash prevents two dozen or so hungry larvae from defoliating your plants. You will need to continue to monitor your plants until they have finished bearing beans.

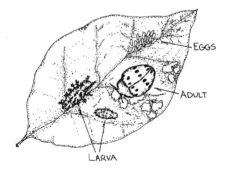

MEXICAN BEAN BEETLE

Q. My tomato seedlings got cut off at the base last year. Did birds do this?

A. It is likely that cutworms were to blame. Although not a terribly common problem, it can be very annoying when a cutworm strikes. Since you had a problem in the past it would be wise to take precautions next season. Protect the plants by curling a rolled up piece of stiff paper around the stems, sticking it down into the soil a couple of inches deep. Alternate methods include sticking several short, straight, sticks around the stem stockade style, wrapping the stems with several layers of newsprint before transplanting into the ground, or sinking a paper cup or empty can two inches into the soil around the stem. If you do find a plant that has been cut at the base, dig around in the dirt nearby; you will most likely come up with a gray or brownish caterpillar which is the larvae of the cutworm moth.

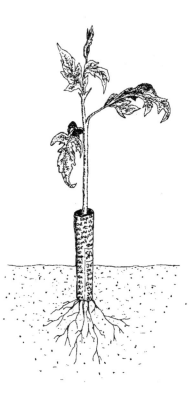

Q. How can I prevent the cabbage butterfly worms from eating my broccoli?

A. Those fat, green worms would be rather cute and amusing were it not for the fact that they can give your broccoli, cabbage, and cauliflower more holes than a golf course. If time and patience are in abundance, they can be hand picked from the plants and destroyed. If picking worms is not your cup of tea, however, there are other organic controls for this pest.

Covering broccoli with lightweight floating row covers will prevent the cabbage butterfly from laying its eggs on the plants. This barrier method also works well to prevent an infestation of cabbage maggots. Cabbage maggot adults lay their eggs on the soil surface near the cabbage plants, and the larvae feed on the roots of the plants, causing them to wilt and eventually die. Floating row cover prevents the adult from laying the eggs near the base of the plant, just as it prevents the adult cabbage butterfly from placing her eggs on the broccoli stems and leaves.

For about the past ten years gardeners have been able to buy a wonderful product called *Bacillus thuringiensis*, or BT for short. BT is a bacterial pest control that kills the caterpillars that ingest it, but is harmless to both people and other beneficial insects. BT will kill other butterfly larvae that eat it, however, so you will want to confine the use of this product to the targeted vegetable, in this case your broccoli. BT can also be sprayed on other plants that are being attacked by caterpillars, although it is most effective on caterpillars when they are young. It does not kill slugs.

Other microbial biological controls of a similar nature are BTI (*B.t. israelensis*), that kills the larvae of fungus gnats, blackflies, and the larvae of mosquitoes in water. BTSD (*B.t. san diego*) kills the larvae of some of the leaf-eating beetles such as Colorado potato beetle, black vine weevils and elm leaf beetles. Like most biological control methods, BT does not work instantly, but it is very effective nevertheless. BT is available in many forms, including dusts and liquids; the concentrated liquids get diluted with water and are applied with a sprayer. Read the directions on the labels to decide which form is right for you.

Q. My summer squash was growing beautifully, when all of a sudden it started to wilt and die. I know that it wasn't either under-or over-watered. My neighbor thought it was the squash vine borer. What can I do to prevent this from happening next year?

A. It is frustrating when a plant that is known for being so prolific in the garden suddenly dies. Because the larvae and the pupae of the squash vine borers over-winter in the soil, once they make an appearance in your garden you will most likely always have them. Squash vine borer adults are small, clear-winged moths, about an inch in length. They resemble a wasp without the wasp's waist. Adults emerge in spring and lay eggs on the stems of the squash plants, usually on the underside near the base of the plant. The larvae bore into the stems of the plant, and feed in the stalks, causing the plant to wilt and die.

Floating row cover placed over the plants early in June will prevent the moths from laying their eggs on the stems. The cover must either be removed to allow the bees to pollinate the plants, or the flowers must be hand pollinated. Another approach is to use some of the botanical pesticides during the time the insects are active. Put some rotenone or pyrethrum (or a combination of the two) dust on a garden glove and smooth it on the stems of the plant. A liquid spray can also be used. Care must be taken to apply this over the entire stems, particularly underneath near the base of the plant. It is best to apply these products in the evening when the bees are no longer active, and take care to spray them on the stems only. Applications must be made weekly during the month of July and the first two weeks of August.

I have also heard of people covering the ground under the vines with aluminum foil, shiny side up. The shiny foil is said to reflect the sky, confusing the moth. I have also heard of gardeners who wrap a soft cloth around the stems of the plant to prevent the eggs from being laid on the plant itself. Since I have not tried these methods or seen them done, I am unsure how effective they are.

If a squash plant suddenly starts to wilt and a borer is suspected, try to locate where in the stem the larvae is feeding. A sharp knife can be used to cut the borer out, and the stem can then be buried in the soil to grow new roots. Keep the newly buried stem watered, and protect as well as possible from further attacks.

Q. I had a terrible problem with flea beetles last year. How can I keep them from killing my young plants?

A. Flea beetles chew many small holes in the leaves of plants, and are particularly troublesome in the early spring. Young plants can be severely stunted or killed by this pest. If crops are planted very early it may be best to cover them with floating row cover until they are large enough to better withstand an attack. Lightly dusting some crops with wood ash seems to help as well. Beneficial parasitic nematodes can be purchased that will help control flea beetles by attacking their larvae. The biological controls such as neem, pyrethrum, rotenone, or sabadilla may also be used, following the directions for flea beetle control.

Q. Several of the tomatoes I picked were cracked. Why does this happen?

A. Tomatoes crack when the plants receive a large amount of water after the tomatoes have become ripe and fully formed; their skin isn't as elastic at that point and the large amount of water makes them burst at the seams, so to speak. There are varieties that are resistant to doing this, if it seems to be a constant problem. Regular watering will help, especially if the tomatoes are almost ripe. If a large amount of rain is forecast, the ripest tomatoes can be picked before the storm.

Q. The tomatoes that I grew last year had a big black spot on the bottom of each of them. How can I prevent that from happening again?

A. The symptom that you describe is called blossom end rot, a condition that sometimes occurs in summer squash as well. It is caused by a calcium deficiency but it does not mean that you need to add more calcium to the soil, unless a soil test shows your dirt to be calcium deficient. You may need to lime your soil, however, so take a soil sample into the extension office to have the pH level tested. The most common cause of blossom end rot is water stress. Letting the young tomato plants dry up early in life, and while the fruits are forming, will cause this condition. Be sure to water your tomato plants regularly and deeply. Other disturbances of the roots, such as tilling the soil too close to the plant, will cause the plant to have difficulty taking up enough water, resulting in blossom end rot. Mulch around the tomato plants to hold in moisture evenly, and to prevent weed growth, which will eliminate the need to till the earth near the root systems. Tomatoes with blossom end rot can still be used after cutting the end spot off.

Q. Some of the first tomatoes that were ripe on my plants were malformed and scarred on the bottom. What caused that?

A. This condition is called Cat-facing, and it is caused by cool weather extending into early summer. If your tomato plants are flowering and the nights are below 50°, covering them in the evening may help. Flowers that are fertilized later, after the night temperatures have warmed, should bear normal looking fruit. Cut out the malformation and use the fruit as usual. Heirloom varieties of tomatoes are particularly prone to cat-facing.

Q. My tomato plants got what my sister calls "Blight." They had spots on the lower leaves, and the entire plant went downhill in a hurry. How can I keep this from happening next year.

A. It sounds like your tomato plants had Early Blight, a common fungal problem that effects the leaves and even the fruit. The fungus over-winters in the soil, traveling to the plants when rain or water from a sprinkler splashes from the ground onto the plants. Be sure to remove all dead foliage and fruit from plants that had early blight, and throw it away. Seek out tomato varieties that are resistant to early blight, such as Mountain Fresh, Mountain Supreme, and Plum Dandy. Legend is a variety that is resistant to late blight.

Next year, plant your tomatoes in a different location if possible. Mulch around the tomatoes and water with soaker hoses, preventing as much as possible the splashing of water from the ground onto the leaves. Removing the lowest leaves so that there is a greater distance between the ground and the first set of leaves will also help. If you see the spots beginning on the lower leaves again, re-move the affected leaves and spray the rest of the plant with a sulfur fungicide.

A "least-toxic" fungicide for the control of tomato leaf-spot dis-eases is now on garden center shelves; it is a combination of insecticidal soap and copper. The soap (which kills insects by smoth-ering them) helps coat the leaf and hold the copper on the foliage. The key to success with this and other fungicides is to use it before you see signs of disease, and apply it regularly throughout the sea-son. Follow the directions on the label.

Q. My tomato plants were stunted and wilted last year, beginning with yellowed leaves. Just as the tomatoes that were on the plant started to get ripe, the plant died. Is this likely to happen again?

A. Anyone with a similar problem should take a large piece of the stem from such a plant into the Cooperative Extension for a defi-nite diagnoses. It sounds like your plant had Fusarium or Verticillium wilt. These fungal diseases produce similar symptoms, and once your plants have them there is nothing that you can do to save them. Clean up all diseased plant material and do not put it in your compost. Next year, plant one of the many varieties of toma-toes that are resistant to these diseases. Look for labels or seeds with the designation F1, F2, and V, which indicates resistance to these diseases. Celebrity is a popular, disease-resistant variety.

Q. The tomato seedlings in my garden were attacked by a small, striped bug that ate them as soon as I planted them. Help!

A. The Colorado potato beetle is the culprit here. A pale bug with ten black stripes down the length of its body, it loves to eat young tomato foliage, as well as the plants of potatoes, eggplants and even nicotiana and petunias! Look for their orange eggs on the under-side of leaves and squash them. The potato beetle larvae is fat, orange and almost Shmoo-shaped, with black dots up its sides.

Plants are most vulnerable to these pests when they are small. Seed-lings can be covered with floating row cover to protect them until midsummer. Potato beetles are themselves the food of other insects, so encourage these beneficial insects to be in your garden by planting flowers nearby. This pest's larvae are killed by BT San Diego. Weekly applications of pyrethrum, rotenone, or neem are also effective.

Hand picking the adults, larvae, and eggs off the plants is sometimes all that is needed. When you give the plant a shake, the larvae and adults fall off easily, making it easy to collect them on a sheet spread around the stem of the plant.

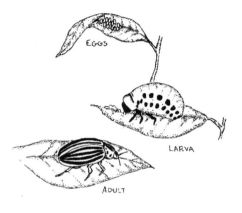

COLORADO POTATO BEETLE

Q. I want to plant some fruit trees and berry bushes in my yard. How do I know what varieties will do well? Are they all pretty much the same?

A. Taking some time to do a bit of research will pay off by leading you to varieties that will grow well, be disease resistant, bear fruit at the right time, and most important of all, taste good. Choosing disease resistant-varieties is the first, and perhaps most important, step for gardeners interested in Integrated Pest Management. (Even gardeners who couldn't care less about IPM are usually interested in saving time and money; choosing disease-resistant varieties does both.) Once you have decided on which types of fruit you want to grow, call or visit the Cooperative Extension and ask for the information sheets on these particular fruits. The Extension bulletins list varieties that grow well in Massachusetts, as well as giving the characteristics of both the plants and the fruit.

Q. How and when do I prune my raspberry bushes?

A. Raspberries and blackberries bear fruit on second-year canes, so you want to prune to remove the canes that had fruit this past year, and prune back the newly grown canes so that they will branch out and have more berries. You can prune these brambles in the late fall or early spring. Cut the older canes to the ground and remove them from the bed. Then cut the new canes down to about four feet tall.

Q. I have just planted some blueberries; do I need to prune these bushes, and if so, when and how do they get pruned?

A. Very small blueberry bushes can be left to grow the first two years, although they will benefit if you remove any weak, short, thin growth. The plant may bear a few berries, which is fine, but you want to encourage the plant's energy to go into its overall growth at this time, not into the berry production. Berries form on the end of a shoot's growth; flower buds are rounded and leaf buds are smaller and pointed. A flower bud will produce 5 to 8 berries in a cluster. After the fourth year the annual pruning, done in the early spring, can include the removal of one or two of the oldest canes, cutting them to the ground. Any dead wood should be removed, as well as fruiting twigs that are thin and weak. New canes that grow from the base of the plant will take at least two years to start making branches that have fruiting tips. Pruning is important to these new canes because inadequate sunlight will hinder them from making flowers and fruit.

Q. I planted a beach plum and haven't seen any fruit in three years. What is the problem?

A. Beach plums are one of the fruits whose bushes are self-sterile. This means that they will not pollinate their own flowers for fruit production. In order to get fruit you need to plant at least two more bushes; even then it might be helpful to place a blooming branch from a bush growing in another location into a jar of water and set it in the middle of your bushes. Even with this set up, beach plums don't set fruit every year as a rule; they bear a crop every three or four years. A cold, wet stretch of weather when they are in flower will also play a role in poor fruit production since there are fewer insects out pollinating in the rain.

Be sure your beach plums are planted in a sunny location. Although they grow and bear fruit in the driest, sandiest soil with no one caring for them, like all fruit-bearing bushes, they will grow even better in soil that has been amended with organic matter and lightly mulched. Prune out oldest growth and weak stems in the early spring to allow sunlight to penetrate the shrub.

Q. I would like to know why my apple tree has never had apples on it.

A. Apples are another example of a self sterile plant. Two or more apple trees are needed in order for pollination and fruit production. Other fruit trees that are self-sterile include most pears, sweet cherries, and Japanese plums. Sour cherries, European plums, and peaches are self-fertile, so these trees can be planted singly and still bear fruit. Call the Master Gardeners at the Extension Service and tell them what type of apple tree you have. (Hotline number included in Chapter 8.) They will send you information about which trees would be good pollinators for the one that you already have.

Q. I planted strawberries but got only one short crop of berries. Is there a variety of strawberry that produces berries all summer?

A. Strawberries that produce berries all summer are called "day neutral" since they produce berries independently of the number of hours of sunlight available. There are several varieties of day neutral berries available, including Tristar and Tribute.

Q. How can I keep my strawberries from molding on the plant?

A. Pick and throw out any berries that you see with mold on them. Placing a layer of mulch around the plants should help; if the berries are kept off of the damp ground the air circulation will keep them from molding. Pine needles or hay make a good mulch for strawberries because they allow a lot of air flow as well as good drainage.

Q. I planted grapes on an arbor near by back door, but the vine never has any fruit on it. The leaves are often covered with a powdery substance by late summer; could this cause them not to bear fruit?

A. The powdery substance is powdery mildew, a fungus that grapes are especially prone to get in the summertime. The mildew itself won't prevent fruit production, but may be part in parcel with what is keeping grapes off your vine. In all likelihood your plants are not in a location that is sunny enough. Grape vines need 150 to 180 days of bright sun in order to bloom. If there are mature trees near your arbor, or if the house shades the vines for half of the day, they are not getting the sun that they need to produce. An open, sunny and airy location will help your vines to bear grapes as well as resist the powdery mildew. Move the vines to another location if possible, and plant a vine that thrives in part shade on the arbor.

~6~

LAWNS

LAWNS

I will honestly admit right from the start that the growing and tending of a lawn is not an activity that holds my attention for long. I am of the "if it's green, mow it" school of turf care, although occasionally I do declare war on one weed or another in the mix of grass and clover that makes up my lawn. I recognize the beauty of a thick, healthy patch of grass, however, especially since it provides such a nice background for all of the other plants that *really* capture my interest. I know that there are many who want to have a lush, weed-free lawn, and for these folks I am pleased to give information that will help people plant and maintain healthy turf.

Q. Which type of grass seed should I use when I plant my new lawn?

A. When choosing a grass seed it is important to be aware that each type of grass has its own cultural needs. Your choice of seed will depend on the location of your lawn and what type of maintenance you are willing to put into it.

Kentucky Bluegrass is the type most often used for sod. It is popular because of its rich blue-green color, and because it forms nice, even sod. The greatest disadvantage of this grass is that it requires more fertilizer and lime. Kentucky Bluegrass grows best in the full sun, with a soil pH of 7.0. It needs fertilizer three to four times a year, and likes ample water.

Fescues are not as fussy as the bluegrass. Red fescue grows best in part shade, and will stand longer periods of drought because it has a deeper root system than bluegrass. Tall fescues are tolerant of low moisture and less fertility, but their clumping nature makes them less attractive for the home lawn. Tall fescue is often planted along highways and other places that require a low-maintenance grass. Fescues tolerate a pH level from about 5.5 to 7.0, and require two applications of fertilizer per year in order to look their best. Tolerant of a lot of foot traffic, fescues are resistant to diseases and insect pests.

Perennial ryegrass is a bunch grower that grows well in full sun and tolerates some shade. It grows well in most soils and is tolerant of a range of pH levels from 5.8 to 7.4. Two applications of fertilizer per year is adequate for this plant. Ryegrass is quick to grow, moderately tolerant of drought, and has a high resistance to insect problems and disease.

You needn't decide on just one of these grasses for a new lawn; there are mixes available that combine two or more of them. The better mixes include 20% bluegrass along with the fescue and perhaps some ryegrass. Check the labels when you purchase the seed.

Endophytic grasses are becoming more widely available as people learn the advantages of planting this grass seed that resists insect attacks. These grasses, usually fescue or ryegrass, contain a fungus that kills or repels common insects that attack lawns. The fungus does not hurt the grass; this fungus is a symbiotic form, meaning that its presence benefits both the organism and its host. Endophytic grasses repel sod webworms, chinch bugs, and certain aphids among others. Unfortunately they do not kill or repel grubs. When planting a new lawn, it is worthwhile seeking out these grasses; although endophytic grasses won't solve all insect problems, they will provide a good deal of protection and will minimize the necessity for more toxic, and expensive treatments.

There are also many types of grasses that are bred to be disease-resistant. Homeowners who have been persistently troubled by a turf disease may want to seek out a grass seed that is resistant to that disease. The book "Common-Sense Pest Control" (See Bibliography) contains an extensive list of disease-resistant varieties.

Q. When should I lime my lawn?

A. The ideal time to lime a lawn is in the early fall. Since it takes a while for the lime to break down and effect the soil's pH, applying lime in the fall means that the pH will be right in the spring when the lawn needs to be able to fully make use of nutrients in the soil. Although lime can be applied any time during the year, most people start thinking about the health of their turf in the springtime when the grass is starting to get green. Whether it is done in the spring or the fall, a soil test will tell how much lime is needed if indeed it is needed at all.

Q. When should my lawn be fertilized?

A. Lawns should receive an application of fertilizer in early May and early September. If a third application is needed a "winter" fertilizer, it contains less nitrogen, can be spread in early to mid-November. Do not apply your lawn fertilizer too early in the spring. On a warm April day it is tempting to get going on your lawn maintenance, but the nitrogen you apply so early may wash away with the spring rain before the grass can really make use of it. It is preferable to wait until the soil is warm and the grass is actively growing, and it's also better to use too little fertilizer than too much. An excess of nitrogen encourages a lush but weak growth spurt, leaving the grass more susceptible to diseases.

To assure an even distribution of fertilizer over the lawn, set the spreader for half of the concentration that you are ultimately going to apply. Run the spreader in even rows first horizontally across the grass, then again vertically. The spreader is set for half the concentration because the spreader will be covering the same area twice; going over the lawn two times from different directions makes it less likely that any one area will be skipped entirely. Any areas that are inadvertently skipped would be less green, giving the lawn a streaked appearance.

Spreading fertilizer over a dry lawn, and watering it in well immediately after spreading, will prevent both the leaves and roots from being 'burned' by the fertilizer. The use of an organic lawn fertilizer eliminates the risk of fertilizer burn as well. There are many fine organic lawn fertilizers on the market.

Q. How can I keep my lawn healthy?

A. In addition to providing the right soil pH and the correct amount of fertilizer, a healthy lawn is maintained by proper mowing and watering. Grass that is cut too short will be stressed; larger leaves provide greater support to the root system. More leaf shades the ground as well, keeping it cooler and retaining moisture longer. Weed seeds that need light to germinate will have a harder time getting a foothold in a lawn that is long enough to shade the soil surface. Grass should be cut no shorter than two inches, and two and a half to three inches is preferable.

Although the blades of grass are wounded when they are mowed, the plants will recover more quickly if the cut is clean. Dull mower blades leave a ragged cut, and tend to shred the grass; grass that is wounded is more vulnerable to disease. Mowing with a sharp blade minimizes the damage and the spread of any pathogens. Always mow grass that is dry, because mowing wet plants spreads disease-causing organisms.

Frequent cutting is not only less stressful to the plants, but the short cuttings can be left on the lawn as it is mowed. These pieces benefit the lawn by returning the nitrogen and organic matter to the soil. If the lawn is allowed to grow too long between cuttings, the pieces will be large enough to clump together, smothering the growing grass; smaller pieces dry quickly and decompose on the soil surface. The cuttings do not contribute to the thatch layer. If the grass clippings are not disappearing within a week after the grass is cut, it is possible that the thatch layer is too thick for the clippings to get down to the soil. (See the next question about thatch.)

Healthy lawns are watered deeply, but not often. Automatic sprinklers that are set to water lawns every day or every other day, keep only the surface of the soil damp. This means that the plant's root systems are shallow—why should they grow down deep if the soil is dry down there? Shallow root systems are not able to withstand short periods of drought should the sprinklers fail, or should water restrictions be imposed in your area. Watering for a longer period of time will soak the soil well and the turf will grow deep, strong roots.

Watering deeply is best done every five to seven days, depending on the weather. Watering more often is too much of a good thing; more water invites fungi and other diseases. Moss, mold, and mushrooms will flourish in a lawn that is kept too wet. Lawns need about an inch of water every week. Placing cans around the yard when the sprinklers are running will allow you to see how long it takes for an inch of water to fall on the lawns. Watering should be done early in the day so that the leaves dry quickly. Never water the lawn in the evening.

Q. What is thatch and how do I know if I have too much of it? Should a lawn have thatch removed every year?

A. Thatch is primarily composed of roots and stems that have not broken down. Some leaf material also contributes to this layer that builds up on the surface of the soil. Although a small amount of thatch is a normal part of any lawn, too much of it inhibits the normal flow of air and water. It prevents the grass clippings from reaching the soil, where they decompose. Thatch forms a barrier that prevents water from sinking into the soil, and provides a place for insects and diseases to grow. Bluegrass forms a layer of thatch more quickly than other types of grass, and the overuse of chemical fertilizers contributes to the problem. Organic fertilizers contain microorganisms that help break thatch down.

Some lawns will need thatch removed every other year, others less often. Because the process is stressful to the lawn, it should not be done unless it is needed. Cutting a plug of grass that includes grass, thatch, and soil will enable you to see how thick the layer of thatch is. Check to see if the thatch layer is more than 3/4 of an inch thick. If so, the lawn needs to have the thatch layer removed. Although most people have their thatch removed in the spring, fall is a better time for this process since spring de-thatching encourages the germination of crabgrass seeds in the lawn. Removing the thatch should always be done before any lime or fertilizer is spread.

Soils that have become compacted over time promote a greater build-up of the thatch layer. Core aeration breaks up this compacted soil, which helps prevent the formation of thatch.

Thatch is not only unhealthy for the lawn, but requires time and money to have it removed. Good lawn management means less thatch, which means less time and money spent on its removal. Practices that encourage the presence of microorganisms that break down thatch are the proper use of organic fertilizers (don't fertilize too much), frequent mowing or the use of a mulching mower, and refraining from the indiscriminate use of pesticides and fungicides. Pesticides kill the beneficial insects and earthworms that help keep a healthy, balanced lawn. Likewise, fungicides kill fungi that are beneficial, as well as any that are not.

Q. I need to replant my lawn. Is it best to do this in the spring, summer, or fall?

A. Renovation is best done in the month of September. Weed seeds are not germinating then, and the cooler temperatures mean the soil is less likely to dry out while the young plants have shallow roots. It is difficult to keep the soil moist in the hot summer weather, and there is a greater chance for rainfall (which means less watering for you) in the fall. Although new grass may germinate and start to grow if planted later in the fall, it is less likely to live through a cold or dry winter than that which was planted in September. Spring is the second best time to plant, if you can't do it in the fall.

Q. Areas of my lawn are dying, and I think insects are to blame. What can I do about this?

A. Before anything is done an accurate diagnosis is needed. Just as you wouldn't take any medications before knowing what was making you ill, nothing should be done to your lawn before it is known what is causing the problem. Circular areas of dead and dying grass, for example, could mean an infestation of chinch bugs. It could also be a fungus known as brown patch, or it could be caused by a neighborhood dog urinating in the same general area every time it passes by the lawn. Each of these problems are treated quite differently.

One way to tell if you have an insect problem is to pour a drenching liquid on your lawn to force insects out of hiding. Mix two tablespoons of liquid dish detergent to one gallon of water, and pour it over a square-yard sample of turf. Cutworms and webworms will come to the surface. If you have between one to ten larvae per square yard, that is thought to be an acceptable level that the lawn can handle without much damage.

To test for chinch bugs, cut the end out of a large can and drive the can two to three inches into the soil. Fill the can with water, and continue to add water as it drains out. After about 25 minutes the chinch bugs will float to the surface. Acceptable numbers of chinch bugs are about 15 per square foot.

If you can't figure out what is causing the damage, take a sample of the problem area into the Cooperative Extension office where you can not only learn what is doing the damage, but receive information about how to correct the situation or prevent a reoccurrence in the future.

Lawn samples should be approximately one foot square, and at least two inches thick. This may seem like a large chunk of turf to cut out of the lawn, but a large enough piece is necessary to be sure the problem can be seen. (This piece can be taken home and returned to the lawn, watering it well after it has been replaced.) If the damage includes areas of dead or dying grass, cut the sample so that half of it includes the dead area, and half of it includes the live grass around the problem area. Taking a sample that is half damaged and half good increases the likelihood of an accurate diagnosis. An insect feeding on the grass is not likely to be in the areas that are already dead, for example, but it is likely to be found on the edges of the dead area, dining on the fresh, green leaves.

Q. There are mushrooms on my lawn. Should I spray them with something to get rid of them?

A. Mushrooms come and go in the yard and the garden. They don't do any harm, particularly, so it's unnecessary to do anything drastic to get rid of them. They can be raked away or chopped up with the lawn mower if the sight of them doesn't appeal to you. If the soil in the area where they are growing is kept wet by frequent watering, revise the way the lawn is watered; watering deeply, but not as frequently is less likely to provide the ideal growing conditions for mushrooms. Soil that hasn't been tested recently should be taken for a test of the pH, which will tell you if the mushrooms are particularly happy there because the acidity suits them. Changing the pH if needed, and keeping the area a bit drier may solve the problem.

Q. I have moss growing in my lawn. Is this a problem and if so how can I get rid of it?

A. Moss in the lawn is only a problem if it bothers you. I recently read about a man who, having more moss than grass, gave up the fight and began pulling up the few clumps of grass that remained. He was left with a beautiful green moss lawn so lush and unusual that garden tours stop by to see it. He no longer had to battle what was a naturally moist site, and even better, *moss never needs mowing*!

Aside from this "if you can't beat them join them" approach, there are several things that you can do, starting with nothing. If the look of moss mixed with grass doesn't bother you then don't bother fixing it! (Life is short. Put your efforts into what is most important to you.) If every time you go into your yard the sight of the moss annoys you, then by all means spend a weekend changing the situation. Moss likes growing in shady, damp places on compacted soil. If you change any of these conditions in your lawn you will discourage moss growth. Look at the site where the moss is growing and see if it is damp. Perhaps the area needs to be built-up, or the water draining from a nearby slope or building rerouted. If the soil is compacted in that area, consider tilling it with a Rototiller or by hand with a garden fork. Be aware that if the moss is growing under a tree, such tilling might injure tree roots that are close to the soil surface. If you need to loosen the soil under a tree, a light, careful tilling by hand would be best. If shade is a factor in the mossy site, look at the trees to see if selective pruning of a limb or two would bring more light to the area. Often a combination of all three of these conditions, (light, drainage, and compacted soil), is making a happy home for the moss and they all will need to be addressed in order to get rid of the moss. After changing those three conditions be sure to have your soil tested for pH so that you will know if an application of lime is needed in order to establish and maintain a healthy lawn.

Q. The skunks are digging up my lawn and driving me crazy. Why are they doing this?

A. The good news is this: although the skunks are eating an assortment of insects and worms that they find in your lawn, they are also after the Japanese beetle grubs, so the more holes you have in your lawn the fewer Japanese beetles you will see next year. The bad news is this: your lawn looks like hell. The best thing to do is to tolerate the holes the skunks have dug for awhile; they will soon move on to other territory. If there is a large population of grubs in the lawn, however, you may want to do something about them. Not only so the skunks stop coming to your yard for dinner every night, but so the grubs will not do as much damage when feeding on the grass roots.

Presented with evidence of grubs in the lawn, most people will go out and get some of the commonly sold chemical that kills grubs, and they will spread it over their grass. It never occurs to them that in addition to killing the grubs, they are killing all the beneficial insects in their lawn, and most likely killing the earthworms too. When the population of beneficial insects in the lawn are killed, the balance of power is upset, so to speak, opening the door to a host of other problems.

Every lawn contains many, many, insects. Most of them do no harm to either the lawn or to people, but many of them are predators of other insects. Lady bugs, ground beetles, and rove beetles all eat either other insects or caterpillars. Spiders and ants both live in lawns and feed on a wide range of insects there. Small parasitic wasps that do not bite or sting people are active in lawns as well; the larvae of these wasps feed on many caterpillars, aphids, and sawflies. If all these predators are killed, the lawn and garden plants are open to attack from other insects that may arrive and find completely undefended territory.

Earthworms help to convert the layer of thatch to soil as well as improving the soil structure that makes for a healthier lawn. Killing the worms with insecticides will cause thatch to build more quickly, and soil to become compacted. As you can see, when insecticide is used to kill the grubs, what starts out as the pursuit of a healthier lawn becomes just the opposite.

If use of insecticides on the lawn is out, how can Japanese beetle grubs be controlled? The first line of defense is proper watering. Japanese beetles prefer to lay their eggs on lawns that are kept moist. Watering the lawn every five to seven days will allow the top layer of soil to dry out, making it less likely that beetles will lay their eggs there in the first place.

Milky Spore Disease has been sold under several brand names including Doom and Grub Attack. It is a bacteria that effects beetle grubs only, and once applied to the lawn it continues to effect the grub population for a long time. Results are not instant, however, and the instructions must be followed for greatest success with this control.

The second biological control for grubs is Parasitic Nematodes; they are beneficial nematodes that do not attack plants or mammals. They also kill grubs, but they must be applied at a time when the grass is watered regularly, or in a season when it is likely to rain.

For more information about Japanese beetles, see Chapter 9.

Q. I can't afford a high water bill. Do I have to water my lawn? Won't the grass come back when it rains?

A. The most wonderful aspect of grass, to my mind anyway, is that it can go completely dormant if the weather is dry, only to grow again as soon as the rain falls. Although other plants may also grow back from their roots after a period of drought, few recover as quickly or as well.

Not only can you let your grass go dormant, but you might want to reconsider how much area of your yard is planted with lawn in the first place. I will admit here that I am not a fan of spending too much time or resources on the lawn. I admire a sweep of uniform, lush green growth as much as the next person, but basically I think the lawn is an ecological disaster. It requires far more resources than other plants in order to keep it looking good, and takes far too much time to maintain.

I personally believe that the custom of having large, open lawns around every house will slowly die out, and I for one will not grieve. People are less willing to spend time and money maintaining a plant that merely provides a seldom-used carpet around the house. (Be honest now. How often does your lawn really get used? Kids are in school most of the year, most adults work away from their houses, and those that work at home are usually indoors. Even when relaxing, most adults may sit near the lawn, but seldom is it used for anything more than looking at. I venture to say that the majority of lawns are only walked on when they get mowed.) Planting large areas filled with trees, shrubs and ground covers, set off, perhaps, by a small strip of lawn, makes much more sense for a number of reasons. For pure gazing pleasure, give me a grouping of shrubs any day!

Because your shrubs and trees are more likely to suffer long-term damage from a drought, letting the lawn go dormant, but using any water you can on the woody ornamentals, is probably the best approach.

Q. I am interested in planting a lawn that has other plants growing in with the grass. There is a lot of information about how to get rid of various weeds in a lawn, but little about how to add other plants into a lawn. Which plants would make good companions for grass?

A. About the only other plant that has been traditionally encouraged to grow with grass is white clover, *Melilotus alba*. Grass inter-planted with clover makes a lot of sense; clover is one of the plants that has the ability to "fix" nitrogen. That is, it takes nitrogen out of the air and puts it into the soil. Planting clover in a lawn can supply the lawn with as much as 30% of its requirement of nitrogen. Clover is a rich, dark green color, and a low-growing, fast spreading ground cover. It is no wonder that it has been used as a companion to the grasses traditionally planted in lawns.

Other plants that can be introduced into a lawn for variety are the creeping plants that have always been thought of as lawn pests. *Ajuga reptans*, (bugleweed) will spread through (and sometimes choke out) grass with enthusiasm, as will *Lysimachia nummularia* (Creeping jenny), especially in a moist area. Creeping thyme will grow well in dryer lawns. Other ideas can be found in a book of lawn alternatives titled *The Wild Lawn Handbook*. (See Bibliography)

Q. I am interested in planting a wildflower lawn, but several people have told me that it is difficult to do.

A. Books and articles about lawn alternatives are being seen in greater abundance as people decide that they are not interested in devoting so much time and money to lawn maintenance. The alternative that has received the greatest attention by far is the wildflower meadow.

There are two methods of making a wildflower meadow. The first is to plow under or otherwise destroy all plants currently growing in the area and plant wildflower seeds. The soil should be turned up and perhaps amended with topsoil. Directions that come with the wildflower seeds should be followed. Care must be taken to keep germinating seed damp.

Most mixed wildflower seed is a combination of annuals for quick color, and perennials for lasting plants. The main problem with growing wildflowers from seed is that as they are germinating it is difficult to tell which small plants are the flowers and which are the weeds. If you are unfamiliar with what common weeds look like, it is difficult to decide if a particularly fast growing plant is a wildflower or another weed that will soon choke out all the flowers.

The second way to grow a wildflower meadow is to start with what is already there, and plant seeds and plants in selected spots around the area. This method is most successful using wildflowers that you can see are already thriving in the area you live in, with perhaps the addition of perennials know for their ability to take over. (See the list of fast-spreading perennials in Chapter 9) This method will not give you a quick field of flowers, but it ends up in much the same way; the strongest plants that are well-suited for that particular site will do well, and the rest will disappear.

Although I applaud anyone who desires to replace much of their lawn with another grouping of plants, I think that many people will be disappointed with the results of a wildflower meadow, not because it is not beautiful, but because they expect something other than what it is. Articles about wildflower meadows show them in full bloom, with a sweep of flowers, often of several types. Most meadows that are planted deliberately look like this the first year or two after planting, but after that Nature takes over, and Nature has never seen the magazine photos. Usually one or two plants will end up becoming dominant, or one will thrive one year and another the next. This is how wildflowers really behave when they are...well, *wild*. If this natural ebb and flow of flowers, grasses, and general weeds is all right with you then a wildflower meadow may be just the "lawn" for you.

Q. My lawn has patches of grass that seem different then the rest—they are fine in texture and lighter in color, especially in the early morning when the dew is on the lawn. What is this, and where did it come from?

A. What you are describing sounds like bent grass. This fine textured grass is sometimes grown on golf courses. You can tell if the patches of grass in your lawn are bent grass by looking closely at the plants. Bent grass has a bare stem at soil level, with the fine-textured blades of grass growing in a cluster above two or three inches of this bare stem. The grass often looks tattered or ratty when examined closely, because of this bare stem. The seed may have been transported to your lawn by the wind, an animal, or on shoes that have walked on a patch of bent grass elsewhere. To get rid of these patches, you will have to spray it with an herbicide or dig it up with a shovel. Put a top-dressing of topsoil down in the areas you have removed, and re-seed. Be alert for new areas of bent grass, because it is easier to remove when the patches are small.

Q. Every year my lawn gets crabgrass, and I don't like how it looks. I don't want to use the usual weed killers on my lawn. Is there an organic alternative?

A. Crabgrass is an annual grass, meaning that it grows from seed every year. The traditional method of control is to use a pre-emergent herbicide; this prevents the seed from germinating. Recently, studies have shown that corn gluten is an effective pre-emergent, and several companies offer it for use in the home landscape. It is available as a single product from several organic garden supply companies, and is also included along with organic fertilizer in an organic equivalent of "weed and feed" products.

Whether you use corn gluten or one of the traditional chemical pre-emergents, you must apply it in the early spring before the crab-grass germinates. In this area, pre-emergent products are usually applied in early May.

Note that corn gluten will kill germinating seeds of all types; it should not be used in any area where you are starting seeds (grass, annual, or vegetables) that you want to grow.

Keeping your lawn thick and healthy, and mowing it three inches long, will also help keep crabgrass away. The seeds need light to germinate, so a thick, longer lawn will shade the soil surface, preventing light from reaching the seeds.

Q. My lawn looks fine, but there is always a bare area next to the driveway that is filled with a low weed. Is this week choking the grass out?

A. It is likely that the weed is just better equipped to live in the conditions along the edge of the driveway. I would guess that the soil is more compact there, and that because of the heat that the driveway absorbs, that area is also warmer and drier. Pull the weeds out and loosen the soil by digging in some soil amendments or topsoil that is high in organic matter. Replant grass seed and make sure that over time the strip next to the drive gets a little extra water in hot weather. If you think that cars may occasionally be diving over this area, consider installing a border of cobblestones so that the lawn is not being stressed and compacted by automobiles.

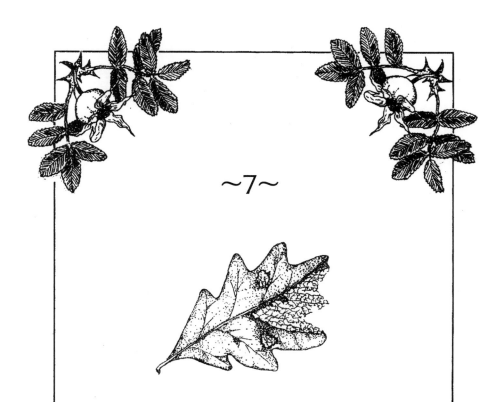

~7~

PESTS, DISEASES, AND CULTURAL PROBLEMS

PESTS, DISEASES, AND CULTURAL PROBLEMS

I know firsthand the disappointment and frustration that a gardener feels when a plant becomes diseased, is eaten by bugs, or just dies "for no reason." It is upsetting that the time and money that went into placing the plant in the yard is for naught, and perhaps even more distressing that something that was enjoyable to watch grow will not be there any longer. Worried that a cherished plant may die, we gardeners often get "twitchy" at the first sign of a hole in a leaf, or a spot of fungus. It is often difficult to know if the symptoms we see call for treatment of some sort, or if a wait-and-see attitude is the best course of action. In the following chapter I have given gardeners and home-landscapers a method for diagnosing potential problems, as well as answering questions concerning specific plant pests and diseases.

Q. Something is wrong with my shrub, so I sprayed it with some insect killer I had on hand. It still looks sick...what should I do?

A. When we suddenly notice that a favorite plant is not doing well, the impulse is to apply anything in the cupboard and hope that it fixes the problem...and fixes it *quickly*. While that impulse is understandable, it isn't very effective, and can even cause more problems down the road. The first thing that should be "taken out of the cupboard" is not an insect killer or fungicide, but a systematic approach to diagnosing the problem.

1. The overall problem may be a sick-looking plant. But what are the specifics? How is the plant different from a normally healthy one? What are the symptoms? (Symptoms are the way the plant is reacting to the problem. Chewed leaves, yellowish foliage, stunted foliage, die-back of branches, overall wilting, and peeling bark are just a few examples of various symptoms.) Holes in leaves can be caused by insects or fungus. Yellowish foliage can be caused by over-watering, under-watering, or nutritional deficiencies, and many plants have yellowing foliage when they shed the oldest leaves as the new growth matures.

2. Next make note of how this plant looks in comparison with other plants in the area. Are several plants showing the same symptoms? Are different types of plants affected or are the symptoms confined to one type of plant?

   Look closely at where the damage is occurring. Is it random, over the entire plant? Is only one side affected, and if so, what is that side facing? (Examples: is the damaged side facing the winter sun, the house, the ocean, or a window?) Is there anything about the location that may be hurting the plant?

3. What has been happening to this plant over time? If the damage spreads over time, either from one part of the plant to another, or from one plant to another plant, it is an indication that the problem is caused by a living organism. This does not have to be an insect; fungi, bacteria, and viruses are living organisms as well.

   Damage that does not spread from damaged tissue to healthy tissue is probably mechanical; something that is not living has caused the problem.

4. Look for signs of what might be causing the problem. Do you see any insects, webs, mold, or fungus? Have there been any large animals in the area? (If animal damage is suspected, rake the area around the plants with a fine rake, and examine the area the next day for tracks.)

5. Think of the human activity in the area as well. Has there been any work on nearby buildings such as window cleaning or house-cleaning, spraying of herbicides, or other substances

dumped onto or near the plant? Was the area cleared with a weed-whacker or lawn mower that may have damaged the bark on the plant? Has the plant been recently watered or fertilized? Has the weather been unusually wet, dry, hot, or cold?

6. Is the plant new in the garden? The most common reason that a new plant fails is improper watering. This is especially true of newly planted shrubs and trees; most people usually remember to water them over the first month or two that they are in place, but they tend to forget the watering three or more months later. It is important to water newly planted shrubs and trees regularly *through the first year* after planting, even into the winter if the ground is not frozen. Do not depend on a brief soaking from an automatic sprinkler system to do the job. Most sprinkler systems don't run for more then twenty minutes, and this does not dampen the soil deeply enough to keep the root ball wet.

7. Was the large shrub or tree a ball-and-burlap plant that was put in recently? It is not uncommon for such plants to have die-back for the first two years. Their roots have been cut, and often they just don't have the roots needed to support all of the foliage and stems. Keep the plant well-watered and don't be tempted to add more fertilizer; a mild application of a fertilizer with a higher middle number once in the spring is sufficient. Too much fertilizer will stimulate growth that there are no roots to support.

8. Was there a drought the previous year or the year before that? Remember that during a drought the root system of a plant is diminished; this can have consequences for up to three years in the future.

Over a period of three or four days, notice what is happening around the plant at many hours of the day and night. Look at the plant with a flashlight right after dark, for example, as well as just before you go to sleep at night. This can be helpful because sometimes the real cause of the problem may only be active on the plant after dark.

If the damage is confined to one branch of the plant, or several branches here or there, follow the damage back to the place where the problem tissue meets healthy tissue. Is there any mechanical reason that the branch or stem is doing poorly from that spot on? (Breaking off the stem or branch where the dying tissue meets the living tissue can sometimes reveal if the cause is inside the stem. Is there a borer living there, for example, or has something girdled the bark at that point?) Is the area where the affected tissue meets healthy tissue sunken, or discolored?

Look at the leaves of the plant. Are they discolored? Are there spots on the leaves, and if so, are they irregular or uniformly distributed? Is the newest growth looking good? Sometimes the damage is on the older foliage, and if the new growth looks good we can assume that the problem occurred in the previous year.

If the leaf margins are browning, this is often a sign of either moisture stress, or chemicals burning the roots or leaves. Fungal spots are usually round, and often are ringed, or darker in the center, gradually yellowing toward the edge. Fungal spots can be on the leaf veins or on the tissue between. Bacterial leaf spots are often stopped by the leaves' veins. The color of bacterial leaf spots is usually uniform, and often makes the leaf appear first water-soaked, then dried and papery thin. Fungal problems are far and away more common than bacterial infections on plants. Physicians are told "if you hear hoof-beats, think first of horses, not zebras," meaning that they should think first of the most common cause of the symptoms that they see. In regard to leaf spot, think of fungi first.

Notice if the leaves have damage that is random or wide/spread. (Random damage is more typical of insect attack.) The color of the leaves is also important. Are they uniformly green, or yellowed? Yellowed veins with green tissue in between indicates virus disease or herbicide damage. If the leaf tissue is yellowing but the veins remain green, this is chlorosis, which is usually a nutrient deficiency.

The following examples illustrate how this systematic approach works:

I noticed that a dwarf Alberta Spruce in my yard was getting brown on the bottom of the plant. A closer look showed me that the needles on one side of the plant, toward the bottom, were brown and dried. Another spruce that is planted nearby showed no signs of dead areas, and the upper part of the affected tree showed no damage. I knew that the plant had been watered over the last dry spell, and I was unaware of anything that might have been spilled on the tree.

Over the next few days there was some spreading of the dying area, but it was mostly confined to the same place. A closer look revealed several types of insects in the tree, but none were especially near the browning area, and the other, healthy tree showed the same diverse insect population.

I began to watch the tree in the early morning and at dusk, and on the second day I saw the neighbor's dog padding through the yard on her "rounds." She stopped very briefly by the spruce to sniff it, and then lifted her leg to mark the tree with urine...right on the dying area. Bingo! I put some large branches around the spruce and the bushes on either side of it to keep the dog away from them. In a week or two, when she had altered her habits, I took the branches away. The branches that had browned did not recover, and I had to cut them out the following year to improve the appearance of the plant.

My neighbor noticed that her Euonymus was losing its leaves. She didn't get around to looking at it closely until the following week, when she noticed that another plant was looking the same way. An examination of other plants in her yard told her that only the Euonymus were affected. She had kept all the shrubs well-watered so she knew that they weren't drying up. Looking closely at one of the plants, she saw that the stem was covered with small, white things, and the plant felt sticky. My neighbor called the Master Gardeners at the Cooperative Extension, and learned that her shrubs had Euonymus Scale, a common pest of this shrub. They told her to spray with Horticultural (Superior) Oil. The plants looked more dead then alive at that point, so rather than treat the scale, she decided to dig the shrubs up and replace them with a variety of shrub that was not prone to problems.

A friend noticed that one section of her yard wasn't looking very good. Looking at the plants closely revealed that all the plants that were declining were in one area, that was near the corner of the house. Every plant that looked ill had stunted leaves, and some seemed to be wilting even though my friend had watered recently. Because the problem seemed confined to one area, she decided that something specific to that spot was causing the problem, and because in all cases the entire plant was effected she suspected that something was wrong with the roots. When one of the plants was dug up and examined, my friend saw that the roots were beginning to rot. Looking closely at the house, she realized that the drainpipe drained all the runoff from the roof to that spot, and because her house is in an area where the soil is clay, the water wasn't being drained away quickly enough. She dug the rotting shrubs up, and is currently deciding what to do to correct the drainage problem.

After going through the process of close examination you may be able to diagnose and treat the problem yourself. If the situation is still puzzling, a sample of the problem can be taken to the Cooperative Extension Service or your local garden center. The information from your close observations will help others give you an accurate diagnosis and suggestions for treatment.

Q. When I look to see what is eating my plants I usually see lots of different bugs. How can I tell what is making holes in my plants?

A. Sometimes it is possible to tell what is eating your plants by the type of damage caused. Having a general idea of what may be eating your plant will help you know what to look for as you search for the insect responsible for the damage.

If *large* amounts of the leaves are gone, suspect caterpillars. They have such large appetites that they can make leaves disappear almost overnight. Look around the area where the chewing has been going on for signs of caterpillar droppings. (These are usually small, black pellets.) Look nearby the new, fresh damage for the caterpillar responsible.

Random holes in leaves are usually caused by beetles or grasshoppers. Larger, random holes, both on the edges and in the center of plant leaves, are often caused by slugs. Look at these plants at night with a flashlight to see if night-feeding insects or slugs are to blame.

Light-colored trails that wind through the leaf tissue are caused by leaf miners. Insects have laid eggs on the surface or underside of a leaf, and the larvae eat their way into and through the leaves. It is pointless to spray the plant when the larvae are active inside the leaves, because the insecticide does not reach them. Leaf miner damage is usually a cosmetic problem anyway, and they do not kill the plant.

Plants with leaves that are rolled are infested with leaf tiers. The insects roll a leaf around themselves for protection. Leaves that have been skeltonized may have been attacked by Japanese beetles, or sawfly larvae.

Before deciding an insect is responsible for damage to your plant, be sure to examine the plant at night as well as at different times of the day. Insects that are near the plants during the day often get blamed for damage done the night before.

Q. If I know my plant has been attacked by insects, will any insecticide kill the bugs?

A. Even after a problem is identified as insect-caused, a rush to any old insecticide may be doing more harm than good. If the damage is noticed after the insect has come and gone, spraying with an insecticide will not only be a waste of time and money, but will result in the death of many beneficial insects as well. Killing the insects that prey on other insects will lead to an imbalance that may cause problems later on. Some insects only eat plants during one part of their life cycle, and if damage is noticed after they have completed that stage of their growth, it is pointless to spray at that time.

Before automatically reaching for a pesticide, determine whether the pest is still active on the plant or not. There may be a non-chemical way to control the problem, or possibly changes in cultural practices that would reduce it to a tolerable level. (By cultural practices I mean how the garden is cared for. Examples would be controlling mildew on asters by not watering with an overhead sprinkler, or reducing the grub population by keeping your lawn dry, and therefore less attractive to beetles laying eggs.) Some insect problems may be relatively minor, and the damage that they do tolerable. If this is the case, doing what you can to attract any natural controls, such as birds or beneficial insects, makes more sense than using a pesticide.

Making note of when the damage has occurred will help to keep the problem under control in coming years. Insect deterrents such as Hot Pepper Wax, can be applied before the insects attack the plant in the future, for example. Most botanical insecticides are most effective when applied early in the insects' life cycle. Knowing when the problem is likely to reoccur allows you to get the jump on it the following year.

Finally, if you determine that an insecticide is absolutely necessary, find one that specifically targets the insect that is causing the problem, and use it according to the directions on the package.

Q. What is the horticultural oil that is recommended for use against certain insects, and how do I use it?

A. For many years people with fruit trees have sprayed them in the early spring with a product called Dormant Oil. It is called Dormant Oil because it must be sprayed on the trees before they break dormancy. This oil helped control pests on fruit trees by smothering any that had over-wintered in the bark of the tree. The oil was too heavy, however, to be used after the leaves had opened.

Superior oil, often called horticultural oil, is more highly refined than dormant oil, so it is possible to use it on plants that have leaves. It may be sprayed on plants anytime the temperatures are below 90°, using it when the temperatures or humidity are high might damage the plants. There are some oils on the market that are being offered as horticultural oils, but they are in truth the regular dormant oil that is mixed at a lower concentration. The superior oil is better for use on plants past the dormant stage. Look for a product that clearly states that it is the highly refined horticultural oil. The brand of superior oil that I am most familiar with is called Sunspray, but there are several on the market.

Horticultural oils are mixed with water and sprayed on plants with a pressure sprayer. They work by smothering the insects, not poisoning them, so they do not harm birds, earthworms, or other insects that are not hit with the oil spray when it is applied. Because the oil suffocates the insects it is sprayed on, pests do not develop a resistance to it.

Recent studies have also found a mixture of horticultural oil and baking soda to be a good fungicide for the treatment of mildew and black spot. It has proven effective against these fungi if used on a regular basis, particularly before the disease gets well established. See the question about leaf spot for more about treating fungal disease.

Q. One of my shrubs is covered with a blackish, powdery substance. What is wrong with it?

A. The dark gray substance is sooty mold. It is found on a variety of plants when they have an infestation of an insect that sucks the plant juices from the leaves of the plants. Because these insects are sucking the juices, not eating away the leaves, their presence often goes unnoticed. They excrete excess sap, which is called honeydew, and this sometimes gives the plant a sticky coating. The sooty mold grows on the excess sap that the insects secrete. The first notice that you have that the plant is infested with these insects may be when you touch the plant and notice that it is sticky, or when you notice the sooty mold.

Try to determine which insect is causing the problem by closely examining the stems and the underside of the leaves. Most sucking insects can be killed with applications of horticultural oil, but a definitive identification should be made before treating any plant with any insecticide. The sooty mold is not harmful, and it will go away when the insect problem is cleared up.

Q. I have several trees that have lichens on them. Should I be doing something about this?

A. The lichens are not harming your trees. Lichens are not parasitic plants, but rather use the tree only for their base of operations. Plants that get their nourishment from the air and rainfall, but live on another plant, are called epiphytes. There is some thought that a tree covered with lichens is a tree that is not in the best of health, but it is not the lichens that are causing the problem. Keep the trees as healthy as possible by fertilizing them in the spring and providing supplemental water during periods of drought.

Lichens are very sensitive to air pollution, so you can take some comfort in knowing that their presence indicates that your air is fairly clean.

Q. How can I get rid of the poison ivy that grows on the edge of our yard?

and

Q. My property is full of a green thorny vine that my neighbors call Cat Brier. How can I get rid of it?

A. I have placed these two questions together because the problems are very similar and the answer to both questions is the same. Poison Ivy is a pest plant because of the rash it gives to those who come in contact with it. Cat Brier is a pest because it takes over any area it can, and its thorny vines make it impossible for anyone except Br'ar Rabbit to walk where it grows. Many gardeners and homeowners want to rid their property of these invasive vines.

It is possible to eradicate most pest plants by cutting them off at ground level. New shoots will be sent up from the roots, and these must be cut off as soon as they appear. Since the leaves of a plant feed the root system, the constant removal of the leaves will eventually starve the roots and the plant will die. Getting rid of vines such as poison ivy, cat brier, and bittersweet using this method takes patience and persistence.

Hand removal of poison ivy poses special difficulties because of the irritating oil contained in all parts of the plant. Not only will contact with the leaves cause a rash, but contact with the stems and roots will as well. Those removing the plant will need to cover their body well, making sure to keep plastic bags on their hands when they take off their clothing and put it in the washing machine. (Clothes should be washed well with hot water and detergent.) Plastic garbage bags can also be pinned or tied over hands and arms (wear gloves and long sleeves as well) while placing the pieces of vine in trash bags. Never send poison ivy through a shredder or burn it; the irritating oil can travel through the air and land on any person in the vicinity. Anyone with a heightened sensitivity to poison ivy should not try to remove the plants.

If the hand control method seems out of the question, chemical controls are available. These too take some patience and persistence, however, since they must be carefully applied and reapplication may be necessary. Most herbicides kill any plants that they land on, so care must be taken to only apply them to the pest plants. (Read all herbicide labels carefully and follow the directions for application.) Vines such as cat brier and poison ivy are usually intermingled with trees and under-story plants that will need to be protected. If there aren't too many catbrier or bittersweet vines you could apply an herbicide by hand, using a paint brush to coat the leaves. Be sure to use such products according to directions, and apply them on a clear, windless day. Repeat applications may be necessary, so monitor the area just as you would if hand cutting the vines back. Reapply herbicides to new shoots as they appear.

Q. When I was weeding in my perennial bed recently I noticed a bunch of long orange-colored thread-like stuff winding in and among some of my plants. What is this silly string?

A. The dreaded dodder has moved into your perennial bed. Dodder is a parasitic plant that grows from seeds in the ground, and attaches itself to another plant. Once attached to a new food source, the roots are dropped and the stringy stuff lives off the juices of the other plant. Dodder blooms in the early spring, scattering seeds on the ground. After finding and removing the dodder from the garden, the garden must be watched closely for new, emerging plants. It is easiest to get rid of before it grows so large that it is firmly entwined around the stems of other plants.

If you catch it soon enough, assiduous attention to hand removal can be enough to rid the garden of this pest. Some perennial stems may have to be cut out of the garden if every piece of dodder can't be removed. If the dodder is well established, the host plant may need to be cut out completely. Herbicides work on dodder, but it can be difficult to apply without also killing the host plant; if you are going to kill the host plant as well, you may as well forgo the herbicide, dig the plant up, and throw the whole mess out, dodder and all.

Dodder grows with abandon in cranberry bogs here in Massachusetts, so gardeners should be aware that if they take soil or mulch material from bogs they may be inviting the parasitic dodder to live in their gardens as well. It can also appear out of nowhere. I had an invasion of dodder myself, even though nothing in my garden has ever been near a cranberry bog. I was able to remove it by hand, carefully peeling every little bit of stem away from all the plants that I could, and cutting the one bee balm that was completely infested off at the ground. I have not, knock on wood, had it in my garden again.

Q. A glob of bright yellow-orange goo appeared in my garden the other day. It grew across the mulch very quickly and soon covered half of a low-growing shrub. I scraped most of it away with a shovel...what is it and will it come back and hurt my plants?

A. This fungus alarms many gardeners because of its rapid growth and shocking color. Come to think of it, the texture is pretty alarming as well! My son calls it Alien Vomit, and that is a fair description. It is actually a type of slime mold that is feeding on micro-organisms in the mulch or soil. For all of its dramatic looks and behavior, it is harmless stuff. At most it might smother a young seedling simply by growing over any small plants in the area. Usually it comes and goes without doing any harm. This fungus most often occurs on areas that have been mulched with wood chips, although I have seen it growing on bare earth, low-growing shrubs, and cement walls. It can be lifted easily with a shovel and turned under the mulch, or washed away with the garden hose. I left mine where it was; it was so bright orange, grew so fast, and looked so gross, that it had great entertainment value for my nine-year-old! I usually see at least one batch of it every year; it has never hurt any of my plants, and it is always a source of great amusement.

Q. My lilac and some of my perennials were covered with a grayish dust last summer. They just looked terrible. What I can I do to prevent it this year?

A. The fungus that you describe is powdery mildew. While very unsightly, it rarely does permanent damage. Shrubs, vines, and perennials may be weakened slightly, but the problem is largely cosmetic on established plants.

When choosing plants for the garden, choose mildew-resistant cultivars, or plants that are not prone to mildew at all. Mildew should be controlled early on plants that are susceptible, with treatment begun before the plant shows signs of infection. Plants that have been prone to mildew in the past can be sprayed with a mix of horticultural oil and baking soda. (See next question for details.)

Antitranspirants have been shown to be successful as well. These products have traditionally been used on evergreens to keep them from losing too much moisture in the winter. The slight barrier that they provide over a leaf also prevents the mildew from getting established. Antitranspirants are sold at garden centers as well as through the mail from garden supply companies. They should be applied *before* mildew gets established on the plants.

Plants that are already showing signs of mildew may be treated with sulfur spray. Care must be taken to spray the tops and bottoms of the leaves, following the directions for the timing of several applications. Sulfur spray is most effective if used early, before the mildew gets a good foothold on the plant.

In addition to sulfur, a new product is on the market for the control of mildew. Called Erase, it is made from Jojoba oil, so it is a good least toxic solution for plants that already have mildew. It is most effective, I have found, when used on mild cases.

It may be impractical to spray large shrubs like lilacs, but a strong stream of water from a garden hose may be just as effective at controlling mildew on these bushes anyway. Studies have shown that when this washing process is started before any sign of mildew appears, it pushes the spores off the leaves before they become attached. Hose the bush down with a heavy stream of water, repeating the process twice a week. Such treatment should not be used on perennials or roses, because keeping the foliage wet will encourage other fungi to grow on these plants.

I have spoken to several gardeners who have noted that mildew is worst when the air is humid but there has been little strong rainfall. Mildew thrives in damp conditions, but hard rain washes the spores off the leaves.

Q. I was told that some of my plants have leaf spot. What is this, and how should I treat it?

A. Leaf spot is an umbrella term used to describe the symptoms that you see when a plant has a fungal condition or, more rarely, a bacterial problem. It is called leaf spot because you see spots on the leaves. (Who is buried in Grant's tomb?) A leaf spot usually starts out yellow and darkens to brown or black over time. (Sometimes these small spots blend together causing the entire leaf to become yellow and brown.) Fungi are themselves small plants that live on other plants. Because they are taking their nourishment from the host plant, the host plant is weakened when the fungi are present in sufficient numbers. There are many fungi that can cause leaf spot, and whether you treat a plant or not depends on how serious the problem is. Some fungal leaf spots cause a dropping of all the foliage, which stresses and weakens any plant. Other leaf spots are mainly cosmetic.

The first line of defense for fungal problems is, of course, to plant plants that are resistant to such problems. There are many lovely trees, shrubs, perennials and annuals that are not prone to fungal diseases; those who don't want to be bothered monitoring and treating their plants should seek out disease-resistant plants from the start.

Fungi are always with us, and as stated before, many of the fungi in the environment are helpful. Even fungi that cause problems can be present in small numbers on an otherwise vigorous, healthy plant. There is always an acceptable level of damage. Many plants, when looked at carefully, will have a bit of leaf spot that does not seem to spread quickly and isn't causing too much of a problem. When this is the case it is best to just ignore it, removing those few leaves that are infected and throwing them in the trash. Since fungi over-winter in the soil, cleaning fallen leaves from around a plant with even a small amount of leaf spot will help keep the situation under control in the coming years.

Plants with more than a touch of leaf spot should be treated with a fungicide. Most fungicides are most effective if applied early, before the fungus is solidly established on the plant. If you have had a fungal problem on a plant in the past, spraying that plant before it shows symptoms the following year will go a long way toward controlling the problem. Continue to regularly use any product that you choose, according to the directions.

The following fungicides are considered the safest for the gardener and the environment:

Sulfur - Available as a wettable powder, dry powder, or in a liquid form that is usually combined with soap, sulfur has long been considered one of the best products for the control of fungus. Liquid sulfur is combined with soap to help the sulfur stick to the leaves of the plant; liquid sulfur with soap sticks well to all parts of the plant, including the underside of leaves.

Copper or Bordeaux Mix - Bordeaux mix is a combination of copper and lime, accidentally discovered by grape growers in France to be effective against mildew and other fungi. Copper-based fungicides are available without the lime as well. Because copper is toxic to fish, Bordeaux mix and other copper fungicides should always be used with caution and they are best avoided for anyone living near a stream, pond, or lake. Always use copper, and other fungicides, according to the directions on the package.

Horticultural Oil and Baking Soda - Research has shown this combination to be effective at preventing fungal spores from getting established on a plant, as well as checking fungal diseases already in the garden. Use the following mixture:

> 1 Tbsp. baking soda
> 2 1/2 Tbsp. Ultra-Fine Horticultural Oil
> 1 Gallon of water

Spray plants prone to fungal problems every other week mid-April through July, then weekly in August and September. Do not spray when weather is very hot and humid. Continue to use cultural practices that discourage fungal growth. (Watering in the morning only, increasing air circulation where needed, and cleaning up all fallen plant debris of diseased plants or those prone to fungal problems.)

Bacillus subtilis – A newly available biofungicide that is a bacterium that either destroys or out-competes pathogens. One brand is called Serenade, and it may be used to prevent or control a variety of fungi, rusts and bacteria.

Antitranspirants - These products coat the leaf of a plant, preventing fungi from getting established, so they should be applied *before* there is a problem. Sold under the names of VaporGard and Wilt-pruf, among others, antitranspirants were originally made to help a plant retain water over the winter. Another type of antitranspirant is made from wax. One brand name currently available is Hot Pepper Wax, which is a product that combines the antitranspirant properties of wax with the insect-repelling quality of hot peppers.

All of the fungicides are most effective the earlier they are used. If plants that are prone to fungal problems are sprayed early in the season, fungi have a harder time getting established in the first place. Do not spray one type of fungicide within three weeks of another, however, because some will damage plants if used in combination with others. They should also not be used when the temperatures are over 90°, since this may also result in damage to the leaves of the plant.

Q. Can I combine an insect killer with a fungicide in my sprayer so that I can deal with two problems at one time?

A. This is something that I used to wonder about myself, since I like to be as time-efficient in the garden as possible. I knew that it wasn't good to combine harsh chemical insecticides and fungicides, but how about the botanical ones? Well, upon doing a bit of research I found out that these can't be combined in a sprayer either. The combination of some fungicides and insecticides can cause damage to the plants, or render each other useless. (Mixing the Bordeaux mix with BT for example, makes the BT inactive. Mixing sulfur with oils can burn plant tissues.) It is probably a good thing that such combinations are not possible. If it were safe to mix them we would all be tempted to dump everything in the sprayer, even if it wasn't needed at the moment. It would be even more tempting to spray what wasn't really necessary.

Two products already combine insecticidal and fungicidal qualities, however. Hot Pepper Wax fights fungus as an antitranspirant, and the hot pepper deters insects. Horticultural oil smothers insects and discourages fungal infestations as well. Other home combinations should be avoided, and package directions followed for every product used.

• • •

Q. Some of the oak trees in my yard have small, white, almost fuzzy round things on the ground under the trees. They are about the size of a raisin. What are they?

A. It sounds like a type of oak gall. There are many types of galls that appear on oak trees. The two found most frequently in this area are a very round, light brown gall just a bit smaller than a golf ball, and one that looks like a *tiny* peach. Galls are made by various insects laying their eggs in the plant tissues; they rarely harm the trees. If your tree is severely infested you may want to spray it with horticultural oil early in the spring, to kill any large amount of insects that have wintered over in the trees. Raking up any galls that fall to the ground, or pruning any branches that are particularly heavy with galls is also an option. Galls from other trees should be taken to the extension and identified, particularly if they are present in large numbers.

Q. What should I do about the tent caterpillars that I see in the crotches of the trees on my property? The caterpillars ate many of the leaves on the apple tree last year.

A. Eastern tent caterpillars can almost defoliate a tree when they are present in large numbers or when the tree is small. Trees usually recover from such an attack, but can be weakened by defoliation. Examine trees that were infested last year for any egg masses that may be present on the twigs or small branches. Egg clusters are black shiny masses that the adult moths have glued to the tree, generally encircling the twigs. They will be visible in the trees from late summer through the winter, and can be cut out and disposed of any time.

Trees currently infested with the caterpillars can be sprayed with BT, which is especially effective when the caterpillars are small. Nests can be removed in the early morning or late evening when all of the caterpillars have returned to the "tent." Remove them with a stick, broom, or scraping them off the tree with your hands. (Wear gloves and place a plastic garbage bag over your hands, scooping the mass into the bag. Be prepared to be grossed out—the nest full of caterpillars and their droppings is not a pretty sight.)

Small infestations of caterpillars are usually controlled by predators; birds, toads, and other insects eat tent caterpillars, and others die from adverse weather conditions or diseases.

Q. How can I control Japanese beetles?

A. Japanese beetles can be kept under control by using several non-chemical means, and usually a combination of approaches works the best. The Japanese beetle lays its eggs in the lawn, and the grubs eat the roots of the grasses during the fall and early spring. Adult beetles emerge from the turf in mid-summer to feed on other plants, most notably roses.

Japanese beetles may be killed in the grub stage with the products discussed in Chapter 6. (See the question about skunks digging up the lawn.)

Traps for Japanese beetles have been popular for many years, but many people don't realize that by hanging a trap near their garden they are actually luring many more beetles into the garden than they are trapping. A trap is most effective if hung far away from the area where Japanese beetles are a problem. On small properties it may be better to forego a trap entirely.

Hand picking the beetles off the plants that they are attracted to is perhaps the best strategy for removing them from small gardens. I have found that a new group of beetles can usually be found in the same place where they have been resting and mating the day before. Examine the plants in the early morning or late evening, removing and destroying any new beetles. If you are reluctant to grab them with your bare hand, they are usually easily knocked into a container of soapy water or water with a small amount of vegetable oil in it. Heavily infested plants can be cleared in one motion by shaking the plant, knocking all of the beetles onto a sheet or cloth spread at the base of the plant. Scoop up or shake the beetles from the sheet into a can or bucket of soapy water.

Other practices can discourage Japanese beetles from making your yard their paradise. Keeping the use of chemical pesticides to a minimum will insure that native insect predator populations are kept high. Encouraging birds in your yard by planting shrubs and trees, and keeping a bird bath filled with fresh water will also help.

Several birds, including cardinals and catbirds, feed on adult beetles. Because the adult Japanese beetles prefer to lay eggs on moist soil, keeping your lawn dry in mid-summer will discourage them from egg-laying in that area.

None of these measures are a quick fix, but they will help maintain a healthy environment overall. We have learned the wisdom of this approach over the years, and now it is time to remind ourselves that the days when we thought that "the only good bug is a dead bug" are over. Insects only raise a white flag and fall over dead in pesticide commercials. Real life is much more complicated; we are now relearning the wisdom of it being so.

Q. The earwigs are eating up my garden. What can I do about them?

A. If your garden is a bare soil (not mulched) vegetable garden full of young seedlings, than it is possible that the earwigs are doing the damage that you think they are. But if the damage you see is in a maturing vegetable garden, or a mulched flower garden, it is unlikely that earwigs are the culprits. Earwigs should be demonstrating in our gardens with placards reading "I've been framed!"

Many people are convinced that earwigs are a pest in the garden because they are present in great numbers, they are crawling around the garden during the day when people are working in their gardens, and most importantly, they look creepy. We blame all kinds of damage on earwigs because, lets face it, they are ugly, menacing-looking bugs.

In reality, the earwig is, in most cases, a beneficial insect in the garden. Earwigs eat decaying plant matter, other insects, and occasionally young seedlings. They do seem to love dahlia and buddleia foliage, and will feast on over-ripe fruit such as tomatoes. If your garden has many seedlings and not much else, than the earwig may eat the young plants because nothing else is available. But give them some decaying mulch, a variety of plants that occasionally shed leaves, and a diverse insect population, and they leave the growing plants alone.

The damage attributed to earwigs is often done by slugs, or night-feeding beetles. If a plant is being eaten, look at that plant with a flashlight at dusk and again two or three hours later. If nighttime checking does not reveal another pest eating your plants, and you are sure that earwigs are the culprit, then they can be trapped in damp newspapers that have been rolled into tubes and placed in the garden. The papers can be lifted from the garden in the early morning, and destroyed. Be sure that the earwigs are not convicted on circumstantial evidence, however. They are most often a beneficial insect in our gardens.

Q. Something was eating large holes in some of my annuals and perennials. When I checked the garden with a flashlight at night I saw lots of slugs. How can I get rid of them?

A. Slugs and snails are always present in the garden, but when their numbers grow or when they have a particular fondness for one type of plant, then action must be taken. You have done the definitive test for the presence of slugs; taking a flashlight into the garden about two hours after it has gotten dark will reveal how much of a slug problem there is, and which plants are currently being eaten. Slugs tend to prefer certain plants in the garden, and this makes their removal a bit easier, it not less slimy. The ornamental kale that I plant in my cottage garden every fall serves as a trap crop for the slug population there. They are drawn to the kale like pins to a magnet, and I spend ten minutes every night removing any that are crawling across the kale's leaves.

The best way to reduce the slug population is to hand-pick them off the plants at night. I hold a small plastic carton and a flashlight in one hand, and use the other hand to pick off the slugs and drop them into the carton. If you object to the slimy feeling of the slugs you can wear thin plastic gloves or pick them up with blunt-ended tweezers. The slugs in the carton can be dumped *far* away, emptied into the toilet, or fed to ducks if you or a neighbor have them. Stepping on them or mashing them with a trowel is also an option.

Slug poison that is non-toxic to insects and other animals is now available; it is iron phosphate mixed into a food bait. The iron poisons the slugs, but dissolves into iron fertilizer if not eaten. Sold under the names Sluggo and Escar-go, it is a good organic slug control for the garden.

Slugs like to hide in cool, damp places during the day, so creating such a place is an ideal way to trap them. Smooth boards, curved pieces of flower pots, and emptied out grapefruit rinds are all ideal when placed under the shady side of plants. Pick them up in the morning and dispose any slugs that are hidden there, replacing the traps to catch another batch the next day.

Saucers of beer are the most widely known traps for slugs and snails, probably because the idea of a tipsy slug is rather amusing; in truth though, a smooth board or grapefruit rind catches the same number of slugs as a saucer of brew, without having to share your beer with a mollusk. The sight of a dish of beer with several slugs drowned in it, or worse, the family dog drinking that dish of beer slugs and all, can turn a person off to a generally appealing beverage.

Barriers to keep slugs from climbing onto plants work if used along with hand-picking to keep the situation under control. Slugs have soft, vulnerable bodies, so placing anything sharp around their favorite food will deter them. Ashes, ground eggshell, diatomaceous earth, and even plain sand have been reported to work. The disadvantage of this method is that the barrier material is less effective if it gets wet, so it must be reapplied after a rain. In areas such as the Cape and Islands, where the mornings are often foggy and damp, such barrier materials are less effective. Seaweed and eel grass repels slugs when laid around plants as mulch, perhaps because it still contains a small amount of ocean salt on its surface.

Copper is another barrier that slugs will not cross because the copper interacts with the slug's skin, causing a toxic reaction that is rather like an electrical shock. Thin sheets of copper can be nailed around the board edges of raised bed gardens making a fairly permanent slug barrier. The natural greening of the copper does not make it less effective, and would make a very classy looking raised bed! Care must be taken to trim foliage that hangs down around the edges. Plants that hang over the edging provide a ramp for slugs, enabling them to cross over the copper strip.

Q. The gypsy moth caterpillars attacked one of my trees and did a lot of damage to the foliage. Will this hurt the tree, and will they be worse next year?

A. Trees can survive an attack that removes some or even all of the foliage as long as it does not happen repeatedly, which would eventually starve the roots, and provided that the tree has not already been stressed by other conditions. Gypsy moth populations come and go, and any trees that are killed after being defoliated by the moth larvae were weakened or already dying from another cause. When the gypsy moth populations are high it is easy to panic, and people often wonder if the trees will be damaged permanently. Trees are very resilient, however, and most will show no sign of the infestation a couple of years down the road.

If there are only a few trees in your yard that were attacked, look at the bark of those trees closely in the fall for the gypsy moth egg cases. These are usually about an inch and a half to two inches long, and half as wide. They are golden brown in color, and a bit fuzzy. Gypsy moths lay their eggs on the bark of trees, stone walls, garden furniture, deck railings, and just about everywhere else! Look around any slightly sheltered surface and scratch off any egg masses that you see. Burn them, or place them in a plastic bag and throw them away.

Trees that are especially small, or that were defoliated the year before can be protected the following season by spraying the tree with BT. Begin applying the BT when you first notice small holes in the leaves or see the young caterpillars. Gypsy moth larvae are small when young, and most people are not aware that they are out and feeding because the damage is minimal at first.

Roberta Clark, Cooperative Extension Specialist in the Landscape and Nursery Program, tells me that an easy way to remember when to first apply BT is to watch for the shad bush blooming. Shad bush (*Amelanchier* or serviceberry) is the bush or small tree with the small, lacy white blossoms that is seen blooming along roadsides and in the woodlands in the spring. In most years the shad bush blooms about the same time that the gypsy moth eggs hatch. Applying the BT ten to fourteen days after the hatch, and again ten days later, will kill the caterpillars. Only the young larvae are vulnerable to BT, however, so spraying early in the spring is the most effective way to protect your trees. If the caterpillars are large when they are first noticed, BT will not be an effective treatment.

Single trees that are too big to spray can be protected with sticky traps that are rolled around the trunks of the trees, catching the caterpillars as they climb up to feed. Make sure that these traps are applied with the sticky side *out*, so that the sticky material does not get on the bark of the tree. Bands of folded burlap can also be wound around the tree. The caterpillars crawl under the folds in the cloth to hide, making it possible for you to collect and destroy them.

The best way to insure that your trees will recover from a gypsy moth attack is to keep them as stress-free as possible the rest of the year. A tree that has been well-watered during a drought, and fertilized in the early spring will be healthy enough to withstand a heavy infestation of the larvae. Natural controls of gypsy moths keep their numbers at tolerable levels most of the time, and a healthy tree with recover if defoliated by a heavy population in any particular year.

Q. Just about every year I battle some small animal in my garden. One year it's voles, then skunks, and the next year rabbits or squirrels. I'm getting fed up!

A. Landscaping and gardening can be a frustrating activity, partly because we expect to have full control over "our" property. In truth, however, we share our property with a myriad of creatures who regard the property as theirs, and they view our plantings not as beautiful landscaping but as their food and shelter. As gardeners and homeowners, successful gardening (not to mention peace of mind) is accomplished best when we take a "if you can't beat them, join them" attitude. This does not mean, however, that we need to abandon the garden and let the critters take over, but that we need to work with nature instead of fighting it.

The first way we can help keep small animals in check is to encourage natural predators. Foxes, skunks, bobcats, coyotes, raccoons, crows, snakes, owls, and even cats prey on small animals of all types, keeping populations from overrunning the area. Yet as we construct suburban style living situations we often discourage these natural predators from making our neighborhoods their home. When we leave some wild spaces in a development, or even in our own yards, we are leaving areas that predators can live in, and these predators are garden allies.

Skunks are my favorite example of an animal that is commonly thought of as a pest, but is in reality a valuable predator. Many homeowners worry about the skunks that pass through their yard every night. These animals are annoying when they take up residence under the back porch, or when they spray the family dog, but aside from these smelly inconveniences they are an asset to our neighborhoods. Skunks not only eat Japanese beetle grubs, but a large part of their diet is small rodents such as mice. Keeping the dog inside after dark is a small price to pay for a "better mousetrap."

When landscaping our yards, we can plant larger areas of trees, shrubs, and perennials; growing more of these plants and less lawn not only means less maintenance for the gardener, but a larger habitat for predators as well. Using a wide variety of plants in our landscaping not only gives us a more interesting, beautiful yard and garden, but provides us with plantings that are less likely to be decimated by animals and insects. If a rabbit takes a sudden liking for your petunias, and all you have planted are petunias, the entire garden will be wiped out. This is a simplistic example, but the principle is the same for gardens, shrub borders, and trees. When an animal or insect attacks a particular plant, the entire garden will not suffer if you have put in a diverse selection of plants.

Planting time is not only an occasion to plant variety, but it is also the time to learn which plants are less desirable to the local wildlife. Beautiful gardens can be designed using plants that rabbits, deer, and woodchucks would just as soon leave alone. Interplanting these plants along with those that are more desirable will often discourage critters from choosing the flower bed as their personal five star restaurant.

Finally, placing plants in areas that are less accessible to the wildlife can mean the difference between watching your favorites grow or watching them disappear. If the annuals and perennials are being devoured by small animals, plant them in window boxes or in containers on the deck. Deer are less likely to munch a shrub that is planted right next to the house than they are one that is planted at the far end of the yard. Placing plants that entice wildlife as close to human activity as possible discourages the animals' extended nibbling.

Q. The squirrels are digging up the bulbs that I plant. What can I do?

A. Squirrels, chipmunks, and even skunks are known to drive fall bulb-planters crazy. Sometimes a chipmunk will take a bite or two from the bulb, but usually the bulb is left unharmed, lying in a pile of dirt near the hole. These animals are usually looking to see if the ground has been disturbed by something else; they are attracted by the loose soil, and they dig, looking to see if a tasty treat may be just underneath that inconveniently placed bulb at the bottom of the hole. They shove the bulb aside to get a better look and...oh bother. Nothing there. Off they go to look under the next bulb.

There are repellents sold at every garden center that deter animals from coming near the newly planted bulb. Powdered hot red pepper works as well; sprinkle some on the bulb, and some on the ground where the bulb is planted. Some gardeners swear that a combination of ground red pepper and garlic powder is effective. You could also use animal repellants sold in garden centers such as Bobinex or Fermented Salmon Spray.

Most small animals seem less interested in daffodils, snowdrops, and crocus than other bulbs, although the variety never seemed to deter them from digging them up in my garden.

After planting and replanting dozens of bulbs one fall, only to find them on the surface again every morning, I finally resorted to laying a physical barrier over the bulbs that I had just planted. After cutting sections from a roll of chicken wire, I placed a section over the newly planted bulbs, weighting it down with large rocks or logs. Since I usually plant bulbs in groups anyway, it was possible to place a short length over each newly planted group. I left the chicken wire over the bulbs for about three weeks, allowing time for several rains to settle the soil around the bulbs. This method has been very successful for me, and I am able to use the same sheets of wire again and again, storing them in a dry place when they are not needed.

Q. The deer eat most of my perennials. How can I keep them away? Are there plants that they won't eat?

A. Gardeners who start out thinking "Bambi!" when they first see a deer in their yard, usually end up thinking "Venison!" after the second or third visit from these lovely creatures. They are indeed lovely creatures...with very large appetites. The problem with a list of plants that deer don't eat is that the deer also don't *read*. Just as soon as you are convinced that they will leave a certain plant alone they will eat it down to the nubs...usually right after you have purchased and planted twelve of them. Barberry bushes are usually included in lists of shrubs that the deer won't eat, but I have known deer to eat barberry bushes, thorns and all, even though they hadn't shown the slightest interest in them for over ten years! That said, I will include a list of plants that deer resist, as well as listing some strategies to discourage them from general garden grazing.

Human smells seem to repel the deer, so many people have had success hanging bars of highly scented soaps from the limbs of their fruit trees. The soap can be left in the wrappers. Soap could also be nailed to wooden stakes and placed in perennial gardens. (There is a product waiting to be developed here. Scented soap in plain olive green wrappers permanently attached to wooden stakes of the same color, available in several lengths. Wrappers made of recycled paper, of course.) Since deer are herbivores, scattering blood meal around the perennials, or spraying them with diluted fish emulsion, may deter them for awhile. This needs to be renewed after a rain however, and since blood meal is pure nitrogen, using it on your beds over and over again will stimulate too much leaf growth on the plants. It is therefore only a short-term solution.

Deer seem to dislike the smell of rotting eggs as well. Spraying plants with a spray made by beating an egg into one to two gallons of water, with the addition of a teaspoon of dish soap or a spreader/ sticker product from the garden center, will encourage the deer to dine elsewhere. The rotten egg smell is not noticeable to humans; it needs to be reapplied every two or three weeks, depending on the amount of rainfall.

Other odoriferous deer repellents include putting human smells in the garden. Gardeners who have access to hair clippings from beauty salons and barber shops can scatter these clippings around or even lightly on top of the plants. I used to hang the T-shirt that I wore while working in the garden on a stake in the middle of the garden as a minimal scare-crow of sorts. Walking the family dog around gardens leaves a scent that helps keep the deer away as well. The problem with any of these methods is that they have to be renewed again and again. The deer seem to know when you and your dog are away for the weekend; invariably there will be signs that the deer have feasted while you were away.

The most permanent way to keep deer out of a garden is to install an electric fence. This can be a minimal two strands of wire, or a regular wooden fence with an electric wire strung a foot or two above the top rail. I have also seen properties where the homeowner fenced in the entire property with a high fence, leaving the driveway as the only opening. (Be sure to check local zoning laws before putting up any fence.) Although the deer could come in the driveway, they didn't usually do so.

My garden in the Berkshires was right on the deers' path from the fields to a stream. When we moved away, we took down the electric fence that was protecting the large perennial bed. I visited recently and noted that although several plants were eaten to the ground, and some chewed halfway down, there were several that the deer left alone. From this experience I have compiled a list of plants that in my experience, the deer don't eat. This list is not complete, of course, and it is based solely on what I grew in my perennial garden where I used to live. Although there is no guarantee that the deer won't *ever* eat these, I think it fair to say that in all likelihood they do not like the following: *Aconitum carmichaelli* (monkshood), *Cassia marilandica* (wild senna), *Dicentra spectabilis* (bleeding heart), *Iris sibirica* (Siberian iris), *Lysimachia clethroides* (gooseneck loosestrife), *Monarda didyma* (bee balm), *Peony lactiflora* (peony), *Salvia officinalis* (garden sage), *Stachys byzantina* (lamb's-ears), and *Solidago* hybrids (goldenrod). For a more complete list of plants commonly thought to be less desirable to the deer, see Chapter 9.

Plants with scented foliage, such as feverfew and marigolds, are usually left untouched when deer come to the garden. Deer always left the stiff ornamental grasses in my yard alone as well, so planting several clumps of *Miscanthus* will not only give the perennial bed winter interest, but will fill out the bed with a lovely clump of green that the deer will not eat. Those who share their property with the Bambi family may want to plant their flower garden with many *Allium* and herbs.

Q. When my annuals started disappearing I started watching the garden at dawn. I discovered that rabbits are responsible. What can I do?

A. Deterring rabbits is similar to deterring the deer. You can use a barrier, scent deterrents, or grow plants that they seldom touch. The best method should be determined by deciding which is most feasible for the type of garden that you need protected. A rectangular vegetable plot is most easily fenced, for example, while fencing a long, curved flower bed would not only be difficult, but unattractive as well.

The same smells that repel deer also deter rabbits. In a recent study, the animal repellant called Bobinex was found to be the most effective of those tested. I have also had good success with fermented salmon spray made by The Coast of Maine. Blood meal, human odors, and the urine of large animals all discourage them, although these odors must constantly be renewed and perhaps changed once in a while. Because rabbits use their sense of taste and smell to decide if they like a plant or not, spraying vulnerable plants with homemade repellents made of garlic, hot peppers, or fish emulsion can be an effective deterrent. Using a spreader/sticker soap will help these sprays stay on the plants for a longer period of time.

Vegetable gardens are best protected by fencing. (See the next question about keeping out woodchucks.) Chapter 9 contains a list of perennials that rabbits usually avoid.

Q. A woodchuck started visiting my vegetable garden, and the garden disappeared almost overnight! Help!

A. Of all the critters that drive gardeners crazy, I think the most frustrating is the woodchuck. They will eat many plants down to the ground, strip the leaves off of others, and even rip plants out of the ground as they eat. I have heard that woodchucks avoid spicy things such as cayenne pepper, so when I was plagued by a groundhog one year I misted all my plants with a Tabasco and hot pepper mix. The woodchucks seemed to think it was Mexican Night, and ate with gusto just the same. I could almost hear them call for margaritas!

The "country cure" for a woodchuck has always been to shoot the animal. Now that there is less space between neighbors, and most people don't have shotguns, this is not even an option. (It is against the law to fire a gun a certain number of feet from your neighbor's house. Check with local law enforcement to find out what is current law.) Those who are reluctant to destroy an animal are in a bit of a bind because even if the animal is trapped alive, it is illegal to transport the animal off your own property. What is the besieged gardener to do?

Because woodchucks feel most secure when provided with cover, mowing a strip around the gardens, or mulching around your beds will help. Anyone with the space might want to let a field of plantain, white clover, asters, and hawkweed flourish as far from the gardens as possible. These are favorite woodchuck foods, and they may keep the woodchucks distracted and in another area.

Fencing is probably the best protection from hungry woodchucks. ("Hungry woodchuck" is almost redundant!) A low electric fence is one option; two electric wires may be better than one. Place the first wire about six inches from the ground, and the next six inches from the first. Weeds must be kept trimmed underneath and around the wires, to prevent the wires from shorting out on contact with the weed stems.

An alternative fence is one that is made of wire mesh that is buried one to two feet under the soil, and attached to the fence posts up to three feet from the ground with the remaining 18 inches to two feet left unfastened and angled outwards. The buried section prevents the animals from tunneling under, the middle section forms the main barrier, and the flopping top keeps them from going over the wire.

Adding two electric wires above the wire mesh will make the fence a deer deterrent as well. Those who are only troubled by rabbits can use chicken-wire, making the buried portion 12 to 18 inches below the surface, and two feet fastened to the posts, with a foot left loose at the top.

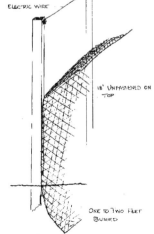

ELECTRIC WIRE

18" UNFASTENED ON TOP

ONE TO TWO FEET BURIED

Q. Small animals have eaten the bark off some of my shrubs. How can I prevent this in the future?

A. Mice and voles will eat the bark from shrubs and trees, particularly in the winter when other food is scarce. They can be discouraged from this practice by providing a less hospitable environment, or with the help of physical barriers.

Push any mulch that is around the shrubs and trees back from the trunk or stems, so that small rodents will be less inclined to nest next to the plantings. Cutting any low branches that provide cover next to the ground will help as well. Because mice and voles are so vulnerable to larger predators, they like to stay as hidden as possible; keeping the area around trees and under shrubs open and clear will mean that the critters will have little cover to hide in.

Chances are that this will be enough to encourage the small animals to stay away from your shrubs and trees, but if not, wire mesh (hardware cloth) can be wrapped around the trunks of trees and stems of shrubs. This protection should be examined twice a year to be sure that it is not digging into the plant as it grows. Voles can be discouraged from tunneling next to shrubs and trees by leaving a 12 inch ring of sand around the base of the plant. If the sand is 6 to 8 inches deep it creates an area encircling the plant where tunnels and burrows are likely to collapse.

As with other animal problems, encouraging the presence of natural predators will help control mice and voles.

Q. My perennial bed is over run with weeds. Is there any product I can use that will kill them quickly?

A. If you sprayed the bed with herbicide, the weeds would die quickly, but so would all your perennials. Products such as Preen and its organic counterpart, corn gluten, are pre-emergents. These prevent weed seeds from germinating, but they do not kill established, perennial weeds. (You should always use pre-emergent products with care in the perennial garden; they can stunt or damage some plants, particularly if used at rates higher than what is recommended on the label.) For established, perennial weeds there is no product that is as safe or effective as hand pulling. If some clumps of perennials are too ingrown with weeds, it is best to dig those out and put them in the compost or brush pile. After you have dug and pulled what you can, mulch with a two inch layer of bark mulch, and go on a regular weed patrol to pull out young plants as they appear.

Q. My hemlocks are covered with white, cottony fluff. Is the cottony stuff a problem? They are also looking rather thin.

A. Yes, the white fluff is a problem. It is hemlock wooly adelgid, a cigar-shaped insect that is most active in cold weather. Wooly adelgid weakens healthy hemlocks, and it can kill a stressed tree in three to five years. Begin monitoring hemlocks in February, and spray infested trees with horticultural oil in the spring and fall. If your trees are large you might need to hire an arborist to spray them. In addition to spraying, keep your trees as healthy as you can. Because hemlocks prefer moist soil, spreading compost and mulch around the base of the plants will help strengthen them. Do not fertilize afflicted hemlocks, however, because this makes them more susceptible to the adelgid.

Q. A bright red insect destroyed my oriental lilies last year. Help!

A. The Asiatic lily-leaf beetle, which is bright red with a black head, arrived on the scene a few years ago, much to the dismay of gardeners who love lilies. This beetle and its larvae are active from the moment the lilies poke up in the spring until late in the season.

Unfortunately, there is no good control for this pest. Handpicking seems to be the least toxic and most effective, although not an easy or pleasant means of control. To discourage their enemies, the lily-leaf larvae carry their excrement on their backs, making gloves a necessity for hand control.

Neem is the least toxic control for the beetle, but it must be applied regularly throughout the season because it stops the beetle from feeding but does not instantly kill the pest.

The lily-leaf beetle attacks true lilies (Asiatic and Oriental) and Fritillaria but does not bother daylilies. Gardeners who are unwilling to handpick or spray regularly with Neem should avoid planting lilies in the future.

Q. I see so many moths in my yard in the winter!
Q. Small green caterpillars are eating my trees – someone said they are the Winter Moth larvae... help!

A. Winter Moths fly and mate in the winter, and their eggs hatch out in the early spring. The larvae of this pest is very destructive, particularly to apple, cherry, maple, and birch trees, as well as roses and blueberries. This small green caterpillar eats oak leaves and the foliage of other trees as well.

What to do? Before bud-break, spray the trunks and branches of vulnerable plants with Horticultural oil. This may help smother some of the winter moth eggs. (As an alternative, dormant oil spray can be applied before bud break) At bud break and as the leaves grow, spray plants with Bt or a product that contains Spinosad. Use these products according to the directions on the label. Large specimen trees may have to be sprayed by a certified arborist. Because this pest is new to the northeast, it remains to be seen how damaging it will be over time.

Bt and Spinosad may also be used for infestations of other types of caterpillars.

~8~

RESOURCES

RESOURCES FOR GARDENERS

Q. What is the Cooperative Extension Service?

A. The Cooperative Extension Service is a joint program of the U.S. Department of Agriculture, state universities, and in some locations, county governments. The Barnstable County Extension Service is funded by all three. Residents of the Cape and Islands are fortunate that the county helps support the CES, since this provides for the availability of staff and programs that are a tremendous resource for people in this area.

Begun in 1914, the CES was created as a way to get information from the land grant colleges, where the latest research in agriculture was being done, to the farmers who could benefit from that research. Over the years the work of the Extension Service has broadened to serve those who live in more urban settings as well. The staff at the CES helps farmers, green-industry business people, home gardeners, and the general pubic by providing information on a wide range of subjects including horticulture and food and water quality. The CES also administers the 4H program for children.

Because of the large number of gardening questions that come into the CES from home gardeners, the Master Gardener program was created. Many Extension offices nationwide run a training program for avid gardeners who, upon being accepted into the program, have agreed to give a set number of hours of volunteer time in exchange for the intensive horticultural training received.

After completing their training, the Master Gardeners begin

209

doing horticultural related service work in their community. In Barnstable County, members of the Master Gardeners Association staff a "hotline" to answer the public's questions about gardening. Other Master Gardeners' activities include: speaking about plants and gardening to local organizations, presenting programs in the schools, testing soil samples for pH both at the Extension offices and at special soil clinics offered at a variety of cape locations, maintaining demonstration gardens at the Barnstable County fairgrounds, and the production of television programs about gardening, that are shown on local public access stations.

> The Barnstable County Cooperative Extension phone number is: (508) 375-6690
> The Master Gardener hotline number is: (508) 375-6700
> U-Mass Extension web site: http://www.umass.edu/umext

The Extension Service publishes a number of bulletins and information sheets that are free of charge. Master Gardeners who answer the calls coming into the hotline will often send the caller printed information relating to their inquiry. People may also come into the Extension office to see which material will be most helpful to them.

Q. What sort of questions can the Master Gardeners answer for me?

A. Any questions concerning plants and gardening can be phoned into the hotline. Those starting a garden for the first time need basic advise about which plants will do well in their location, or the best way to prepare the soil for planting. Experienced gardeners may be puzzled about a situation that they have not encountered before. People often bring plants and insects into the office for identification. Many are curious to know if an insect that they have noticed on their plants is harmful or beneficial, and others want to know what in heck is eating their broccoli. If the answer to the question is not immediately known, the Master Gardeners will research the problem, and get back to the caller with a response, either by phone or through the mail. Many questions can be answered over the phone, but it is sometimes necessary for a sample of the plant or insect in question to be mailed to the Extension, or brought into the office.

The address of the Extension Service office is:

Cooperative Extension Service, Barnstable County
Deeds and Probate Building
P.O. Box 367
Barnstable, MA 02630

Q. How can I have my soil tested for *more* than the pH level?

A. The Soil Testing Lab at the University of Massachusetts will test soil samples for levels of available plant nutrients and abnormally high levels of toxic heavy metals, as well as for pH. For a slightly higher fee they will test for organic matter or soil texture. Complete information about the variety and cost of tests available will be mailed to you upon request. Write or call the Soil Testing Lab for information.

Soil Testing Lab
West Experiment Station
University of Massachusetts
Amherst, MA 01003-2082
(413) 545-2311

Q. I am interested in learning more about how to manage problems in my yard and garden in the least toxic way. Where can I get more information about Integrated Pest Management?

A. The Cooperative Extension can provide you with a great deal of information about IPM, particularly as it applies to situations that you may be currently facing. General information, resource material, and updates on current research in Least-Toxic Pest Management can be obtained from the Bio-Integral Resource Center in California. Write or call for a booklet describing their publications and services.

  The Bio-Integral Resource Center
  P.O. Box 7414
  Berkeley, CA 94707
  (510) 524-2567

There is also a book that details the least toxic ways to control pests in the garden and the home. It is titled *Common-Sense Pest Control* (See Bibliography) and it is available at some libraries or through the CLAMS system.

Q. There are so many gardening books available...how do I know which ones will be most helpful?

A. Every gardener has his or her favorite reference materials, and which books you find valuable will depend on what type of gardening you are doing. Asking other gardeners which books they find most useful is a place to start; the Master Gardeners at the Extension Service will be happy to tell you which books are most helpful to them. I also recommend a visit to your local public library. Most libraries have a good selection of gardening books, and books that are not available at your local branch can usually be borrowed from another library through the CLAMS system. Borrowing a book for a week or two will give you time to read through the material and see if it contains information that will be helpful. The Bibliography at the end of this book lists books that I refer to again and again.

Q. Where can I learn more about gardening in this area? Are there gardens that are open to the public?

A. Interest in gardening is *growing* on the Cape and Islands, and there are so many places to learn about plants and stroll through gardens that it is almost difficult to find the time to visit them all. The following is a list of resources for gardeners.

• *Public libraries:* Aside from the books inside, many public libraries have lovely plantings on their grounds. Contact the library in your area to inquire about any new or mature plants that surround the library building.

- *Garden centers and Nurseries:* Many garden centers plant the area around their yard and buildings with both seasonal and permanent landscaping. These plantings are a good place to learn what is currently in bloom, as well as how certain shrubs and trees look as they mature.

- *Botanical Trails of the Historical Society of Old Yarmouth:* Located off Route 6A behind the Yarmouthport post office are trails leading through 50 acres that include wildflowers and an herb garden. For information call the Historical Society of Old Yarmouth: (508) 362-3021.

- *Falmouth Historical Society:* Located at the Julia Wood House in Falmouth are three gardens maintained with the help of the Falmouth Garden Club. The formal garden is restored to the home's period, and there is an herb garden and woodland garden as well. Information: (508) 548-4857

- *Green Briar Nature Center:* A wildflower garden containing more than 200 varieties of flowers is planted on this site on Discovery Hill Road in East Sandwich. Wildflowers from North America abound, along with plants from other parts of the world. Separate beds feature plants for meadows, woodlands, and wetlands.
Green Briar Nature Center Wildflower Garden
6 Discovery Hill Road (off 6A)
East Sandwich, MA 02537
(508) 888-6870
www.thorntonburgess.org

- *Thorton Burgess Museum:* A lovely herb garden in the shape of a Victorian nosegay is located next to the museum in Sandwich.
Thorton Burgess Museum
 Route 130
Sandwich, MA 02537
(508) 888-4668

- *Spohr Gardens:* Famous for daffodils, this private garden belonging to Charles Spohr is set on the shore of Oyster Pond. Footpaths lead through a perennial garden, rock garden, and rhubarb garden, as well as a collection of millstones and anchors. Mr. Spohr's garden contains mature specimens of shrubs and trees from all

over the world, and is located on Fells Road in Falmouth. Visitors are welcome during daylight hours.
Spohr Garden Trust
45 Fells Road (off Oyster Pond)
Falmouth, MA
Open dawn to dusk
(508) 548-0623

- *Cape Cod Horticultural Society/ Armstrong-Kelley Park:* Based in Osterville, the Cape Cod Horticultural Society is open to individuals who have an interest in horticulture. The group meets at the Osterville Public Library, and at each meeting a speaker presents a talk on a variety of garden-related topics. The Horticultural Society also maintains Armstrong-Kelley Park, which is located on Main Street in Osterville. The park contains a wide variety of shrubs and trees, a display garden of heaths and heather, and a rhododendron walk that is planted with 150 rhododendrons and azaleas. The park is open to the public, free of charge, during daylight hours. For more information call Dr. Carl Mongé, (508) 420-3635
Armstrong-Kelly Park
Main Street (across from Swifts Grocery)
P.O. Box 934
Osterville, MA 02655

- *Memorial Gardens of St. Mary's Episcopal Church:* These gardens are located on over two acres of land in Barnstable. There are formal gardens and a wildflower meadow, and all are open to the public during daylight hours.
Gardens at St. Mary's Church
3055 Main St. (Rt. 6A)
Barnstable, MA 02630
(508) 362-3977
www.stmarys-church.org

- Several other churches on the Cape welcome visitors to their gardens. They include:
Church of the Messiah, Church Street Woods Hole
Corpus Christi, Quaker Meeting House Rd. Sandwich

St. Joseph's Church, Millfield Street Woods Hole
Church of the Holy Spirit, Monument Road Orleans

• *Polly Hill Arboretum:* Originally a sheep farm that was acquired by Polly Hill's family in 1926, this garden began with Polly's interest in growing trees from seed. In the mid-1950's, Polly Hill began experimenting with hybridization and plant hardiness. The long list of plant selections resulting from her work include: rhododendrons, azaleas, camellias, viburnums, magnolias and lilacs. Today, visitors to the arboretum can see the results of Polly's efforts, new plantings, and mature specimens of shrubs and trees from around the world. Throughout the year, classes, lectures, and special programs are offered at Polly Hill, making this a horticultural resource for visitors and island residents alike. Day visitors who do not wish to take their car to the Vineyard will appreciate the bus that takes visitors from the ferry in Vineyard Haven up to the arboretum.
Polly Hill Arboretum
809 State Road
West Tisbury, MA 02575
(508) 693-9426
www.pollyhillarboretum.org

• *Mytoi:* This garden (pronounced "mee-toy") is on Chappaquiddick Island and was given to the Trustees of Reservations in the early seventies. Originally planted by Mary Wakeman, Mytoi is now open all year without charge.
   Visitors to this island property usually comment on the sense of solitude and meditation that permeates the gardens. As this garden developed, the approach was an unusual mix of native plantings and oriental style, blending a Japanese design sensibility with the wind-swept island environment.
Mytoi
Dike Road
Chappaquiddick Island
Martha's Vineyard, MA
(508) 627-7689
www.thetrustees.org

- *Heritage Plantation:* Formally the estate of Charles O. Dexter, who was internationally known for his rhododendron hybrids, these 76 acres are a treasure for gardeners and anyone who strolls through the lovely landscaped grounds. Thousands of rhododendrons bloom in May and June, and there is a daylily bed, hosta garden, heather display, herb garden, and a perennial bed. This is a good place to see trees and shrubs (all labeled) that have grown to maturity. The Heritage Plantation also sells plants from the garden gift shop, holds an annual plant sale, and runs programs of interest to gardeners throughout the year; contact them for details.
  Heritage Plantation
  Grove and Pine Street
  Sandwich, MA
  (508) 888-3300
  www.heritageplantation.org

- *Ashumet Holly and Wildlife Sanctuary:* Extensive plantings of American holly, that was propagated by Winifred Wheeler, the state's first commissioner of agriculture. Other types of holly and woodland plants are abundant on this forty-five-acre parcel located in Hatchville. (508) 563-6390

- Cape Cod, Martha's Vineyard, and Nantucket are filled with conservation lands, parks, and sanctuaries, each of which contain abundant inspiration for the gardener. When planting our yards and gardens we are working in partnership with nature, so she should always be our first teacher. While most people are drawn to natural landscapes, gardeners in particular are inspired and renewed by visiting such areas.

   Most town conservation commissions publish a map of local conservation lands that are open to the public. These are either free or available for a minimal fee. Several books contain lists of the many nature trails and sanctuaries on the Cape and Islands. (See Bibliography) Among the many sanctuaries that should not be missed are the Sandy Neck Conservation Area in Barnstable, the Wellfleet Bay Wildlife Sanctuary in Wellfleet, the Cape Cod National Seashore, and Cedar Tree Neck on Martha's Vineyard.

- *Garden Tours:* Most garden clubs run garden tours in the summer. For a small fee you are given a map showing the location of the gardens included on the tour. The gardens included are of all sizes and styles, and are usually designed and planted by the owner. Garden tours are a wonderful way to become better acquainted with which plants grow well in this area, as well as seeing plants that are favorites of that particular gardener. Information about garden tours usually starts appearing in the newspapers in May or June.

  For the past several years the Provincetown Art Association has offered a "secret garden tour" as a benefit fundraiser. It is usually held in July. Contact the Art Association for information.
  Provincetown Art Association
  460 Commercial Street
  Provincetown, MA 02657
  (508) 457-1750

- There are many magazines about gardening that are available by subscription, over the counter at bookstores and garden centers, and at local libraries. Especially worthwhile for gardeners in our area are the following:

- *People, Places & Plants* is a magazine that focuses on gardening in New England. It features stories about area gardeners and growers, and concrete information about plants and gardening. Contact them at:
  People Places & Plants
  173 Gray Road
  Falmouth, ME 04105
  (207) 878-4953
  www.newenglandgardening.com

- *The Avant Gardener* is a horticultural news service that contains short articles about plants, tools, current research, and books of interest to gardeners. It is available from the Horticultural Data Processors, Box 489 New York, NY 10028.

- *Garden Clippings* is a newsletter put out by the Massachusetts Cooperative Extension Service. It is filled with timely articles of interest to home gardeners, and contains a sheet of information written by the Cape Cod Horticultural Extension Agent. This bulletin contains news about plants that do well on the Cape and Islands, information about common garden pests that are currently active and how gardeners can best cope with them, and seasonal reminders about garden tasks and activities. *Garden Clippings* is mailed to local gardeners eight months a year. For information about subscriptions call the Barnstable Cooperative Extension at: (508) 375-6690 or click on "publications" at the web site: http://www.umassgreeninfo.org

- *Wildcare:* These are the folks to call with questions about the wildlife in your yards and neighborhood. They do not remove woodchucks or skunks from your property, however, nor do they have any better answers for control of woodchucks than I do! They will answer questions about such matters as whether a particular animal behavior is normal, or what to do about injured animals or wildlife in distress. Wildcare can be reached at 896-5273.

- Massachusetts Audubon Natural History Help Line: A place to call with your questions about animal behavior, handling wild animal problems, or dealing with injured wildlife. (781) 259-9506 x7416

- Other addresses and phone numbers of interest to gardeners are:
Poison Control: (800) 682-9211
Poison Control, Boston: (617) 232-2120
For questions about the possible toxicity of plants.
Animal & Health Inspection Service (APHIS)
USDA APHIS
Plant Inspection and Quarantine
Room 4, Customs House
Boston, MA 02109
Local number for the APHIS at Otis: (508) 563-9309

- The APHIS is the agency that can tell you if you can move a particular plant from country to country or state to state. If you want to move to California and take your houseplants with you, or if you want to send some of your garden produce to a friend overseas, they can tell you if your plans are possible.

- Spring Plant Sales: Many of the organizations listed above and most garden clubs hold spring plant sales that raise the funds needed to maintain their gardens or fund scholarship programs. Because these sales often offer plants donated from local gardeners, as well as from the garden that is holding the sale, they are an excellent place to buy plants that are tried and true performers, perennials with established root systems, and unusual varieties that may not be available at local garden centers. For details, contact the organization in question in the spring. Information about plant sales begins appearing in local papers in April.

PLANTS AND PRODUCTS BY MAIL

There are many wonderful plant and seed catalogs available to entertain and tempt the gardener throughout the winter months. Most of the large, glossy, color catalogs are available free, and addresses and phone numbers for these companies are boldly advertised in gardening magazines from November until June. I have chosen to list only a few lesser-known catalogs here, partly because the larger catalogs are widely advertised, and partly because many of the plants that they carry are available locally. (Locally available plants are usually larger, and there is no shipping fee!) I realize that this list is far from complete. Most of these catalogs are from companies I have ordered from again and again; others are from sources that I have not yet tried. (I have to restrain myself. If I purchased every plant that appealed to me, my bank account would be bare and my property would be even more of a jungle than it already is!) Even if I do not order from a particular catalog I usually learn quite a bit just from reading it.

Most of these nurseries charge for their catalogs; I have included this information as I know it, but be aware that the price may change over time. Please call or write for current information, and be aware that address and phone numbers may change over time.

Antique Rose Emporium
9300 Lueckemeyer Rd.
Brenham, TX 77833
(979) 836-9051
www.weareroses.com
Catalog: free
Old-fashioned roses

Donaroma's Nursery
P.O. Box 2189
Edgartown, MA 02539
(508) 627-8366
catalog: free of charge
Good list of perennials

Fairweather Gardens
P.O. Box 330
Greenwich, NJ 08323
(856) 451-6261
www.fairweathergardens.com
catalog: $4.00
Great selection of plants, many unusual or hard to find.

Forest Farm
990 Tetherow Road
Williams, OR 97544-9599
(541) 846-7269
www.forestfarm.com
catalog: $4.00
Large *selection of trees, shrubs, and perennials. Many unusual plants - a catalog to keep by your bedside.*

Heronswood Nursery Ltd.
7530 288th Street NE
Kingston, WA 98346
(360) 297-4172
www.heronswood.com
catalog: $5.00
Trees, shrubs, vines, perennials, and grasses, many of them unusual. My favorite winter read.

J.L. Hudson, Seedsman
Star Route 2, Box 337
La Honda, CA 94020
cannot be reached by telephone
catalog: $1.00
seeds for many annual and perennial plants

Niche Gardens
1111 Dawson Road
Chapel Hill, NC 27516
(919) 967-0078
www.nichegdn.com
catalog: free
Shrubs, perennials, and grasses - specialty is native plants.

Rockspray Nursery
Box 693
Truro, MA 02666
(508) 349-6769
www.rockspray.com
catalog: no charge
Heaths and Heathers - although it is a "local" nursery, it is worth
requesting the catalog for research before you go. Large selection.
Visit if you can, but mail order is good for those pressed for time.

Roslyn Nursery
211 Burrs Lane
Dix Hills, NY 11746
(631) 643-9347
www.roslynnursey.com
catalog: free
Large selection of Rhododendrons and Azaleas, that are their spe-
cialty - unusual perennials, shrubs and trees

Shady Oaks Nursery
112 10th Ave. S E
Waseca, MN 56093
507-835-5033
www.shadyoaks.com
catalog: $4.00
Plants for shade gardens including many wildflowers and natives.

Underwood Shade Nursery
P.O. Box 138
North Attleboro, MA 02763
www.underwoodshadenursery.com
Catalog $3.00
Plants for shade gardens

Siskiyou Rare Plant Nursery
2825 Cummings Road
Medford, OR 97501
503-772-6846
www.siskiyourareplantnursery.com
catalog: $3.00
Specialists in rock garden and woodland plants, - offers other pe-
rennials and shrubs as well

Singing Springs Nursery
8802 Wilkerson Road
Cedar Grove NC 27231
www.singingspringsnursery.com
Call or email them to request a catalog. Singing Springs special-
izes in unusual annuals and tender perennials. I have ordered
from them for several years and have always been pleased with
the size of the plants I've received.

Avant Gardens
710 High Hill Road
North Dartmouth, MA 02747
(508) 998-8819
www.avantgardensne.com
Rare and unusual annuals, tender perennials, and shrubs. Order
by mail or on-line, but be sure to visit their demonstration gar-
dens later in the summer. A short drive from the Cape and worth
the trip.

One Green World
28696 S. Cramer Road
Molalla, OR. 97038-8576
(800) 418-9983
www.onegreenworld.com
Fruits, nuts and berries; specialists in edible landscaping.

Bluestone Perennials
7211 Middle Ridge Road
Madison, OH 44057

(800) 852-5243
www.bluestoneperennials.com
catalog: free
small (less expensive!) perennials; good selection of popular varieties

Tomato Growers Supply Company
P.O. Box 2237
Ft. Myers, FL 33902
(888) 478-7333
www.tomatogrowers.com
catalog: free
Tons of tomatoes, including heritage varieties and other veggies too.

Territorial Seed Company
P.O. Box 158
Cottage Grove, OR 97424-0061
(541) 942-9547
www.territorialseed.com
Vegetable and flower seeds with emphasis on organic seed and heritage varieties.

Chiltern Seeds
Bortree Stile
Ulverston, Cumbria
LA12 7PB
England
www.chilternseeds.co.uk
Catalog: free
If you are having trouble finding a source for the seeds for a particular plant, write and ask for this catalog! A seed-starters heaven.

WEB SITES

Since this book was first written, gardeners have gained access to a wonderful tool in the form of the internet. Many gardeners now go to the web to find everything from seeds to information; garden bulletin boards and chat rooms provide "over the garden fence" information twenty-four hours a day, in all seasons. In fact, if we took the time to explore all the plant related information that is on the internet we would never get into the garden!

My home on the web? **www.gardenlady.com.** I update my site quarterly or whenever the garden isn't demanding all my time.

I have included just a few sites here that I find useful. Do keep in mind that these addresses change with some frequency.

www.gardenreview.com *Reviews of garden tools*

www.mastercomposter.com *Composting information*

http://plant-disease.orst.edu *Diseases of plants*

http://plantpropagation.com *Propagating plants*

www.findmyroses.com *Locating particular roses*

http://web.aces.uiuc.edu/weedid *Weed identification*

www.wvu.edu/~agexten/ipm/intify/insectid.htm *Identify insects*

www.arboristsite.com *Arborist site with articles & chat about trees*

www.massorganic.org *Web site of the Mass. organic gardeners*

http://webgarden.osu.edu *information and problem solving*

~9~

PLANT LISTS

PLANT LISTS

PLANTS FOR EXPOSED SEASIDE CONDITIONS

Amelanchier canadensis (Shadbush/Serviceberry)
Ammophila breviligulata (American beachgrass)
Cytisus scoparius (Scotch Broom)
Eleagnus umbellata (Autumn Olive)
Eragrostis (Weeping Lovegrass)
Hippophae rhamnoides (Sea Buckthorn)
Juniperus (Junipers most species, including Red Cedar *J. virginiana*)
Ligustrum (Privet most species)
Myrica pensylvanica (Bayberry)
Pinus mugo mughus (Mugho Pine)
Pinus thunbergii (Japanese Black Pine)
Prunus maritima (Beach Plum)
Qiercus sp. (Oaks, including white, black, and red oaks)
Rhus typhina (Staghorn Sumac)
Robinia pseudoacacia (Black Locust)
Rosa rugosa (Rugosa rose)
Taxus cuspidata (Yew)

TREES FOR LESS EXPOSED SEASIDE PLANTING

Acer sp. (Maples, including Norway, Red, and Sycamore)
X Cupressocyparis leylandii (Leyland Cypress)
Gleditsia triacanthos (Honey locust)

Heptacodium miconioides (Seven-son Flower)
Ilex opaca (American Holly)
Malus sp. (Crabapples)
Pinus sp. (Pines, including White, Austrian, Scotch, and Blue Spruce)
Salix sp. (Willow)

SHRUBS AND VINES FOR LESS-EXPOSED SEASIDE PLANTING

Akebia quinata (Akebia vine)
Berberis thungergii (Barberry)
Buddleia sp. (Butterfly Bush)
Campsis radicans (Trumpet Vine)
Chamaecyparis obtusa (Hinoki Falsecypress)
Clethera alnifolia (Summersweet)
Comptonia peregrina (Sweet Fern)
Cotoneaster sp. (Cotoneasters, several cultivars)
Euonymus alata (Burning Bush)
Hydrangea macrophylla (Bigleaf Hydrangea)
Hydrangea peteolaris (Climbing Hydrangea)
Hibiscus syriacus (Rose of Sharon)
Ilex crenata (Japanese Holly)
Ilex glabra (Inkberry Holly)
Kolkwitzia amabilis (Beauty Bush)
Ligustrum sp (Privet)
Lonicera sp. (Honeysuckle)
Parthenocissus tricuspidatta (Boston Ivy)
Polygonum aubertii (Silver-Lace vine)
Potentilla fruticosa (Bush Cinquefoil)
Pyracantha sp. (Firethorn)
Rosa sp. (Roses – bush, ramblers, and climbing)
Spireas sp. (Spirea)
Vaccinium corymbosum (Highbush Blueberry)
Viburnum sp. (Viburnums including Arrowwood,Witherod, Tea, European Cranberrybush, and American Cranberrybush)
Weigela hybrids (Weigela)
Wisteria sp. (Wisteria)
Yucca filamentosa (Yucca)

Seaside Groundcovers and Grasses

Arctostaphylos uva-ursi (Bearberry)
Calluna vulgaris (Heather)
Chasmanthium latifolium (Sea-Oat grass)
Cotoneaster horizontalis (Creeping Cotoneaster)
Deschampsia caespitosa (Tufted Hair grass)
Hedera helix (English Ivy)
Juniperus horizontalis (Creeping Juniper)
Juniperus procumbens (Japanese Juniper)
Miscanthus sinensis (Miscanthus grass)
Molinea coerrulea (Variegated Moor Grass)
Panicum virgatum (Switch Grass)
Pennisetum alopecuroides (Fountain Grass)
Rosa wichuraiana (Memorial Rose)
Spartina alterniflora (Smooth Cordgrass)
Spartina patens (Salt-meadow Cordgrass)
Thymus sp. (Thyme)

Under-used or Unusual Annuals or Tender Perennials

Agrostemma githago (Corn Cockle)
Clerodendrun ugadense
Cuphea ignea
Dicliptera suberecta
Dolichoes lablab (Hyacinth Bean)
Emilia javanica (Tassel Flower)
Euphorbia marginata (Snow-on-the-Mountain)
Fuchsia triphylla 'Gartenmeister'
Lagenaria vulgaris (Ornamental Gourds)
Nicotiana alata (Flowering Tobacco)
Nigella damascena (Love-in-a-Mist)
Osteospermum many cultivars
Perilla frutescens (Beefsteak Plant)
Plectranthus species and varieties
Scabiosa atropurpurea (Scabiosa)
Solanum species and varieties (Ornamental Peppers)
Strobilanthes dyeranus (Persian Shield)

Tagetes tenuifolia (Signet Marigold)
Thithonia rotundifolia (Thithonia)
Verbena bonariensis
Verbena hybrids

RELIABLE, LITTLE-MAINTENANCE ANNUALS

I list these by common name because many are so seldom called by their botanic names that to do so here seems confusing.
Blue Horizon Argeratum
Sweet Alyssum
Wax Begonia
Blue Salvia
Cleome
Marigold
Scaevola
Impatiens

DROUGHT-TOLERANT ANNUALS

Brachycome iberidifolia (Swan River Daisy)
Cleome pungens (Cleome or Spiderflower)
Cosmos bipinnatus (Cosmos)
Gaillardia pulchella (Blanket flower)
Gazania rigens (Treasure flower)
Gomphrena globosa (Globe Amaranth)
Helianthus annuus (Sunflower)
Helichrysum petiolantum (Licorice Plant)
Pelargonium hybrids (Geraniums)
Perilla frutescens "crispa" (Beefstake Plant)
Portulaca grandiflora (Portulaca)
Portulaca oleracea (Purslane)
Rudbeckia hirta (Black-eyed Susan)
Scaevola saligna (Scaevola)

DROUGHT TOLERANT PERENNIALS

Achillea hybrids (Yarrow)

Ajuga reptans (Bugleweed)
Ameria maritima (Sea Thrift)
Anthemis tinctoria (Golden Marguerite)
Arabis procurrens (Rockcress)
Artemisia sp. (Artemisia)
Asclepias tuberosa (Butterfly weed)
Aster novi-angliae (New England Aster)
Aster tataricus (Tartarian Aster)
Aurinia saxatilis (Basket-of-Gold)
Baptisia australis (False Blue Indigo)
Cassia marilandica (Wild Senna)
Chrysanthemum nipponicum (Nippon Daisy)
Coreopsis grandiflora (Tickseed)
Coreopsis verticillata (Threadleaf Coreopsis)
Echinacea purpurea (Purple Coneflower)
Echinops species (Globe Thistle)
Epimedium species (Barrenwort)
Eringium hybrids (Sea Holly)
Euphorbia species (Spurge)
Gaillardia grandifloria (Blanket flower)
Gaura lindheimeri (Wand Flower)
Helianthus spp. (Sunflower)
Hemerocallis hybrids (Daylily)
Kniphofia uvaria (Red-Hot Poker)
Lavandula angustifolia (Lavender)
Lychnis chalcedonica (Maltese Cross)
Lychnis coronaria (Rose Campion)
Malva moschata (Musk Mallow)
Oenothera missourensis (Missouri Primrose)
Perovskia atriplicifolia (Russian Sage)
Phlox subulata (Moss Phlox)
Potentilla sp. (Cinquefoil)
Rudbeckia species (Black-eyed Susan)
Salvia officinalis and varieties (Sage)
Santolina species (Santolina)
Saponaria ocymoides (Soapwort)
Sedum species (Stonecrop/Sedum)
Solidago hybrida (Goldenrod)

Thymus species (Thyme)
Verbascum species (Mullein)
Yucca filamentosa (Adam's Needle)
Most ornamental grasses

PERENNIALS FOR MOIST CONDITIONS

Aruncus dioicus (Goatsbeard)
Astilbe species (Astilbe)
Astrantia major (Masterwort)
Chelone obliqua (Turtlehead)
Cimicifuga racemosa (Snakeroot)
Darmera peltata (Umbrella Plant)
Eupatorium fistulosum (Joe-Pye Weed)
Ferns (most species)
Filipendula rubra (Meadowsweet)
Hibiscus moscheutos (Swamp Mallow)
Incarvillea delavayi (Hardy Gloxinia)
Iris ensata (Japanese Iris)
Lythrum salicaria (Purple Loosetrife)
Myosotis scoipioides (Forget-me-nots)
Rodgersia aesculifolia (Roger's Flower)
Tradescantia virginiana (Spiderwort)
Trollius europaeus (Globeflower)
Viola species (Violet)

ANNUALS FOR SHADE (PT: part shade S: full shade)

Begonia x *semperflorens-culorum* (Wax Begonia) PT/S
Begonia tuberhybrida (Tuborous Begonia) S
Browallia speciosa (Browallia) PT
Caladium hybrids (Caladium) S
Cleome pungens (Spiderflower) PT
Coleus hybrids (Coleus) PT/S
Impatiens wallerana (Impatiens) PT/S
Lobelia erinus (Lobelia) PT
Tropaeolum majus (Nasturtium) PT
Viola species (Pansies and Johnny Jump-ups) PT/S

PERENNIALS FOR SHADE (PT: part shade S: full shade)

Aconitum species (Monkshood) PT
Ajuga species (Bugleweed) PT
Alchemilla mollis (Lady's Mantle) PT/S
Anemone x *hybrida* (Japanese Anemone) PT
Astilbe species (Astilbe) PT
Asarum species (Wild Ginger) S
Aster cordifolius (Blue Woods Aster) PT
Aquilegia vulgaris (Columbine) PT
Brunnera macrophylla (Brunnera) S
Cimifuga racemosa (Snakeroot) PT/S
Chasmanthium latifolium (Sea-Oat grass) PT
Chelone lyonni (Turtlehead) PT
Companula persicifolia (Bellflower) PT
Convallaria majalis (Lily of the Valley) PT/S
Cypripedium species (Ladyslipper) PT
Dicentra species (Bleeding Heart) PT
Doronicum cordatum (Leopard's Bane) PT
Digitalis species (Foxglove) PT
Epimedium species (Barrenwort) PT/S
Eupatorium purpureum (Joe Pye Weed) PT
Galium odoratum (Sweet Woodruff) PT/S
Geranium macrorrhizum (Bigroot Geranium) PT
Hemerocallis hybrids (Daylily) PT
Hosta species & hybrids (Hosta) PT/S
Heuchera sanguinea (Coral Bells) PT
Iris sibirica (Siberian Iris) PT
Lamium maculatum (Dead Nettle) PT/S
Liatris species (Gayfeather) PT
Ligularia x *przewalskii* (Rocket Ligularia) PT/S
Lilium especially oriental hybrids (Lily) PT
Liriope muscari (Lilyturf) PT/S
Lunaria annua (Moneyplant) PT/S
Lythrum salicaria (Purple Loostrife) PT
Masus reptans (Mazus) PT/S
Mertensia virginica (Virginia Bluebells) PT/S
Myosotis scorpioides (Forget-me-Not) PT/S

Persicaria 'Firetail' PT
Phalaris arundinacea (Ribbon Grass) PT
Phlox divaricata (Woodland Phlox) PT
Phlox stolonifera (Creeping Phlox) PT/S
Platycodon grandiflorus (Ballon Flower) PT
Polemonium caeruleum (Jacob's Ladder) PT
Polygonatum odoratum "Variegatum" (Solomon's seal) PT/S
Primula vulgaris (Primrose) PT
Pulmonaria saccharata (Lungwort) PT
Rudbeckia 'Goldstrum' (Black-eyed Susan) PT
Stylophorum diphyllum (Wood Poppy) PT/S
Thalictrum species (Meadowrue) PT
Tiarella cordifolia (Foam Flower) PT/S
Tradescantia species (Spiderwort) PT/S
Tricyrtis hirta (Toad Lily) PT/S
Trollius species (Globeflower) PT
Valeriana officinalis (Common Valerian/Garden Heliotrope) PT
Viola labradorica (Labrador Violet) PT/S
Waldsteinia ternata (Barren Strawberry) PT/S
Ferns, most species including:
Blechnum pennamarina (little hard Fern) PT/S
Dryopteris filix-mas (Male Fern) PT/S
Polypodium species
Polystichum acrostichoides (Christmas Fern) S
Polystichum braunii (Hardy Shield Fern) PT/S
Polystichum setiferum (Soft Shield Fern) PT/S

LONG-BLOOMING PERENNIALS

Alchemilla mollis (Lady's Mantle)
Achillea species (Yarrow)
Agastache 'Blue Fortune' (Blue Fortune Anise Hyssop)
Aquilegia canadensis (Canadian Columbine)
Aster novi-angliae "Alma Potschke" (New England Aster)
Aster tataricus (Tartarian Aster)
Coreopsis auriculata "Nana" (Dwarf Tickseed)
Coreopsis grandiflora (Tickseed)
Coreopsis verticillata (Threadleaf Coreopsis incl. "Moonbeam")

Echinacea purpurea (Purple Coneflower)
Gaillardia x *grandiflora* "Goblin" (Blanket flower)
Gaura lindheimeri (Gaura)
Heuchera species (Coral Bells)
Hemerocallis "Stella de Oro" (Stella de Oro Daylily)
Lathyrus latifolius (Perennial Sweet Pea)
Lysimachia clethroides (Gooseneck Loosestrife)
Oenothera speciosa (Evening Primrose)
Oenothera missouriensis (Missouri Primrose)
Persicaria 'Firetail'
Perovskia atriplicifolia (Russian Sage)
Platycodon grandiflorus (Balloonflower)
Rudbeckia fulgida "Goldsturm" (Blackeyed Susan)
Rudbeckia nitida (Golden Coneflower)
Salvia x *supurba* (Hybrid Sage)
Scabiosa caucasica (pincushion Flower)
Sedum "Autumn Joy (Autumn Joy Sedum)
Verbascum chaixii (Chaix Mullein)
Verbena bonariensis
Viola labradorica (Labrador Violet)
Viola x *tricolor* (Johnny Jump-Up)

PERENNIALS BY BLOOM PERIOD

Some of the many perennials popular on the Cape and Islands, listed
in the approximate month of bloom. (Plants may begin blooming
late in the month listed, or at the beginning of the following months,
depending on the weather.) I have starred (*) plants that have foliage that looks good both before and after they bloom.

APRIL
Arabis species (Rock and Wall Cress)
Chionodoxa luciliae (Glory-of-the-snow)
Crocus sp. (Crocus)
Galanthus nivalis (Snowdrop)
Mertensia virginica (Virginia Bluebells)
Narcissus (Daffodils)
Primula several varieties (Primrose)

Pulmonaria augustifolia (Lungwort)
Tulipa (Species Tulips)

MAY
**Aurinia saxatilis* (Basket-of-Gold)
**Ajuga reptans* (Bugleweed)
Convallaria majalis (Lily-of-the-Valley)
Dicentra spectabilis (Bleeding Heart)
Doronicum caucasicum (Leopardbane)
**Epimedium species*
Euphorbia sp. (Spurge)
Fragaria x *frel* "Pink Panda" (Pink Panda Strawberry)
**Iberis sempervirens* (Candytuft)
Lunaria biennis (Moneyplant)
Mazus reptans
Muscari botryoides (Grape Hyacinth)
Nepeta mussini (Nepeta)
Papaver nudicale (iceland Poppy)
Phlox divaricata (Sweet William Phlox)
**Phlox subulata* (Moss or Creeping Phlox)
**Tiarella cordifolia* (Foamflower)
Trollius europaeus (Globeflower)
Tulipa (Tulips)
Viola sp. (Violets and Johnny-Jump-Ups)

JUNE
**Alchemilla mollis* (Lady's Mantle)
Allium species (Allium)
Alyssum saxatile (Goldentuft)
Anthemis tinctoria (Golden Marguerite)
Aquilegia sp. (Columbine)
Aruncus dioicus (Goat's Beard)
Asarum europaeum (Wild Ginger)
Astrantia major (Large Masterwort)
**Baptisia australis* (Blue False Indigo)
Catananche caerulea (Cupid's dart)
Camassia cusickii
Centaurea species (Cornflower/Mountain Bluet)

Cerastium tomentosum (Snow-in-Summer)
Companula carpatica (Carpathian Bellflower)
Campanula glomerata (Bellflower)
Companula persicifolia (Peach-leaved Companula)
*Companula poscharskyana (Serbian Bellflower)
Centranthus ruber (Red Valerian)
Cornus canadensis (Bunchberry)
Cypripedium species (Lady's Slipper)
Delphinium in variety
Dianthus in variety (Pinks)
Dictamnus albus or *fraxinella* (Gas Plant)
Digitalis in variety (Foxglove)
Filipendula rubra (Meadowsweet)
*Geranium in variety (Hardy Geraniums/Cranesbills)
Geum species
Gypsophila repens (Creeping Baby's Breath)
Incarvillea delavayi (Hardy Gloxinia)
Iris germonica (Bearded Iris)
*Iris siberica (Siberian Iris)
Linum perenne (Flax)
Lupinus x "Russell Hybrids" (Lupine)
Lysimachia punctata (Yellow Loosestrife/Circleflower)
*Nepeta Six Hills giant/Superba
Oenothera in variety (Sundrops/Evening Primrose)
Paeonia in variety (Peony)
Papaver orientale (Oriental Poppy)
Phlox stolonifera (Creeping Phlox)
Polemonium caeruleum (Jacob's-ladder)
*Polygonatum species (Solomon's-seal)
Salvia in variety (Salvia/Sage)
Scabiosa caucasica (Caucasian Scabiosa)
*Stachys byzantina (Lamb's Ears)
Thalictrum aquilegifoilum (Meadowrue)
Thermopsis caroliniana (Carolina Thermopsis)
*Thymus (Thyme)
Tradescantia x *montana* and *virginiana* (Spiderwort)
Trollius europaeus (Globeflower)
Verbascum chaixii (Verbascum)

Verbascum x *hybridum* (Verbascum)
Veronica in variety (Speedwell)

JULY
Achillea in variety (Yarrow)
Allium in variety
Asclepias tuberosa (Butterfly Weed)
Astilbe hybrids
*Calluna vulgaris (Heather)
Cimicifuga racemosa (Bugbane)
Coreopsis grandiflora (Tickseed)
Coreopsis verticillata (Threadleaf Coreopsis includes "Moonbeam")
Echinacea purpurea (Purple Coneflower)
Echinops ritro or *sphaerocephalus* (Globe Thistle)
Erngium amethystinum (Sea Holly)
Euphorbia corollata (Spurge)
Filipendula rubra (Meadowsweet)
Gaillardia grandiflora (Blanketflower)
Gaura lindheimeri (Gaura)
Geum quellyon (Geum)
Gypsophila paniculata (Baby's Breath)
Heracleum sphondylium montanum (Giant Cow Parsnip)
Helianthus x *multiflorus* and *helianthoides*
*Hemerocallis in variety (Daylily)
*Hosta in variety (Plantain Lily)
*Iris ensata (Japanese Iris)
*Lavandula agustifolia (Lavendar)
Liatris spicata (Gayfeather)
Ligularia dentata or *przewalskii* (Ligularia)
Lilum in variety (Lily) first Asiatics, then Trumpets and Orientals
Lobelia cardinalis (Cardinal Flower)
Lychnis cahlcedonica (Maltese-cross)
Lychnis coronaria (Rose Campion)
Macleaya cordata (Plume Poppy)
Malva alcea (Hollyhock Mallow)
Malva moschata (Musk Mallow)
Monarda in variety (Bee Balm)
Penstemon in variety

Phlox paniculata (Garden Phlox)
Platycodon grandiflorum (Balloon Flower)
Rudbeckia fulgida including "Goldstrum" (Black-eyed Susan)
Sedum in variety (Stonecrop)
Sidalcea malviflora (Mallow/Miniature Hollyhock)
Stokesia laevis (Stokes' Aster)
Stokesia lilacina grandiflora (Stokesia)
Veronica in variety (Speedwell)
Yucca filamentosa (Yucca/Adam's-Needle)

AUGUST
Adenophora confusa (Ladybells)
Boltonia asteroides "Pink Beauty" (Pink Boltonia)
Cassia hebecarpa (Wild Senna)
Ceratostigma plumbaginoides (Leadwort/Plumbago)
Chelone lyoni (Pink Turtlehead)
Dicentra scandens
Eupatorium coelestinum (Hardy Ageratum)
Hemerocallis hybrids (Daylily)
Hibiscus moscheutos (Rose Mallow)
Hosta in variety (Plantain Lily)
Kniphofia uvaria (Poker Plant)
Lilium Oriental hybrids (Oriental Lily)
Liriope muscari (Blue Lilyturf)
Perovskia atriplicifolia (Russian Sage)
Physostegia virginiana (Obedient Plant)
Rudbeckia hirta (Black-eyed Susan)
Salvia azurea (Blue Sage)
Santolina incana (Lavender Cotton)
Verbena bonariensis

SEPTEMBER
Aconitum carmichaelii (Monkshood)
Anemone hupehensis or x *hybrida* (Japanese Anemone)
Aster x *frikartii*
Aster novi-belgii (New England Aster)
Boltonia asteroides "Snowbank" (White Boltonia)
Chrysanthemums in variety

Cimicifuga simplex (Bugbane)
Colchicum speciosum
Delphinium in variety (when cut back after first flowering)
Eupatorium coelestinum (Hardy Ageratum)
Fragaria x *frel* "Pink Panda" (Pink Panda Strawberry) second bloom
Gaura lindheimeri (stem is cut down by half after first bloom)
Helenium autumnale (Sneezeweed)
**Miscanthus sinensis* (Silver Grass)
*Pennisetum in variety (Fountain Grass)
Salvia pitcheri (Great Azure Sage)
*Sedum spectabile "Autumn Joy"

OCTOBER
Aconitum fischeri wilsoni (Violet Monkshood)
Aster tataricus (Tartarian Aster)
Chrysanthemum in variety
**Chrysanthemum nipponicum* (Nippon Daisy)

FAST-SPREADING PERENNIALS

Perennials that spread quickly may be desirable in a contained space, or when a large garden needs to be filled quickly; they are also useful for groundcovers. Anyone with limited space, however, should think long and hard before putting the following plants into their garden; they will fill in quickly, but they will need to be divided fairly often. Those that spread so quickly that many people consider them invasive are marked with an asterisk (*). These garden thugs may be best planted together in a semi-wild space where they can slug it out among themselves.

Ajuga reptans (Bugleweed)
Achillea most varieties (Yarrow)
Anemone tomentosa (Grape-leaf Anemone)
Artemisia stelleriana (Dusty Miller)
Cerastium tomentosum (Snow-in-Summer)
Ceratostigma plumbaginoides (Leadwort/Plumbago)
Coreopsis verticillata (Threadleaf Coreopsis)
Eupatorium coelestinum (Hardy Ageratum)

Filipendula rubra (meadowsweet)
Fragaria x *frel* "Pink Panda" (Pink Panda Strawberry)
Galium odoratum (Sweet Woodruff)
Helianthus most varieties (Perennial Sunflower)
*Houttuynia cordata (Chameleon Plant)
Lamium maculatum (Spotted Dead Nettle)
*Leonurus cardiaca (Motherwort)
*Lysimachia clethroides (Gooseneck Loosestrife)
Lysimachia nummularia (Creeping Jenny)
Lysimachia punctata (Yellow Loosestrife)
Macleaya cordata (Plume Poppy)
Mentha most varieties (Mint)
Monarda didyma (Bee Balm)
Oemothera speciosa (Evening Primrose)
Physostegia virginiana (Obedient Plant)
**Polygonum cuspidatum (Mexican Bamboo)
Thermopsis montana (Mountain Thermopsis)
Tradescantia x *andersoniana* (Spiderwort)
Valeriana officinalis (Valerian or Garden Heliotrope)
Viola labradorica (Labrador violet)

GROUNDCOVERS FOR SUNNY SITES

Ajuga reptans (Bugleweed)
Arctostaphylos uva-ursi (Bearberry)
Calluna vulgaris (Heather)
Cerastium tomentosum (Snow-in-Summer)
Cotoneaster horizontalis (Creeping Cotoneaster)
Fragaria x *frel* "Pink Panda" (Pink Panda Strawberry)
Geranium sanguineum (Cranesbill Geranium)
Hedera helix (English Ivy)
Juniperus horizontalis (Creeping Juniper)
Juniperus procumbens (Japanese Juniper)
Lysimachia nummularia (Creeping Jenny) in moist locations
Phlox subulata (Moss Phlox)
Parthenocissus quinquefolia (Virginia creeper)
Rosa wichuraiana (Memorial Rose)
Thymus sp. (Thyme)

GROUNDCOVERS FOR SHADE (PT: part shade S: full shade)

Ajuga reptans (Bugleweed) PT
Asrum canadense (Wild Ginger) PT/S
Ceratostigma plumbaginoides (Plumbago) PT
Chrysogonum virginianum (Green and Gold) PT
Epimedium hybrids (Epimedium) PT/S
Ferns, most species including:
Blechnum pennamarina (little hard Fern) PT/S
Carex 'Ice Dance'
Convallaria majalis (Lily-of-the-Valley) PT/S
Dryopteris filix-mas (Male Fern) PT/S
Polypodium species
Polystichum acrostichoides (Christmas Fern) S
Polystichum braunii (Hardy Shield Fern) PT/S
Polystichum setiferum (Soft Shield Fern) PT/S
Galium odoratum (Sweet Woodruff) PT/S
Hedera helix (English Ivy) PT/S
Hosta all varieties PT/S
Hydrangea anomala petiolaris (Climbing Hydrangea) PT/S
Lamium maculatum (Spotted Dead Nettle) PT/S
Liriope muscari (Lily Turf) PT/S
Mazus reptans (Mazus) PT
Pachysandra terminalis or *procumbens* (Pachysandra) PT/S
Vinca minor (Vinca/Periwinkle/Myrtle) PT/S
Viola labradorica (Labrador violet) PT

VINES FOR SHADE

Actinidia arguta (Kiwi vine) PT
Akebia quinata (Akebia) PT
Aristolochia durior (Dutchman's Pipe) PT
Clematis 'Nelly Moser' PT
Dicentra scandens PT/S
Hedera helix (English Ivy) PT/S
Hydrangea anomala petiolaris (Climbing Hydrangea) PT/S
Lonicera sempervirens (Honeysuckle) PT/
Parthenocissus quinquefolia (Virginia Creeper) PT/S

Parthenocissus tricuspidata (Boston Ivy) PT/S

SHRUBS FOR FOUNDATION PLANTINGS

Shrubs listed grow to four feet or under, and require little pruning to keep a lovely shape. (In other words, you won't have to shear them into cubes and balls in order to prevent them from blocking the windows.)

Abelia x *grandiflora* 'Sherwood'
Berberis thunbergii 'Crimson Pygmy', 'Compacta', 'Sparkle', or 'Nana' (Barberry - compact forms)
Buxus microphylla (Littleleaf Boxwood)
Chamaecyparis obtusa 'Nana' or 'Nana Gracilis' (Hinoki Falsecypress)
Cotoneaster apiculatus (Cranberry Cotoneaster)
Cotoneaster horizontalis (Rockspray Cotoneaster)
Euonymus alata 'Gracilis' or 'Rudy haag' (Compact Burning Bush)
Fothergilla gardenii (Dwarf Fothergilla)
Hydrangea macrophylla (Bigleaf Hydrangea)
Ilex crenata low forms such as 'Green Island', 'Helleri', or 'Tiny Tim' (Japanese Holly)
Ilex glabra 'Compacta' (Inkberry)
Juniperus chinensis low-growing varieties such as 'Sarcoxie', *sargentii* 'Glauca', or 'Sea Green'
Juniperus conferta (Shore Juniper)
Juniperus horizontalis (Creeping Juniper)
Kalmia latifolia 'Elf' or other dwarf form (Mountain Laurel)
Kerria japonica 'Picta'(Kerria)
Leucothoe fontanesiana (Drooping Leucothoe)
Mahonia aquifolium 'Apollo', 'Compactum', or 'Mayhan Strain' (Oregon Grapeholly)
Picea abies 'Nidiformis', 'Procumbens', or 'Pumila' (Norway Spruce)
Pieris japonica 'Compacta' (Japanese Pieris)
Pinus mugo 'Compacta' or 'Mops' (Dwarf Mugo Pine)
Prunus laurocerasus 'Otto Luyken' (Cherry Laurel)
Rhododendron Low-growing varieties such as *R. canadense, R.* 'P.J.M. hybrids, *R. smirnowii, R. yakusimanum,* and the many evergreen Azalea hybrids.
Skimmia japonica (Japanese Skimmia)

Spiraea (any of the compact varieties)
Taxus cuspidata 'Densa' ot 'Aurescens' (Japanese Yew - compact varieties)
Taxus x *media* low varieties such as 'Chadwickii', 'Andersonii', or 'Densiformis' (Anglojap Yew)
Thuja occidentalis (Eastern Arborvitae - several small or dwarf varieties.)
Viburnum carlesii 'Compactum'
Yucca

Shrubs that Bloom in the Summer

Buddleia davidii (Butterfly Bush)
Caryopteris x *clandonensis* (Bluebeard)
Clethra alnifolia (Summersweet)
Hibiscus syriacus (Rose-of-Sharon)
Hydrangea macrophylla (Bigleaf Hydrangea)
Hydrangea paniculata (Peegee Hydrangea)
Hydrangea quercifolia (Oakleaf Hydrangea)
Potentilla fruticosa (Cinquefoil)
Spirea x *bumalda* (Bumald Spirea)
Vitex agnus-castus (Chaste Tree).

Shrubs for Shade (PT: part shade S: full shade)

Abelia x *grandiflora* (Abelia) PT
Berberis thunbergii and *Berberis* x *mentorensis* (Barberry) PT
Calycanthus floridus (Common Sweetshrub)
Clethra alnifolia (Summersweet) PT/S
Cornus alba (Tartarian Dogwood) PT
Enkianthus campanlatus (Redvein Enkianthus) PT
Fothergilla all species PT
Hamamelis virginiana (Witchhazel) PT/S
Hydrangea macrophylla (Bigleaf Hydrangea) PT
Hydrangea quercifolia (Oakleaf Hydrangea) PT/S
Ilex crenata (Japanese Holly) PT/S
Ilex x *meservae* (Meserve Hollies) PT
Itea virginica (Sweet Spire) PT

Kalmia latifolia (Mountain Laurel) PT/S
Kerria japonica (Kerria) PT/S
Leucothoe fontanesiana (Leucothoe) S
Mahonia aquifolium (Oregon Grape Holly) PT/S
Pieris japonica (Japanese Pieris) PT/S
Prunus laurocerasus (Cherry Laurel) S
Rhododendron species PT/S
Rhodotypos scandens (Jetbead) PT/S
Rhus typhina (Stagehorn Sumac) PT
Skimmia japonica (Skimmia) PT/S
Viburnum most species PT

FAST GROWING SHRUBS

Callicarpa japonica (Japanese Beautyberry)
Cornus alba (Tartarian Dogwood)
Cytisus coparius (Broom)
Elaeagnus umbellata (Autumn-olive)
Forsythia x *intermedia* (Forsythia)
Ligustrum species (Privet)
Philadelphus coronarius (Sweet Mockorange)
Sorbaria sorbifolia (Ural Falsespirea)

CAREFREE SHRUBS

Berberis x *mentorensis* (Mentor Barberry)
Calycanthus floridus (Common Sweetshrub)
Chamaecyparis species (Falsecypress)
Clethra alnifolia (Summersweet)
Euonymus alatus (Burning Bush or Winged Euonymus)
Fothergilla gardenii (Dwarf Fothergilla)
Hydrangea quercifolia (Oakleaf Hydrangea)
Ilex glabra (Inkberry)
Itea virginica "Henry's Garnet" (Virginia Sweetspire)
Juniperus chinensis (Chinese Juniper-various cultivars)
Juniperus horizontalis (Creeping Juniper)
Kalmia latifolia (Mountain Laurel)
Kerria japonica (Kerria)

Myrica pensylvanica (Northern Bayberry)
Rhodotypos scandens (Jetbead)
Spiraea species (Spirea)
Viburnum dentatum (Arrowwood Viburnum)

SMALLER LOW-MAINTENANCE TREES

Abies concolor (Concolor Fir)
Acer buergeranum (Trident Maple)
Acer campertre (Hedge Maple)
Acer ginnala (Amur Maple)
Acer griseum (Paperbark Maple)
Acer rubrum (Red Maple)
Acer triflorum (Three-flower maple)
Betula nigra 'Heritage" (Heritage River Birch)
Carpinus caroliniana (Ironwood)
Cercidiphyllum japonicum (Katsura tree)
Chamaecyparis pisifera (Sawara Falsecypress)
Chionanthus virginicus (Fringetree)
Cornus kousa (Kousa Dogwood)
Ginko biloba (Ginko)
Halesia carolina (Carolina Silverbell)
Heptacodium miconioides (Seven-son Flower)
Ilex pedunculosa (Longstalk Holly)
Koelreuteria paniculata (Golden Rain Tree)
Maackia amurensis (Amur Maackia)
Magnolia x *loebneri* (Loebner Magnolia hybrids)
Magnolia virginiana (Sweetbay Magnolia)
Malus "Donald Wyman" or *"Professor Sprenger"*(Crabapple)
Oxydendron arboreum (Sourwood)
Pinus cembra (Swiss Stone Pine)
Stewartia pseudocamellia (Japanese Stewartia)
Styrax japonicus (Japanese Snowbell)
Syringa reticulata (Japanese Tree Lilac)

TREES KNOWN FOR RAPID GROWTH

Acer ginnala (Amur Maple)
Betula nigra (River Birch)
Cedrus atlantica glauca (Blue Atlas Cedar)
x *Cupressocyparis leylandii* (Leyland Cypress)
Elaeagnus angustifolia (Russian Olive)
Halesia Carolina (Carolina Silverbell)
Magnolia virginiana (Sweetbay Magnolia)
Picea abies (Norway Spruce)
Quercus palustris (Pin Oak)
Quercus Rubra (Red Oak)
Salix alba (White Willow)
Sophora japonica (Japanese Pagodatree)
Styrax japonicus (Japanese Snowbell)

PLANTS WITH RED/PURPLE FOLIAGE

Plants with red or purple foliage provide a wonderful contrast to
the variety of greens in a shrub or perennial border. The following
plants are known for their lovely leaves, which retain the red/purple
color throughout the season.

SHRUBS AND TREES
Acer palmatum many cultivars
Acer platanoides 'Crimson King'
Berberis thunbergii 'Atropurpruea', 'Crimson Pygmy', or 'Crimson
Velvet'
Betula pendula 'Purpurea' (Purple-leaf Birch)
Betula 'Crimson Frost'
Cercis canadensis 'Forest Pansy' (Forest Pansy Redbud)
Cotinus coggygria 'Purpureus' (Purple Smoke Tree)
Prunus cerasifera 'Atropurpurea,' 'Newport' 'Nigra' (Purple Plum)
Prunus cistena (Purple-Leaved Sand Cherry)
Prunus serrulata 'Royal Burgundy' (Royal Burgundy Cherry)
Sambucus nigra 'Purpurea' (Purple-leaf Elderberry)
Weigela florida 'Java Red,' 'Wine and Roses' or 'Tango' (Weigela)

PERENNIALS

Ajuga reptans several cultivars (Bugleweed)
Anthriscus sylvestris 'Ravenswing' (Purple Leaf Cow Parsley)
Aster lateriflorus 'Prince' and 'Lady in Black' (Calico Aster)
Cimicifuga simplex 'Brunette'
Eupatorium rugosum 'Chocolate'
Euphorbia amygdaloides 'Purpurea' (Purple Leaf Spurge)
Euphorbia dulcis 'Chameleon' (Chameleon Euphorbia)
Geranium pratense 'Midnight Rider' (Purple Leaf Cranesbill)
Heuchera many cultivars including 'Stormy Seas' 'Can Can' and 'Chocolate Ruffles' (Coral Bells)
Imperata cylindrica 'Red Baron' (Japanese Blood Grass)
Lobelia splendens (Red Leaved Cardinal Flower)
Lysimachia ciliata (Purple Leaved Loosestrife)
Ophiopogon planiscapus 'Nigrescens' (Black Mondo Grass)
Penstemon digitalis 'Huskers Red'
Persicaria microcephala 'Red Dragon'
Plantago major 'Atropurpurea' (Red Leaved Plantain)

ANNUALS

Brassica oleracea 'Early Purple Viena' or 'Giant Red' (Japanese Red Mustard)
Dahlia 'Ellen Huston' 'Bishop of Llandaff'
Ocimum Basilicum 'Dark Opal' (Dark Opal Basil)
Pennisetum alopecuroides 'Purpurea' (Purple Fountain Grass)
Perilla frutescens 'Atropurpurea' (Beefstake Plant)
Phormium several varieties
Solanum several varieties (Purple Leaf Ornamental Pepper)

ROSES POPULAR ON THE CAPE AND ISLANDS

Aloha (dark pink flowers – climber)
Betty Prior (pink single flowers – shrub)
Blanc Double de Coubert (white flowers – shrub)
Blaze (red flowers - climber)
Bonica (pink flowers – shrub)
Carefree Beauty (pink flowers – shrub)
Carefree Wonder (pink flowers – shrub)

Carpet Roses (red, pink or white flowers – low shrub)
Dublin Bay (red flowers - climber)
Graham Thomas (yellow flowers)
Knockout (bright pink flowers all summer – shrub)
Meidiland Roses, Pink and Scarlet (shrub)
New Dawn (pale pink flowers – climber)
Sea Foam (pinkish white flowers - shrub)
Sally Holmes (single-flowered - climber)
The Fairy (pink flowers – shrub)

DEER-RESISTANT PLANTS

Plants that the deer are *less likely* to eat.

TREES
Acer species (Maples)
Ilex species (Hollies)
Picea species (Spruce)
Pinus species (Pines)
Quercus species (Oaks)

SHRUBS
Berberis thunbergii (Japanese Barberry)
Cytisus scoparius (Scotch Broom)
Calycanthus floridus (Common Sweetshrub)
Juniperus species (Junipers)
Potentilla fruitcosa (Cinquefoil)
Rhododendrons hybrids excluding Azaleas
Spiraea species (Spirea)
Syringa species (Lilac)

FERNS, VINES, AND GROUND COVERS
Ajuga reptans (Bugleweed)
Althyrium filix-femina (Lady Fern)
Arctostaphylos uva-ursi (Bearberry)
Clematis species (Clematis)
Dryopteris spp. (Wood Ferns)
Festyca spp. (Fescues)

Hedra helix (Ivy)
Miscanthus sinensis (Maiden Grass)
Pachysandra
Vinca minor (Vinca/Periwinkle/Myrtle)

PERENNIALS
Aconitum carmichaelli (Monkshood)
Adenophora confusa (Ladybells)
Allium species (Ornamental Onions)
Aster species (Asters)
Baptisia australis (False Blue Indigo)
Boltonia asteroides (Bolton's Aster)
Cassia marilandica (Wild Senna)
Chrysanthemum parthenium (Feverfew)
Convallaria majalis (Lily of the Vally)
Coreopsis grandiflora (Tickseed)
Dicentra spectabilis (Bleeding Heart)
Echinacea purpurea (Purple Coneflower)
Echinops ritro (Globe Thistle)
Eupatorium purpureum (Joe-Pye Weed)
Iberis sempervirens (Candytuft)
Iris sibirica (Siberian Iris)
Lysimachia clethroides (Gooseneck Loosestrife)
Monarda didyma (Bee Balm)
Papaver species (Poppy)
Peony lactiflora (Peony)
Pulmonaria species (Lungwort)
Salvia officinalis (Garden sage)
Stachys byzantina (Lamb's-Ears)
Solidago hybrids (Goldenrod).
Yucca filamentosa (Yucca/Adam's Needle)

BULBS
Cammassia esculenta
Colchicum spp.
Crocus spp.
Chionodoxa spp. (Glory of the Snow)
Galanthis nivalis (Snowdrops)

Hyacinthus orientalis (Hyacinth)
Narcissus spp. (Daffodils)
Scilla spp. (Squill)

RABBIT-RESISTANT PERENNIALS

Achillea species (Yarrow)
Aconitum species (Monkshood)
Artemisia species (Wormwood)
Aster species (Aster)
Astilbe hybrids (False Spirea/ Astilbe)
Baptisia australis (False Blue Indigo)
Campanula pericifolia (Peach-Leaved Companula)
Cimicifuga species (Snakeroot)
Digitalis species (Foxglove)
Doronicum species (Leopard's Bane)
Epimedium species
Filipendula vulgaris (Meadowsweet)
Geranium species (Cranesbill Geraniums)
Hemerocallis hybrids (Daylily)
Hosta hybrids (Hosta/Plantain Lily)
Iris species
Kniphofia uvaria (Red Hot Poker)
Papaver orientale (Oriental Poppy)
Peony lactiflora (Peony)
Salvia species (Sage)
Stachys byzantina (Lamb's Ears)
Trollius species (Globe Flower)
Yucca filamentosa (Yucca/Adam's Needle)

BIBLIOGRAPHY

Armitage, Allan M. *Allan Armitage on Perennials*. New York: Prentice Hall, 1993.

Armitage, Allan M. *Herbaceous Perennial Plants*. Athens, GA: Varsity Press Inc, 1989.

Ball, Jeff and Ball, Liz. *Landscape Problem Solver*. Emmaus, PA: Rodale Press, 1989.

Clausen, Ruth R. and Ekstrom, Nicolas H. *Perennials for American Gardens*. New York: Random House, 1989.

Daniels, Stevie. *The Wild Lawn Handbook*. New York: Macmillan, 1995.

Dirr, Michael A. *Manual of Woody Landscape Plants*: *Their Identification, Ornamental Characteristics, Culture, Propagation and Uses*. Champaign, IL: Stipes Publishing, 1990.

DiSabato-Aust, Tracy. *The Well Tended Perennial Garden*. Portland, Oregon: Timber Press, Inc, 1998.

Druse, Ken. *Making More Plants*. New York, NY: Clarkson Potter Publishers, 2000.

Foley, Daniel J. *Gardening by the Sea from Coast to Coast*. Orleans, MA: Parnassus Imprints, 1965.

Ellis, Barbara W. and Bradley, Fern M. (eds.). *The Organic Gardener's Handbook of Natural Insect and Disease Control*. Emmaus, PA: Rodale Press, 1992.

Hudak, Joseph. *Gardening with Perennials Month by Month*. Portland, OR: Timber Press, 1993.

Köhlein, Fritz and Menzel, Peter. *Color Encyclopedia of Garden Plants and Habitats*. Portland, OR: Timber Press, 1994.

Massachusetts Audubon Society. *Birding Cape Cod*. South Wellfleet, MA: Massachusetts Audubon Society, 1990.

Nollman, Jim. *Why We Garden*. New York: Henry Holt and Company, 1994.

O'Brien, Greg (ed.). *A Guide to Nature on Cape Cod and the Islands*. Hyannis, MA: Parnassus Imprints, 1995.

Olkowski, William, Daar, Sheila, and Olkowski, Helga. *Common-Sense Pest Control*. Newtown, CT: Taunton Press, 1994.

Pirone, Pascal P. *Diseases & Pests of Ornamental Plants*. New York: John Wiley & Sons, Inc., 1978.

Powell, Eileen. *From Seed to Bloom*. Pownal, VT: Storey Communications, 1995.

Reich, Lee. *A Northeast Gardener's Year*. Reading, MA: Addison-Wesley, 1992.

Taylor's Guide to Perennials. Boston: Houghton Mifflin,1986.
Taylor's Guide to Annuals. Boston: Houghton Mifflin,1986.
Taylor's Guide to Shrubs. Boston: Houghton Mifflin,1987.
Taylor's Guide to Natural Gardening. Boston: Houghton Mifflin,1993.
Taylor's Guide to Roses. Boston: Houghton Mifflin,1995.

University of California. *Pests of Landscape Trees and Shrubs: An Integrated Pest Management Guide*. Okland, CA: ANR Publications - Univ. of California Division of Agriculture and Natural Resources Publication 3359, 1994.

University of Massachusetts Cooperative Extension System Bulletins # C-108, L-165-R, L-278, L-282, L-284, L-302, L-306, L-321, L-324, L-334, L-338, L-365, L-381, L-383, L-384, L-426, L-454, L-494, L-495, L-497, L-500, L-510, L-517, L-518, L-519, L-529, L-530, L-534, L-537, L-539, L-548, L-563, L-598, L-612

University of Massachusetts Cooperative Extension System Publications:

Cultural Practices of Woody Plants by Deborah Swanson, Extension Specialist, CES Plymouth County
Non-Chemical Methods of Insect and Disease Control in the Home Vegetable Garden, CES Worcester County Office
Selection and Maintenance of Plant Materials for Coastal Landscapes by Karl Rask
CES Barnstable County
Trees for Low Maintenance Landscapes by Roberta A. Clark and Deborah C. Swanson, CES Nursery and Landscape Program

INDEX